Academic Inquiry 2

Academic Inquiry 2

Paragraphs and Short Essays

John Scott Jamieson
James Papple

SERIES EDITOR Scott Roy Douglas

OXFORD
UNIVERSITY PRESS

OXFORD
UNIVERSITY PRESS

Oxford University Press is a department of the University of Oxford.
It furthers the University's objective of excellence in research, scholarship,
and education by publishing worldwide. Oxford is a registered trade mark of
Oxford University Press in the UK and in certain other countries.

Published in Canada by
Oxford University Press
8 Sampson Mews, Suite 204,
Don Mills, Ontario M3C 0H5 Canada

www.oupcanada.com

Library and Archives Canada Cataloguing in Publication
Jamieson, John Scott, 1965–, author
Paragraphs and short essays / John Scott Jamieson, James Papple.

(Academic inquiry ; 2)
Includes index.
ISBN 978-0-19-902540-4 (softcover)

1. Report writing.   2. English language–Paragraphs.   3. Essay–
Authorship.   4. English language–Rhetoric.   I. Papple, Jim, author
II. Title.   III. Series: Academic inquiry (Series) ; 2

LB2369.J36 2018   808'.042   C2017-907096-7

Cover images: © iStock/Geber86 (Top); © iStock/M_a_y_a (Bottom)
Cover design: Laurie McGregor
Interior design: Laurie McGregor

Oxford University Press is committed to our environment.
Wherever possible, our books are printed on paper which comes from
responsible sources.

Printed and bound in Canada

1 2 3 4 — 21 20 19 18

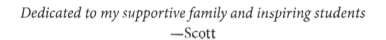

Dedicated to my supportive family and inspiring students
—Scott

My grateful thanks to Scott, and to my family for the tremendous support
—Jim

SCOPE and SEQUENCE

		Unit 1	Unit 2	Unit 3	Unit 4	Unit 5	Unit 6
	Theme	Communication and Culture Studies	Environmental Sciences	Business Studies	International Education	Design	Health Sciences
	Topic	Subcultures and Identities	Environmental Sustainability	Marketing and Consumers	Globalization and Cultural Adjustment	Understanding Processes	Wellness
Exploring Ideas	**Introduction**	Identity Formation Graphic	Frayer Model	Compare-and-Contrast T-Chart	Survey	Design Process Diagram	Wheel Chart
	Fostering Inquiry	Creating Inquiry Questions	Exploring Cause and Effect	Making Comparisons	Responding to Ideas and Information	Analyzing a Process	Framing a Problem
	Structure	Opinion Paragraph	Cause-and-Effect Paragraph	Compare-and-Contrast Paragraph	Summary-and-Response Paragraphs	Process Writing	Problem–Solution Writing
	Language Tip	Using Transition Words and Phrases	Expressing Cause and Effect	Showing Comparison and Contrast	Writing Summary Statements	Using Process Connectors	Introducing Problems and Solutions
Academic Reading	**Vocabulary Skill**	Choosing Words to Learn	Learning Words with Related Meanings	Understanding Word Forms and Suffixes	Understanding Word Forms and Prefixes	Varying Vocabulary Using Synonyms	Using Collocations
	Academic Word List	8 Word Families from the Academic Word List in each unit					
	Mid-frequency Vocabulary	8 Word Families up to the 6K Frequency Level in each unit					
	Pre-reading	Word Cloud	T-Chart	Venn Diagram	Idea Web	Design Process	KWL Chart
	Reading	"Who Are You?"	"Global Sustainability and Prosperity"	"E-Commerce Basics"	"A World of Learning" and "Study Abroad Challenges"	"Making Design Decisions"	"Well-being in Canada"
	Critical Thinking	Distinguishing between Fact and Opinion	Identifying Reasons and Examples	Making Connections between Ideas and Information	Recommending a Course of Action	Identifying Assumptions	Evaluating and Ranking

Topic	Unit 1 Subcultures and Identities	Unit 2 Environmental Sustainability	Unit 3 Marketing and Consumers	Unit 4 Globalization and Cultural Adjustment	Unit 5 Understanding Processes	Unit 6 Wellness
Process Fundamentals						
Brainstorming and Outlining	Listing / Creating a Formal Outline	Cube Brainstorm / Coordinating Ideas in an Outline	Venn Diagram / Parallel Ideas in an Outline	Idea Webs / Outline for Summary-and-Response Paragraphs	Sticky Note Process Map / Process Essay Outline	Split Page Notes Chart / Problem–Solution Essay Outline
Content Skill	Evaluating Information from Websites	Integrating Information from How-To Guides	Integrating Information from Charts and Diagrams	Integrating Information from Reports	Integrating Information from Magazine Articles	Integrating Information from Online Campus Resources
Preventing Plagiarism	Understanding Academic Integrity	Managing notes and integrating quotations	Understanding and Following Citation Styles Carefully	Integrating Summary Statements	Integrating Paraphrases	Using Online Tools to Check Own Writing
Reference Skill	Using APA Style	Citing How-To Guides in APA Style	Citing Information from Charts and Diagrams in APA Style	Citing Reports in APA Style	Citing Magazine Articles in APA Style	Citing Video and Online Resources in APA Style
Format and Organization Skill	Organizing Opinion Paragraphs	Organizing Cause-and-Effect Paragraphs	Organizing with Point-by-Point Format	Writing General-to-Specific Introductory Sentences	Writing an Ask-the-Reader Introduction	Writing a Problem–Solution Introduction
Topic Skill	Writing Topic Sentences	Writing Cause-and-Effect Topic Sentences	Writing Compare-and-Contrast Topic Sentences	Writing Topic Sentences for a Response Paragraph	Writing Process Thesis Statements	Writing Problem–Solution Thesis Statements
Conclusion Skill	Restating	Predicting	Recommending	Integrating an Expert Opinion	Reminding the Reader	Suggesting Other Solutions
Writing Fundamentals						
Composition Skill	Developing Topics and Supporting Ideas	Staying on Topic	Organizing Logical Connections between Ideas	Paragraphing	Maintaining Coherence	Revising and Editing
Sentence and Grammar Skill	Using Simple Past and Simple Present	Moving from Simple to Compound and Complex Sentences	Using Adverb Clauses	Avoiding Sentence Fragments, Comma Splices, and Stringy Sentences	Using Adverbs	Using Adjective Clauses
Unit Outcome						
Writing Assignment	Opinion Paragraph	Cause-and-Effect Paragraph	Compare-and-Contrast Paragraph	Summary-and-Response Paragraphs	Process Essay	Problem–Solution Essay
Evaluation	Opinion Paragraph Rubric	Cause-and-Effect Paragraph Rubric	Compare-and-Contrast Paragraph Rubric	Summary-and-Response Paragraphs Rubric	Process Essay Rubric	Problem–Solution Essay Rubric
Unit Review	Self-Assessment and Vocabulary Checklists					
Learning Strategy	Understanding a Writing Assignment	Helping Yourself Become an Academic Writer	Giving and Receiving Feedback	Participating in Group Work	Developing Effective Time Management Strategies	Reflecting on Learning, and Planning for Future Academic Success

Contents

Unit ① COMMUNICATION AND CULTURE STUDIES
Subcultures and Identities

Unit 2 ENVIRONMENTAL SCIENCES
Environmental Sustainability   39

Unit ③ BUSINESS STUDIES
Marketing and Consumers   75

Unit ④ INTERNATIONAL EDUCATION
Globalization and Cultural Adjustment   115

Unit 5 DESIGN
Understanding Processes   155

Unit 6 HEALTH SCIENCES
Wellness 193

Note to Instructors

Taking an inquiry-based approach, this series fosters academic writing skills that contribute to student success in post-secondary studies. Each unit is based on an academic discipline and opens with an introduction to theme-related content that prepares students to think about ideas within that discipline. At the heart of each unit, students develop personalized Unit Inquiry Questions to guide their study; these questions are inspired by each student's personal interest and curiosity. The process promotes higher-order thinking skills, encourages student curiosity, and resists simple yes or no answers. The Unit Inquiry Questions put an active learner-centred focus on content and prime students for dynamic engagement with unit materials, concepts, and skills.

Student writing skills are developed using a language-through-content approach to composition instruction, with each unit focused on one rhetorical writing pattern and one academic discipline. At the core of each unit is an authentic reading, such as an excerpt from an undergraduate textbook that students might typically encounter in a post-secondary setting. These readings provide a springboard for the inclusion of informative content in student writing and promote effective writing skills. Within each of the core academic readings, students are exposed to key vocabulary from the Academic Word List (AWL) along with pertinent mid-frequency vocabulary (MFV); these words are introduced to students in pre-reading activities and recycled throughout the unit to foster a greater depth and breadth of lexical usage in student writing.

Additionally, the rich contextual framework within each unit provides an opportunity for the recycling of skills and the spiralling of concepts. Each unit also emphasizes the fundamentals of the writing process as well as key composition and grammar skills, according to the demands of the unit content and writing assignments. These fundamentals are supported by special skills boxes focusing on thinking critically, developing learning strategies, and preventing plagiarism. Furthermore, all the process and writing fundamentals are accompanied by focused activities, opportunities for meaningful writing practice, and multiple writing models to provide comprehensible input to students as they gather ideas to answer their Unit Inquiry Questions and complete their own writing projects.

The final writing assignment in each unit is based on students' personalized Unit Inquiry Questions and the rhetorical pattern explored in the unit. Numerous opportunities for controlled writing output are provided throughout the unit until the final assignment is written as a culmination of the language and content knowledge gained throughout the unit. The final writing assignment is supported with evaluation and review activities to reinforce student learning and mastery of the unit outcomes.

Robustly supporting the content in the student books, the *Academic Inquiry* companion website (teacher's resource) is a rich source of supplementary materials. Online, teachers can find teaching notes, pacing guides, adaptable practice materials for each unit's learning objectives, answer keys, additional sample writing models, editing activities, and printable versions of the evaluation rubrics. Teachers will also find extension activities in the form of genre-based academic writing tasks (such as journal entries, lab reports, and case studies) and integrated tasks (such as surveys, short presentations, and posters). Finally, teachers have access to writing prompts suitable for timed exam purposes. Teachers can contact their local Oxford University Press sales and editorial representative for access to the password-protected teacher's resource.

Note to Students

Writing for academic purposes can seem like a difficult task; however, it doesn't have to be impossible. *Academic Inquiry* breaks down the task of academic writing into manageable parts. Each unit has carefully structured activities. You develop your academic writing skills step by step until you have the confidence to handle academic writing tasks on your own.

This textbook series takes an inquiry-based approach to learning. Each unit focuses on a core academic discipline, and you are encouraged to decide for yourself what specific area within that discipline you want to write about. This approach puts you in control of your learning. You find answers to your own questions. You develop your own writing topics.

Each unit opens with an opportunity to explore ideas connected to a topic within a specific academic discipline. Then you develop a question about that topic. It is a meaningful question based on your own curiosity. Throughout the unit, you have opportunities to find answers to this question—your Unit Inquiry Question.

Next, you work on expanding your vocabulary. New vocabulary supports your ability to express your ideas effectively and precisely. The new vocabulary is introduced in the context of academic readings, similar to those found in college and university settings. These readings also help you find ideas for your writing.

After you have read and responded to the readings in each unit, you have the opportunity to explore the unit topic in greater detail. You brainstorm and develop your chosen writing topic. You consider ways to prevent plagiarism. You make connections to your Unit Inquiry Question. You cover the structure and elements of quality academic writing, as well as critical thinking skills, learning strategies, vocabulary, and grammar points.

The key to developing these skills is extensive writing practice. Throughout each unit, you revisit and revise your own writing on a number of occasions. You see examples of good academic writing. You have the opportunity to review and rework your Unit Inquiry Question. You then complete the final unit assignment related to your Unit Inquiry Question. The end of each unit includes a writing rubric and self-assessment checklist connected to what you have learned in that unit. These tools help promote your understanding of the elements of effective academic writing.

The *Academic Inquiry* series guides you through the academic writing process. In each unit, you explore academic writing skills one at a time within the context of an academic discipline. In doing so, you will find the process of academic writing to be much less challenging. This style of writing is about communicating your ideas, which takes hard work and practice. However, developing the ability to express yourself clearly and effectively makes all that hard work and practice worthwhile. *Academic Inquiry* will empower you to use your skills and knowledge of the process in your future college and university studies.

Acknowledgements

The authors would like to acknowledge everyone at Oxford University Press who helped with this series and contributed to its publication. In particular, the authors thank the editorial team for their insightful suggestions and tireless dedication to excellence in English language teaching materials.

Oxford University Press Canada would like to express appreciation to the instructors and coordinators who graciously offered feedback on *Academic Inquiry* at various stages of the developmental process. Their feedback was instrumental in helping to shape and refine the book.

Carolyn Ambrose-Miller, Niagara College
Mélanie Barrière, Université de Sherbrooke
Erminia Bossio, Sheridan College
Devon Boucher, Thompson Rivers University
Kim Cechetto, Fanshawe College
Dara Cowper, Centennial College
Susan A. Curtis, University of British Columbia
Jason Doucette, Saint Mary's University
Cynthia Eden, University of Guelph
Giacomo Folinazzo, Niagara College
Sean Henderson, Wilfrid Laurier University
Gilmour Jope, University of the Fraser Valley
Barbara Kanellakos, Dalhousie University
Kristibeth Kelly, Fanshawe College

Vasie Kelos, Seneca College
Daryaneh Lane, University of Waterloo
Fiona Lucchini, Bow Valley College (retired)
Jonathon McCallum, Mohawk College
Angela Meyer Sterzik, Fanshawe College
Kristopher Mitchell, Dalhousie University
Anne Mullen, Université Laval
Thomas O'Hare, Université de Montrèal
Sophie Paish, Dalhousie University
Cyndy Reimer, Douglas College
Shawna Shulman, York University
Ardiss Stutters, Okanagan College
Elham Tavallaei, Centennial College
Jason Toole, Wilfrid Laurier University

UNIT 1

Communication and Culture Studies

Subcultures and Identities

EXPLORING IDEAS

Introduction

Activity A | Discuss the following questions with a partner or small group.

1. Your identity relates to who you are. Who are you? Describe your personality, interests, favourite things, work experiences, and so on.
2. Who or what has had the greatest impact on creating your identity?
3. What other things affect your identity?
4. Do you belong to any groups?
5. How do people show that they belong to a group?
6. Look at the people in the picture at the top of the page. What does the picture reveal about their individual identities? What do you think they have in common? What makes them different from each other?

Activity B | Look at the graphic showing four factors related to a person's identity and read the four statements below it. Match the four factors to the statements by putting a number in the blank in front of each statement. Then write your own identity statement, a sentence or two that describes who you are based on one of the factors in the graphic. Discuss your answers with a partner.

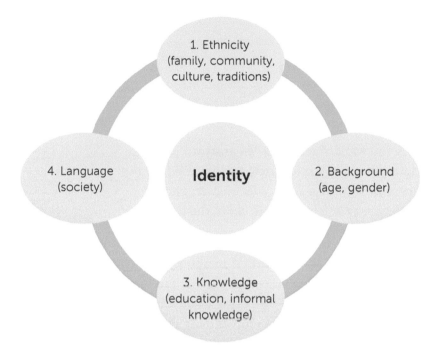

a. _____ Studying in Canada has helped me grow. Now I have many new interests.

b. _____ I am the oldest in my family with four younger brothers and sisters. I think it made me more responsible and taught me to enjoy taking care of other people.

c. _____ When I was little, my mother taught me the traditional arts and crafts that she learned from her grandmother. As a result, I feel connected to my community.

d. _____ I feel like I have a different personality when I'm speaking English—people think I'm a serious person! But when I speak my first language, I'm very funny.

My identity statement:

_____

_____

_____

Activity C | Looking at the graphic in Activity B and your identity statement, which factors do you think have the most influence on a person's identity? Discuss with a partner or small group. Then report your opinions to the class.

Fostering Inquiry

Creating Inquiry Questions

An inquiry question helps you learn about a topic that is important to you. A good inquiry question

- makes you want to search for an answer;
- encourages you to explore new or unfamiliar topics;
- requires more than a *yes* or a *no* answer; and
- may change as you learn more about the topic.

When developing your first inquiry question, start with a question word like *who, what, where, when, why,* or *how.* Thinking about your experiences, knowledge, and interests will help you find new ideas that you want to focus on and investigate further. By creating an inquiry question, you decide what you want to learn more about.

While searching for the answers to your inquiry question, you may think of new questions or ideas. Remember, it is all right to change your inquiry question or to develop a new one. As you move through the units in this book, you will develop many different inquiry questions that will help you learn more about the topics in this book.

Activity A | What do you want to know more about in relation to the topic of identity and the field of communication and culture studies? For example:

- *How does your identity change over time?*
- *How does learning English affect your identity?*
- *Why do people join a group or subculture?*

1. Write two or three questions you are curious about related to identity.
2. When you are finished, compare your questions with a partner or small group.
3. Choose one question to guide you as you work through this unit. It does not have to be the same question as your partner or group. Your question may change as you learn more about your topic.
4. Write your inquiry question in the space provided. Look back at this question as you work through the unit. This is your Unit Inquiry Question.

   My Unit Inquiry Question:

   _____

   _____

   _____

   _____

Activity B | Writing Task: Freewriting | Write for at least five minutes on the topic of your Unit Inquiry Question. Do not stop writing during this time. After five minutes, read what you have written and circle two or three ideas that you would like to explore further.

FREEWRITING TIPS

Process

- Write whatever comes into your head, if it is connected to your topic.
- Start with the ideas that are clearest and easiest to write about.
- Write by hand rather than typing on your computer.
- When you are done, reread your text. Highlight and save any new ideas.
- Don't throw your freewriting away. It will be useful when you start planning your paragraph or essay.

Time

- Set a time limit of five minutes.
- When time is up, take a short break from writing before going back to read what you've written.

Language

- Write without worrying about grammar, vocabulary, or spelling. Ideas are more important than grammar or spelling when you freewrite.
- Don't stop to check the dictionary. If you can't think of the exact word you need, rephrase your idea using whatever words you can and carry on writing.

Structure

Opinion Paragraph

An opinion paragraph follows a common structure that includes opinions, reasons, and evidence (ORE). The first sentence in the paragraph, which expresses the writer's opinion (feelings or reaction to a topic), is called the topic sentence. The body of the paragraph includes reasons, which explain why the writer holds that opinion, and evidence that supports the reasons. Evidence is based on facts and can include examples, statistics, quotations, and summary statements. An opinion paragraph will often end with a restatement of the topic sentence. The figure to the right illustrates how an opinion paragraph can be organized.

Activity A | Read the following opinion paragraph, then discuss the following questions with a partner or small group.

The Greatest Influence on Identity

In my opinion, culture has the greatest impact on a person's identity. From the moment a baby is born, he or she is surrounded by cultural markers, including the songs the baby's family sings or the food the baby is fed. Therefore, children absorb the culture around them while their identity is being formed. As children grow, their culture affects how they act in their families, in their schools, and eventually in their work. It appears that people's identities are shaped by the society in which they live, and culture strongly

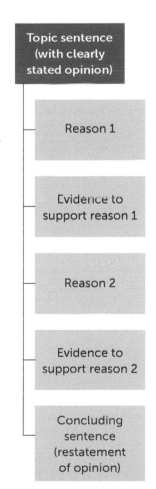

FIGURE 1.1
ORE structure

influences the stories people tell themselves and others about who they are (O'Brien & Szeman, 2014). For example, I was taught as a child to respect my teachers. That is part of my culture. As a result, I have always tried to be a good student. Being a good student is part of my identity. All in all, it seems that culture and identity are clearly connected.

Reference

O'Brien, S., & Szeman, I. (2014). *Popular culture: A user's guide* (3rd ed.). Toronto, ON: Nelson Education.

1. Does the first (topic) sentence express a clear opinion?
2. What reasons are given to support the opinion?
3. What types of evidence follow the reasons?
4. What words or phrases show that this paragraph is an opinion paragraph?
5. What do you notice about the first and last sentences?

Activity B | Read the following sentences and choose the best topic sentence. Then rearrange the other sentences to complete a short paragraph. All the sentences should work together to express a single opinion on the topic.

1. People may adopt a new identity to better reflect how they feel inside.
2. They may dress and act differently from their peers, but they are not necessarily being fake.
3. All in all, taking on a new identity does not mean people are pretending to be someone they are not.
4. In fact, they may be displaying an identity they value, and which better reflects how they see themselves.
5. Take, for example, rural teenagers who seem happier when they adopt an urban identity.
6. They may adopt a new identity because they are happier when the identity they show to the world matches how they feel.

Words and Phrases for Expressing Opinion

When writing an opinion paragraph, you should include words or phrases that let your reader know you are giving an opinion and not presenting a fact. The following expressions help to signal or emphasize to your reader that you are expressing a personal opinion or point of view.

In my experience . . .	Personally, I (don't) think that . . .	I would argue that . . .
In my opinion . . .	I (don't) believe that . . .	As far as I'm concerned . . .
I'm (not) certain/sure that . . .		

Sometimes you want to present a more general opinion rather than simply your own personal opinion. The following phrases can be used to express an opinion that is generally held or that many people share. These general phrases can also be used to express your own opinion in a less direct way.

It is generally accepted that . . .	Generally, people think that . . .	Most would argue that . . .
It is commonly believed that . . .	Some people believe that . . .	It is thought that . . .
Some people say that . . .	It is considered . . .	It is commonly held that . . .

Activity C | Complete each of the following sentences by using an opinion phrase to express a personal opinion.

1. _____ identity comes from a combination of culture and individual personality.

2. _____ individualism is an important aspect of identity.

3. _____ a cultural or subcultural group is defined by its similarities to and differences from other groups.

4. _____ people's identities change as they get older.

5. _____ identity is unique to each person.

Activity D | Complete the following thoughts by using different opinion phrases to express general opinions.

1. _____ group membership is a form of identification.

2. _____ statements such as "we are all the same" tend to ignore the perspectives of subcultures or minorities.

3. _____ how we dress and what we eat can affect our social interaction.

4. _____ the media can reinforce stereotypes about some subcultures.

Activity E | What opinions do you have about the topic you chose for your Unit Inquiry Question? Look back at the ideas you came up with during the freewriting you did on page 4. Write two sentences stating your personal opinion and two sentences stating a general opinion based on these ideas. Then share your sentences with a partner or small group. Be sure to include words and phrases for expressing opinion in your sentences.

Personal Opinions	General Opinions

Activity F | Writing Task: Opinion Paragraph | For each of the opinions you wrote in Activity E, think of one reason and one piece of evidence to support it. Then choose one of your opinions and write a short paragraph that includes an opinion, a reason, and some evidence. Use appropriate transition words and phrases in your paragraph to make the connections between ideas clear for your reader. See the *Language Tip* below to help you.

Activity G | Exchange your opinion paragraph with a partner. Read your partner's paragraph and answer the following questions.

1. Does the first sentence in the paragraph contain a clear opinion? What is it?
2. What reason does the writer give for his or her opinion?
3. What evidence is used to support the opinion?
4. What words and phrases for expressing an opinion does the writer use?
5. Is the last sentence an appropriate restatement of the topic sentence?

Language Tip

Using Transition Words and Phrases

Transition words and phrases help create logical connections between sentences and between paragraphs by signalling to the reader how the ideas are organized. Transitions can have different functions. For example, some transition words and phrases can help show that a writer is expressing an opinion.

Some common transition words and phrases, which can be used in an opinion paragraph, are set out below.

Example	Purpose of Transition Word or Phrase
to start with	to introduce
as well	to add to
for example	to give an example
similarly	to continue the same idea
on the other hand	to change ideas
as a consequence	to express a result or consequence
to sum up	to conclude

Activity H | Revisit your Unit Inquiry Question on page 4. Now that you have learned more about your topic, you may have a better idea of how to answer your question, or you may consider revising it. Use the following questions to guide you in assessing your Unit Inquiry Question.

- What information have you learned that will help you answer your Unit Inquiry Question?
- What information do you still need to answer your question?
- Do you want to change your question in any way?

ACADEMIC READING

Vocabulary

Vocabulary Skill: Choosing Words to Learn

An effective way to develop vocabulary is to focus on learning words (or word families) based on how often, or how frequently, they are used. If you know the 3000 most frequently used word families (all the different parts of speech related to one word) in the English language, you will be able to understand most general writing. These first 3000 words are called high-frequency vocabulary

However, most academic writing also contains mid-frequency vocabulary, which includes words from the 4000 to about the 8000 or 9000 most frequently used word families in English. Word families in this range often include words that are considered more academic. Knowing these words can help you read about and write on various topics.

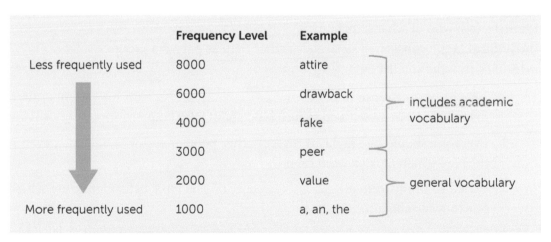

FIGURE 1.2 Frequency table

Activity A | The following words are from the upcoming reading "Who Are You?" on pages 12–13. Some words you will know because they are frequently used and others may be unfamiliar because they are less frequently used. Try to sort the words into two categories—high-frequency and mid-frequency—by guessing which are in the 3000 most frequently used word families and which are in the 4000 to 8000 range. The first two have been done for you. Then choose three words that are unfamiliar to you and that you would like to learn. Discuss with a partner why you chose these words.

inspired	preserving	have	choose
about	reflected	dominant	you
and	number	attire	drawbacks

High-frequency	Mid-frequency
about	inspired

Vocabulary Preview: The Academic Word List

Activity B | The Academic Word List (AWL) is a list of 570 word families that cover about 10 percent of the words found in an average piece of academic writing. Knowing these words can help you write for academic purposes. The following AWL words are taken from the reading on pages 12–13, a textbook excerpt titled "Who Are You?" Read the words and their definitions, then use these words to fill in the blanks in the sentences that follow.

affect (v.): to produce a change in someone or something
aspect (n.): a particular part or feature of a situation, an idea, a problem
culture (n.): the customs and beliefs, art, way of life, and social organization of a particular country or group
dominant (adj.): describing something important or powerful
generation (n.): all the people who were born at about the same time
identity (n.): who or what somebody is
individual (adj.): considered separately rather than as part of a group
minority (n.): the smaller part of a group

1. I have a strong sense of my own _____ because my parents raised me to believe in myself and to feel good about who I am.

2. Everyone should be taught to respect other people's _____, even if they are different from one's own.

3. I tried to brainstorm all _____ of this topic before deciding which one to write about.

4. Timothy surveyed each _____ member of the DIY punk collective to find out why he or she had joined.

5. Only a small _____ of students in the class decided not to hand in their essays.

6. My _____ grew up to believe in diversity and acceptance.

7. The teacher's opinion did not _____ my decision to change my essay topic.

8. The Internet is perhaps the most _____ form of mainstream media now.

Vocabulary Preview: Mid-frequency Vocabulary

Activity C | Read the following sentences, then read the two options that follow. Circle the word or phrase that is closest in meaning to the bolded mid-frequency vocabulary item in each sentence. Note that the correct answer might not fit grammatically into the example sentence.

1. Fighting the HIV/AIDS **crisis** is a major part of Bono's identity.
   a. problem
   b. solution

2. Not every word or idea can be **translated** into another language.
   a. lost
   b. said the same way

3. When meeting a new group, we are often **inspired** to adopt elements of that group's culture.
   a. motivated
   b. surprised

4. One way of communicating your personal taste is through **jewellery**.
   a. books
   b. objects worn as decoration

5. Our **beliefs** change over time depending on who we meet and what we experience.
   a. facts
   b. opinions

6. People may **dye** their hair or change their clothes to better fit in to a new group.
   a. colour
   b. lose

7. Members of minority groups may not see their cultural values **reflected** on television.
   a. shown
   b. removed

8. There can be social **drawbacks** to joining a subculture.
   a. advantages
   b. disadvantages

Reading

The reading "Who Are You?" on pages 12–13 is made up of excerpts from *Living in a Globalizing World*, a textbook that introduces students to basic concepts related to culture. The reading defines identity and explains how our identity shapes our decision making.

Activity A | The word cloud to the right was created from the reading "Who Are You?" The larger the size of the word in the cloud, the more often it occurs in the reading. With a partner or small group, predict the main ideas of the reading.

Activity B | Before reading "Who Are You?", mark the following statements as true (T) or false (F) based on your current understanding of the topic. As you

read the text, think about whether your answers are correct. Paragraph numbers have been provided to help you check your answers after you are done reading.

1. _____ There is a single answer to the question, *Who are you*? (1)

2. _____ People often express their identities through what they wear. (2)

3. _____ The clothes people wear are partly influenced by the groups they belong to. (3)

4. _____ Language has an effect only on your collective identity. (4)

5. _____ Some aspects of collective and individual identities are connected. (5)

6. _____ The media can have an effect on an individual's identity. (8)

Activity C | Read the following textbook excerpt and underline examples of how the author answers the question *Who are you?* When you are done, compare your examples with a partner and answer the questions that follow.

READING

Who Are You?

1   Who are you? You could respond to this question by simply stating your name—asserting[1] your **individual identity** as a single, unique person with your own views, habits, likes, and dislikes. Or, you could answer the question by stating that you are a Canadian, a Ukrainian-Canadian, or a Calgarian. You might also choose to identify yourself as a member of a political party, a teenager, a student, an environmentalist,[2] or a member of a particular religion. Each of these labels[3] places you as part of a larger group, or collective identity.

2   What is the relationship between your individual and your collective identities? Let's look at an example. One way that people express their individual identities is through what they wear. You select items of clothing, **jewellery**, and other **aspects** of your attire[4] based on your individual preferences. You may choose to **dye** your hair or change your hairstyle in order to tell people something about yourself.

3   But your choices of attire are also influenced by the groups to which you belong. For example, you probably pay at least some attention to what other people are wearing, and try to choose clothes that will tell other people something about who you are.

4   Here's another aspect of identity to consider. What language did you learn first, when you were a baby? Whatever language it was, it has likely had an effect on your individual and collective identities. Different languages communicate different ways of seeing the world. Some ideas and understandings of the world cannot be **translated** into another language. So the language you learn as a child becomes part of who you are and how you see things.

5   So now you have an idea of how elements of your identity can be affected by many things. Aspects of your individual identity and of your collective identities are connected, shaping who you are and how you see the world.

Maintaining and Promoting[5] Identities

6   Have you ever felt that you had to give up some aspect of your identity in order to fit in with a group?

[1] to state clearly and firmly that something is true
[2] a person who is concerned about the natural world
[3] a name or phrase that is used to describe somebody/something
[4] the things a person wears
[5] to help something to happen or develop

For example, at one time or another, you may have felt pressured to dress, act, or speak in a certain way in order to fit in. You may not have liked giving up other practices or interests, but reasoned that you would gain more by joining the group than you would by following your own path. Perhaps you felt that no one else shared your interests and points of view, and it was too difficult to go it alone.

7   It's not easy to resist a **dominant** group or way of doing things. This is true for collective identities as well. Some groups have found it difficult to maintain their distinct identities because of growing pressure from outside forces.

8   An important part of preserving[6] a collective identity is the ability to pass aspects of that identity on to the next **generation**. With the increasing reach of media such as television and the Internet, however, today's young people have access to ways of life, **beliefs**, and role models from all over the world, instead of just from their own **culture**. For example, Bono is the lead singer of the Irish band U2. He has worked hard to convince politicians around the world to do something about the HIV/AIDS **crisis** and debt crisis in less developed countries. This rock star's political activism[7] has **inspired** young people worldwide, not just in his homeland of Ireland.

9   While there are some obvious benefits to having more choices, **minority** groups have pointed out that there are also **drawbacks**. What happens if you do not see your culture **reflected** in media? How might this **affect** your sense of identity? What if one culture or group has more money or power than others and therefore is more appealing to young people, who may choose not to be part of a minority?

Source: Perry-Globa, P., Weeks, P., Zelinski, V., Yoshida, D., & Colyer, J. (2007). *Living in a globalizing world* (pp. 25, 30–31). Don Mills, ON: Oxford University Press Canada.

---

[6] to keep a particular quality, feature, etc.; to make sure that something is kept

[7] the act of working to achieve political or social change

Activity D | Discuss the following questions with a partner or small group.

1. According to the reading, what kinds of things contribute to creating a person's identity?
2. What is the difference between individual and collective identity?
3. Have you ever given up aspects of your identity to fit in with a group? How can an individual or a smaller group maintain a unique identity against the pressures of a larger group?
4. Look back at the examples you underlined related to the question *Who are you?* What do you now know about the concept of identity that you did not know before?
5. Are there any ideas discussed in the text that you do not quite understand? Discuss anything you are not sure about.

Activity E | Revisit your Unit Inquiry Question on page 4. Are there any ideas from the reading that will help you answer your question? Share your ideas with a partner or small group. At this point, you may consider revising your Unit Inquiry Question. Use the following questions to help you in assessing your question.

1. How does the information from this reading change your understanding of identity?

2. Which ideas from the reading can be used to help answer your Unit Inquiry Question?

3. What additional questions do you have after finishing the reading?

4. Where could you find more information?

Activity F | Writing Task: Opinion Paragraph | Write a short paragraph giving your opinion on how identity is formed. Before you write, brainstorm ideas by freewriting for five minutes on the topic of identity. Then choose the best ideas from your freewriting to use in your paragraph. Try to include five of the vocabulary words from this unit, but make sure the paragraph is written in your own words.

Activity G | Compare your paragraph to the sample paragraph in Appendix 2, then answer the questions that follow. Share your answers with a partner or a small group.

1. What is the main idea of the sample paragraph?
2. Where did you find the main idea?
3. Does the paragraph use ORE structure? What opinions, reasons, and evidence did you find?
4. What words and phrases signal that the author is giving an opinion?
5. Is there an effective concluding sentence?
6. After reading the sample paragraph, is there anything you would revise in your paragraph?

Critical Thinking

Distinguishing between Fact and Opinion

Writers should always ensure that the reader can easily identify facts and opinions. Facts are statements that can be researched and verified as true. For example, it is a fact that the word *identity* is a noun, and one could verify that fact by looking the word up in a dictionary. Writers find and cite reliable sources to support statements of fact.

Facts (from the reading "Who Are You?")

• One way that people express their individual identities is through what they wear.
• Bono is the lead singer of the Irish band U2.

Opinions are statements that express someone's judgement, belief, feelings, or way of thinking. An example of an opinion is that a person's identity is shaped by early childhood experiences and doesn't really change very much throughout the rest of a person's life. While some may agree with this statement, others may not. When opinions are presented with supporting facts or evidence from experts, they are considered valid opinions.

Opinions (from the reading "Who Are You?")

• It's not easy to resist a dominant group or way of doing things.
• Your language likely affects both your individual and your collective identities.

PROCESS FUNDAMENTALS

Brainstorming and Outlining

Listing

Listing ideas to write about can be an easy way to start thinking about a topic, especially if you find it difficult to come up with ideas. Do not worry about writing too many ideas. In fact, you should try to write as many ideas as you can. After you complete your list, you can narrow the ideas by connecting related ideas in your list or crossing out the ideas that you don't think will be useful for your paragraph.

When you list ideas in a brainstorm, begin with your main ideas and then list supporting ideas or examples that are connected to these main ideas. You may also add in other questions that come up or interesting facts that you find. Read the example listing brainstorm below. Notice how this writer has added many ideas and a few questions or examples to the list. As well, this writer has reviewed the list and crossed out repeated ideas.

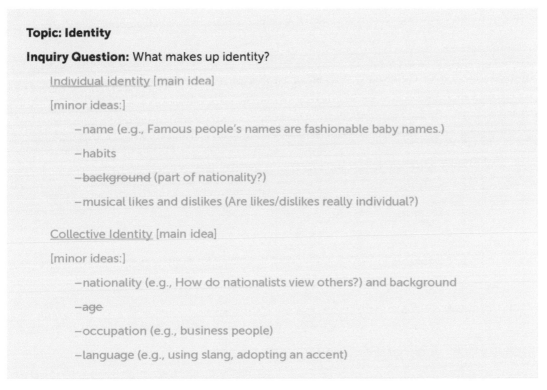

Topic: Identity

Inquiry Question: What makes up identity?

Individual identity [main idea]

[minor ideas:]

    —name (e.g., Famous people's names are fashionable baby names.)

    —habits

    —background (part of nationality?)

    —musical likes and dislikes (Are likes/dislikes really individual?)

Collective Identity [main idea]

[minor ideas:]

    —nationality (e.g., How do nationalists view others?) and background

    —age

    —occupation (e.g., business people)

    —language (e.g., using slang, adopting an accent)

FIGURE 1.3   Example listing brainstorm

Activity A | To help you start thinking about ideas, reread the freewriting you did for your Unit Inquiry Question in Activity B on page 4. Then create a listing brainstorm for your Unit Inquiry Question. Include as many ideas as possible. Can you think of any new ideas not found in your freewriting?

Formal Outline

After brainstorming about a topic, the next step in the writing process is planning how to organize all the ideas you want to include in your writing. An outline helps you organize your ideas. It also helps you to avoid repetition. Finally, it helps you make sure that you include all of your most important ideas.

A formal outline can contain a title, the main idea, supporting ideas, specific details related to the supporting points, and a concluding idea. If you are writing a formal outline for an opinion paragraph, your main idea is your opinion about the topic, and the supporting ideas include the reasons and evidence you have for your opinion. You may also include specific details as evidence, including facts, explanations, examples, and statistics.

Finally, the concluding idea can be a restatement of your main idea. In your outline, the headings and indented sub-headings show the main idea, concluding idea, supporting ideas, and details related to the supporting ideas. You can add as many or as few supporting ideas and details to your outline as needed to support your main idea. Generally speaking, for a short paragraph, two or three supporting ideas should be enough to explain your main idea. Below is an example of a typical outline for a short paragraph of around 100 words.

Title:

I.   Main idea:

   A. Supporting idea:

      1. Detail:

      2. Detail:

   B. Supporting idea:

      1. Detail:

      2. Detail:

   C. Supporting idea:

      1. Detail:

      2. Detail:

II. Concluding idea:

FIGURE 1.4 A general outline for a paragraph

Creating an outline that includes more than just a simple list of points helps you to think more deeply about your topic. Look at the example of a formal outline in Figure 1.5. Notice how this outline uses indenting and labels to show relationships. Roman numerals (I, II) and letters (A, B) show the relationship between the main points and the supporting points. In addition, notice how Arabic numbers (1, 2, 3), show the relationship between each supporting idea and its specific details. Lower case letters are used for examples and statistics. As well, notice how short phrases are used for the supporting points.

Title: Identity Changes and Social Groups

I.   Main idea: People often choose their clothes based on what specific group they identify with.

   A.   Supporting idea: Groups of people with similar hobbies wear certain fashions.

      1.   Detail: Skateboarders like to wear hooded sweatshirts and baggy jeans.

      2.   Detail: Some clothing stores exist just for special groups, e.g., skateboard shops.

      3.   Detail: Sales at specialized clothing stores are growing (almost 7 percent of all sales).

   B.   Supporting idea: Jobs also influence what clothes people wear.

      1.   Detail: Business people might want to wear dark suits to appear professional.

      2.   Detail: College students might dress in casual clothes such as khakis.

   C.   Supporting idea: Nationality might also influence clothing choices

      1.   Detail: Some countries, e.g., Japan, have traditional clothing like yukata and kimono.

      2.   Detail: 10 percent of Canadians wear shorts, even in winter, to show the cold doesn't bother them.

II.   Concluding idea: Clothing can be a good indicator of the groups people belong to.

FIGURE 1.5   Example paragraph outline

Activity B | Reread the paragraph you wrote in Activity F on page 14. Use the information in your paragraph to create a "reverse outline" for your paragraph. A reverse outline is a useful revising technique that allows you to review the first draft of a paragraph and make sure you have included all the necessary points in your draft.

Find the main idea in your paragraph and write it in the outline template below. Remember, in an opinion paragraph, your main idea is your opinion about the topic. Then find and write in your supporting ideas. Your suppporting ideas will include your reasons and evidence for your opinion. You might also have some details related to your supporting ideas such as facts, examples, and statistics. Finally, add your concluding idea to complete the outline. This outline template will help guide you. You may need to add or delete lines, depending on how the outline template fits the paragraph you wrote. If you did not include a title in the first draft, now is a good time to give your paragraph a title.

Title:
I.   Main idea:
   A.   Supporting idea:
      1.   Detail:
      2.   Detail:
   B.   Supporting idea:
      1.   Detail:
      2.   Detail:
   C.   Supporting idea:
      1.   Detail:
      2.   Detail:
II.   Concluding idea:

Activity C | Look back at the listing brainstorm you created for your Unit Inquiry Question in Activity A on page 15. Using ideas from that brainstorm, create an outline for a paragraph that answers your Unit Inquiry Question. Think about your opinion, reasons, and evidence as you include one main idea, at least two or three supporting ideas, and some details in your outline.

Content Skill

Evaluating Information from Websites

Not all the information you find on the Internet is going to be useful for your writing. You need to look carefully at online material to make a decision about whether the information is reliable. A reliable source will often have the following:

- factual information;
- opinions based on facts;
- current information;
- information that is well supported by other people's ideas;
- citations or references; and
- hyperlinks to other reliable sources.

Activity A | With a partner or small group, arrange the following examples into the chart below based on how reliable you think the information on each type of website would be. Discuss your answers with the group.

- a personal web page made by your friend
- an entertainment news website
- a website for a national newspaper
- a university department's web page showing current research
- a company's website advertising their latest product
- [name of website you frequently use] _____.

Most Reliable	1.
	2.
	3.
	4.
	5.
Least Reliable	6.

Activity B | The following article is based on an excerpt of an article from the website of *The Brock Press*, the official weekly student newspaper of Brock University in St. Catharines, Ontario. As you read, think about your opinion of the information given about subcultures. Is this article a reliable source of information that might help to answer your Unit Inquiry Question? Why or why not? Use the guiding questions found after the article to discuss your ideas with a partner or small group.

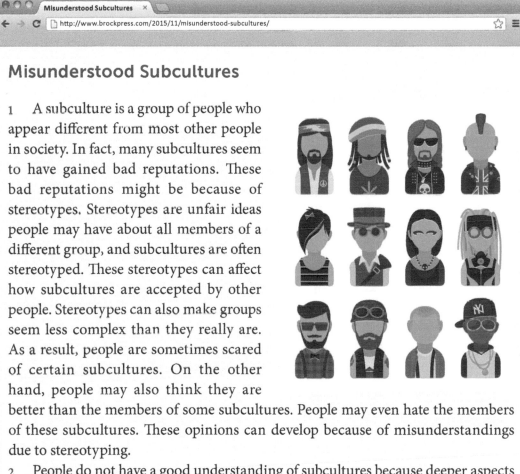

Misundersood Subcultures ×

http://www.brockpress.com/2015/11/misunderstood-subcultures/

Misunderstood Subcultures

1   A subculture is a group of people who appear different from most other people in society. In fact, many subcultures seem to have gained bad reputations. These bad reputations might be because of stereotypes. Stereotypes are unfair ideas people may have about all members of a different group, and subcultures are often stereotyped. These stereotypes can affect how subcultures are accepted by other people. Stereotypes can also make groups seem less complex than they really are. As a result, people are sometimes scared of certain subcultures. On the other hand, people may also think they are better than the members of some subcultures. People may even hate the members of these subcultures. These opinions can develop because of misunderstandings due to stereotyping.

2   People do not have a good understanding of subcultures because deeper aspects of a subculture are often ignored in the media. In the mainstream media, subcultures are not represented in a complex way. The media often relies on stereotypes and typical images. As a result, people do not see what subcultures are really about.

3   Dr. Scott Henderson, the chair of Brock University's Department of Communication, Popular Culture, and Film, says that people usually focus on what is easy to see about a subculture. They may misunderstand what they see. He thinks that we live in a visual culture, and we decide things immediately based on what we see. Thus, we may base what we think about the members of a subculture just on their external images. However, subcultures involve more than just the external images.

Source: Based on Greenwood, S. (2015, November 10). Misunderstood subcultures. *The Brock Press*. Retrieved from http://www.brockpress.com/2015/11/misunderstood-subcultures/

Use these guiding questions to help determine if a source found on the Internet is reliable:

1. Does the source include factual information?
2. Are the opinions based on facts?
3. Is the information current?
4. Is the information supported by other people's expert ideas?
5. Are there citations or references?
6. Are there hyperlinks to reliable sources?

Reference Skill

Using APA Style

Academic writers are expected to use a style of referencing sources that is specific to the subject area in which they are writing. One common citation style that you may encounter is APA. APA stands for the American Psychological Association. This style is typically used in education, science, and psychology (and many other subject areas).

You are not expected to memorize all the rules, but you should become familiar with the style. Some of the basics of APA are presented in this book.

In-Text Citations   If you use another person's words or ideas in your writing, you need to include an in-text citation. An in-text citation is a note in the text that clearly shows which words and ideas come from another person. An in-text citation includes the last names of the authors along with the publication date. If you are using a direct quotation, you also include the page number. Consider the short paragraph below with two underlined in-text citations referring to information from the reading "Who Are You?" on pages 12–13:

Clothing can be very important to some people. One reason people worry about their clothes may be related to identity. Perry-Globa, Weeks, Zelinski, Yoshida, and Colyer (2007) said that people express their identity through their clothing. For example, people who like sports may always wear running shoes and work-out clothes. Other people who enjoy rock music may wear leather jackets and ripped jeans. It seems like "one way that people express their individual identities is through what they wear" (Perry-Globa, Weeks, Zelinski, Yoshida, & Colyer, 2007, p. 25). Clothes are an essential part of some people's identities.

References   If you use words and ideas from another person in your writing, you also need to include a References list that gives full details about your sources. The References list contains one entry for each different in-text citation you used. The

References list is at the end of a piece of academic writing. Here is an example of a reference entry for the book cited in the example paragraph in Activity A on pages 5–6. Notice the different pieces of information needed for an entry in a References list.

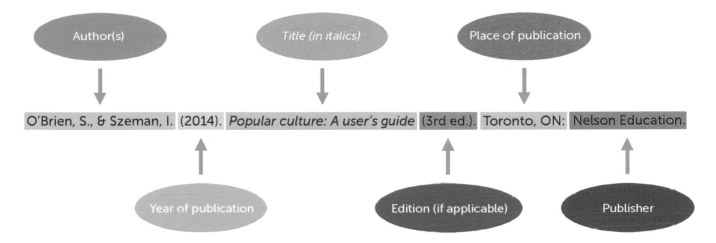

Below is an entry in a References list for the book *Living in a Globalizing World*. The reading on pages 12–13 came from this book.

Perry-Globa, P., Weeks, P., Zelinski, V., Yoshida, D., & Colyer, J. (2007). *Living in a globalizing world*. Don Mills, ON: Oxford University Press.

Below is an entry in a References list for the online article "Misunderstood Subcultures," which was referenced on page 19. A reference entry for a website or an online article requires different information than a reference entry for a book.

Greenwood, S. (2015, November 10). Misunderstood subcultures. *The Brock Press*. Retrieved from http://www.brockpress.com/2015/11/misunderstood-subcultures/

Activity A | Label the following citation for a book with one author with the following: title, author, publisher, place of publication, year of publication.

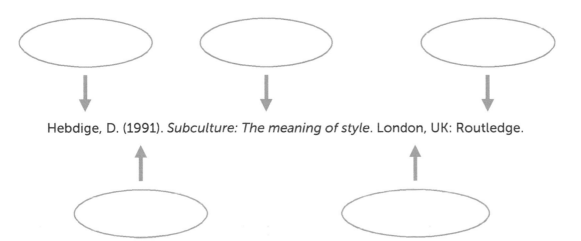

Preventing Plagiarism

Understanding Academic Integrity

Academic integrity means carrying out your studies and completing your work in an honest way. It is not always easy to understand the expectations around academic integrity because in different academic cultures, the rules and expectations might be different. It is very important for you to learn about the academic integrity expectations at your college or university, especially if you are new to studies in Canada.

In Canada, colleges and universities have the following four common expectations around academic integrity.

✓ **Do your own work without extra help.**
Do not copy or purchase assignments and do not submit assignments that you have not completed on your own, unless you have permission to collaborate.

✓ **Cite your sources.**
Clearly reference all ideas and words from outside sources.

✓ **Submit an assignment only once.**
Do not submit the same assignment for two courses.

✓ **Help other students to be academically honest.**
Do not let other students copy your work and report any academic integrity challenges to your instructor to be fair to all students.

Format and Organization Skill

Organizing Opinion Paragraphs

Typically, an academic paragraph is a group of sentences collected around one main idea. An academic paragraph has a clear structure. This structure usually includes a topic sentence, supporting sentences, and a concluding sentence. Opinion paragraphs are academic paragraphs that tell readers what the writer thinks about something based on reasons and evidence. Thus, when you are writing an opinion paragraph, you can use ORE structure (see page 5) to organize the ideas in your paragraph. Your topic sentence will include your opinion. Then your supporting sentences will include the reasons and evidence that support your opinion.

Your academic paragraph may also include the opinions of others to help provide support for your own opinions. Remember that when you include other people's ideas, you must use in-text citations and references. Academic paragraphs can vary in length, but the basic structure will usually remain the same. The chart on page 23 explains the structure and organization of an academic opinion paragraph.

Topic Sentence	A topic sentence is a single sentence that states your opinion on a narrowed topic. It is not necessary that everyone agree with your opinion, but you should have an opinion that can be supported with good reasons and evidence.
Supporting Sentences	The supporting sentences show the reasons you have the opinion presented in your topic sentence. You should also provide evidence to support the reasons for your opinion. For example, you can use examples, facts, quotes, paraphrases of other people's ideas, and summaries of articles as evidence.
Concluding Sentence	A concluding sentence is a restatement of your opinion, using different words and sentence structure than you used in your topic sentence.

Activity A | Examine the following student paragraph on subcultures. Notice the structure and organization of the paragraph. Then discuss the questions below with a partner.

Subcultures are often unfairly viewed by others as a negative influence. — Topic Sentence

Part of this perception most likely comes from the wrong idea that everyone who belongs to a subculture is upset with the mainstream culture. Laura Weibe (2015), an Associate Professor in Communication and Popular Culture, argues in the article "Misunderstood Subcultures," that well-known subcultures get the most media attention because they are the most spectacular. This media attention creates stereotypes that can be harmful to the subculture. Consequently, changing the perception of how subcultures are seen may allow more people to participate in some wonderful groups. — Supporting Sentences

All in all, it is unfair to stereotype all subcultures as having a bad influence on society. — Concluding Sentence

Reference

Greenwood, S. (2015, November 10). Misunderstood subcultures. *The Brock Press*. Retrieved from http://www.brockpress.com/2015/11/misunderstood -subcultures/

1. Is the topic sentence narrow enough given the length of the paragraph?
2. What opinion is presented in this paragraph?
3. Is the opinion something that can be supported with reasons and evidence?
4. What reasons are provided to support the author's opinion?
5. What type of evidence is presented in the supporting sentences?
6. Is the concluding sentence similar to the topic sentence?

Activity B | Writing Task: Opinion Paragraph | Write an academic opinion paragraph giving your own views on subcultures. Use ORE structure to organize your ideas.

Activity C | Exchange your paragraph with a partner and check your partner's paragraph organization using the list of questions below.

1. Does the topic sentence contain a clear opinion?
2. Does the paragraph offer a clear reason for the opinion?
3. Does the paragraph include evidence to support the opinion?
4. Does the paragraph have a concluding sentence?
5. Does the concluding sentence restate the writer's opinion in a way that is different from the topic sentence?

Topic Skill

Writing Topic Sentences

The first sentence in an academic opinion paragraph using ORE structure is usually the topic sentence. Some common problems with topic sentences in opinion paragraphs include

- not stating a clear opinion;
- stating a fact instead of an opinion;
- including too many main or supporting ideas; and
- giving an opinion that cannot be supported with reasons and evidence.

Creating a short answer for your Unit Inquiry Question can help you to produce a topic sentence.

Examples

1. **Inquiry question**: Can the Internet change people's identity?
   Topic sentence: The Internet can have a major effect on how people's identities change.

2. **Inquiry question**: Can identity change over time?
   Topic sentence: People's sense of their identity can change over time because of several factors in their lives.

Activity A | Match each inquiry question below with the most appropriate topic sentence.

Inquiry Questions	Topic Sentences
_____ 1. What kinds of experiences can define people?	a. Identity is flexible and can change based on a number of external and internal factors.
_____ 2. Is identity fixed?	b. Group membership offers many benefits, but it often comes with a loss of individuality.

_____	3. What do people give up when they belong to a group?	c. People have more freedom to be themselves when they do not belong to a group.
_____	4. Why would someone choose not to belong to a group?	d. Negative experiences can define people, but often in surprising and unexpected ways.

Narrowing Topic Sentences

Inexperienced writers may sometimes start with a topic sentence that is too broad. If the main idea of the topic sentence is too broad, it will be hard to cover it in a single paragraph. In an effective academic opinion paragraph, the topic sentence will tell readers what they can expect in the paragraph.

The topic sentence in an opinion paragraph usually has two parts. The topic is what the paragraph is about, and the controlling idea relates to one specific opinion about the topic. If your topic sentence is too broad, you can narrow it down to one topic and one specific controlling idea. However, remember that if your topic sentence is too narrow, you may not have enough support to write an effective paragraph.

Too broad
Students' part-time jobs and hobbies can have a big impact on how they see themselves and who they are friends with.
topics + controlling ideas

Narrowed down
Students' part-time jobs can have a big impact on how they see themselves.
topic + controlling idea

Activity B | Review the following topic sentences and decide which ones are too narrow (N) or too broad (B). Discuss your answers with a partner or small group.

1. Some people think that everyone has an identity. _____

2. It has been said that people today can join many different subcultures. _____

3. Teenagers who are 12 or 13 years old in Toronto who are part of the DIY neo-punk subculture are likely to be rejected by their parents. _____

4. Identity crises hurt. _____

Activity C | Revise the broad and narrow topic sentences in the previous activity to create effective topic sentences better suited for an academic opinion paragraph.

Activity D | Choose one of the following subjects and write three possible topic sentences for it. Then decide which one of your three topic sentences would be best to start an opinion paragraph.

1. language and its influence on identity
2. English language learner identity
3. influence of a group on individual identity
4. influences of friends on identity

Subject #_____

a. _____

b. _____

c. _____

Best topic sentence: _____, because _____

Activity E | The following two paragraphs are missing their topic sentences. Write a topic sentence for each paragraph that best fits with the main and supporting ideas. Then compare your topic sentences with a partner or small group.

1. _____
_____ The reason is that people spend much of their time at work. Being at work for at least eight hours a day affects how people think of themselves and how others think about them. For example, when meeting someone for the first time, you might ask, "what do you do?" The answer is usually tied to a person's work, and might be something like, "I am an accountant," or "I am a teacher." It would be very rare for someone to say something other than their occupation. Clearly, people often see their jobs as one of the most important aspects of their identity.

2. _____
_____ Not everyone likes his or her job. For example, a young university graduate might work as a junior accountant during the day, but spend every weekend mountain biking. She might also belong to a mountain biking club, and shop at stores that sell mountain biking gear. Another person might be a restaurant manager. However, what he really loves is trains. During his vacation, he travels all around the country taking pictures of trains. He then posts those pictures on his blog about trains that he writes in his spare time. Sometimes what people do outside of work reflects their true identities.

Activity F | Look back at the short opinion paragraph you wrote in Activity B on page 23 and identify its topic sentence. If your paragraph does not have a strong topic sentence, write one that expresses a clear opinion that works with the rest of the paragraph. Be prepared to share your topic sentence with the class.

Activity G | Writing Task: Topic Sentence for Unit Inquiry Question | Look back at the listing brainstorm you did in Activity A on page 15 and the outline you created in Activity B on page 17 for your Unit Inquiry Question. Write a topic sentence that contains both a topic and a controlling idea in response to your Unit Inquiry Question. Then compare your topic sentence with a partner or small group, and be prepared to share your topic sentence with the class.

Conclusion Skill

Restating

The last sentence of a paragraph is usually the concluding sentence. This sentence can remind readers of the main idea of the paragraph. The concluding sentence often restates the topic and controlling idea from the topic sentence. In an opinion paragraph, the concluding sentence includes a restatement of the opinion from the topic sentence.

Paraphrasing the topic sentence, or restating an idea in a new and different way, is a useful strategy to create a concluding sentence. Paraphrasing involves using different words and grammar to express the same idea. You can use a thesaurus to help you find synonyms and antonyms of the keywords from your topic sentence. You can also try to use a different sentence structure than in the topic sentence.

Many writers will introduce a concluding sentence with a connector that shows the reader that the paragraph is coming to an end. Common concluding connectors are *in the end, all in all, to sum up, in summary, in short, in conclusion,* and *to conclude.*

Activity A | Write a concluding sentence for each of the topic sentences below. Your concluding sentence should restate the main idea using different words than those in the topic sentence. The first one has been completed for you.

1. Identity is flexible due to several external and internal factors.

   As a result of the many factors that impact our lives, identity is something that frequently changes.

2. Group membership offers significant benefits, even if it may lead to some loss of individuality.

3. Many people spend their lives trying to fit in with others, but people can have more freedom when they do not belong to a group.

4. Negative experiences can help define people, but often in surprising and unexpected ways.

5. Personal identity is partly constructed by our interactions with others.

6. A person in a subculture can maintain his or her individuality within the group.

Activity B | Look back at the short opinion paragraph you wrote in Activity B on page 23 and identify its concluding sentence. If your paragraph does not have a clear concluding sentence, write one that restates the main idea of the paragraph. Be prepared to share your topic sentence with the class.

Activity C | Writing Task: Concluding Sentence for Unit Inquiry Question | Write a concluding sentence based on the topic sentence related to your Unit Inquiry Question you wrote for Activity G on page 27. In your concluding sentence, try to restate the main idea from the topic sentence using different words and sentence structure. Then compare your concluding sentence with a partner or small group and be prepared to share it with the class.

WRITING FUNDAMENTALS

Composition Skill

Developing Topics and Supporting Ideas

Once you have developed your topic sentence and your concluding sentence, you need to think about how you are going to express the supporting ideas. Your supporting ideas can include both reasons and evidence.

An opinion needs to be supported by a reason to gain the trust and support of the reader. A reason tells readers why you have an opinion. For example, if you have the opinion that the media affects how people understand their identity, your reason might relate to the fact that people interact with the media every day. This daily interaction can have a big impact on what people think about themselves.

Evidence provides support for your opinions and reasons. Consider the following paragraph on Japanese animation subculture in Regina, Saskatchewan. The paragraph has been put into a table so you can see how ORE (opinion, reasons, evidence) structure has informed the topic development and supporting ideas.

Title	The *Otaku* Subculture in Regina, Saskatchewan
Opinion (topic sentence)	Although Saskatchewan is far from Japan, being *otaku* (someone who likes Japanese animation and comic books) places you within a popular subculture in Regina.
Reason (supporting sentence)	One reason *otaku* subculture is popular in Regina is that there are fun social events, including Otakupalooza.

Evidence (supporting sentences including facts, examples, and statistics)	Started in 2011, Otakupalooza is an annual convention in Regina. The Facebook page for Otakupalooza has over 295 "likes" and 289 followers, which is pretty good in a small city like Regina. At Otakupalooza, fans can go to workshops, listen to expert speakers, and dress up like their favourite characters from television shows and comic books such as Naruto and Pokémon. There are also games of live human chess, trivia competitions, and costume contests. All of these activities help convention-goers to have a great time, and they don't have to leave Regina to do it.
Opinion Restated (concluding sentence)	All in all, because of enjoyable events like Otakupalooza, there is a happy group of people in Regina who are big fans of Japanese animation.

As you write your own opinion paragraphs, keep in mind your organizational structure. Your reader does not have to agree with your opinion, but you do need to have enough organized support for your arguments to show the reader that your ideas are valid.

Activity A | Read the paragraph below. Decide what reasons or support you would add to the gaps below—more than one answer may be possible. When you are done, discuss your ideas with a partner or small group.

> Youth Subcultures Still Exist
>
> Many parents think that youth subcultures no longer exist, but that is false. Young people today _____. They create online videos of themselves and their interests. For example, _____. There is a vibrant community online where individuals can meet similar people. This has allowed subcultures to expand beyond local neighbourhoods. In conclusion, subcultures haven't gone away; they have simply changed.

Activity B | Writing Task: Opinion Paragraph | With a partner or small group, brainstorm a list of subcultures. Some examples of subcultures include YouTubers, Japanese animation fans, soccer fans (or fans of hockey, baseball, basketball, and so on), country music fans, heavy metal fans, hipsters, gamers, yoga lovers, and punks. Choose one from your list, then brainstorm everything you know about that subculture. Finally, work on your own to write a short paragraph. Remember to support your opinion with reasons and evidence.

Activity C | Exchange your paragraph with a partner. Use the questions below to review your partner's paragraph, then share your answers with each other.

1. Does the paragraph have enough reasons to support the opinion expressed?
2. Are the supporting ideas related to the reasons?

3. Is there variety in the types of supporting ideas presented?
4. Is the paragraph organized in an opinion pattern that you recognize?

Sentence and Grammar Skill

Using Simple Past and Simple Present

Opinion writing can involve a variety of verb tenses. For example, opinion paragraphs could be written in the simple present or the simple past. As you begin to write longer work, you will notice that you need a variety of verb tenses to communicate your thoughts.

Note that opinions are often given in the simple present tense, but as in the examples below, it is sometimes necessary to use the simple past.

Example	Explanation
Simple Present	
1. I believe that language plays an important role in defining a person's identity.	Generally, use the simple present to introduce an opinion.
2. Culture affects how people develop their sense of identity.	Use the simple present to express facts or ideas that are considered accepted truths.
3. It is generally believed that some tattoos are connected to certain subcultures, such as biker gangs.	Use *it is*, *there is*, or *there are* to express general statements or commonly held opinions.
4. There are many different cultural groups living in Canada.	
5. There seem to be a lot more ways for people to express their identity today than there were 100 years ago.	Use *it/there seem(s) to be* to express a less certain idea or situation.
Simple Past	
6. I felt proud to belong to my school chess club when I was younger.	Use the simple past to introduce an opinion that has since changed. It is good to use a time phrase or clause to indicate that this opinion was held in the past.
7. There was a strong traditional Irish community in my city.	Use *there was/were* to express facts, generally accepted truths, or commonly held opinions about the past.
8. There were a lot of social clubs in small towns in the old days.	
9. There seemed to be less pressure on students in the past to belong to a group.	Use *it/there seemed to be* to express a less certain idea or situation in the past.

Generally, it is a good idea in academic writing to be as consistent as possible with your verb tenses. Using one tense within a paragraph or section can help keep your writing clear.

Activity A | Read the following paragraph written by a student on the topic of fashion in subcultures. As you read, pay attention to the verb tenses. Underline the simple present tense and double underline the simple past tense.

Clothing Can Show Subculture Membership

Wearing specific clothing is a popular way for people to show that they belong to a subculture. For example, punk is a subculture that started in the 1970s. At that time, punks were unhappy with the government and with the economic situation. To separate themselves from people who accepted the government and the mainstream culture, they wore clothes that were very different. For instance, some punks used a lot of safety pins on their clothes to show they were different. They also sometimes wore ripped clothing, a lot of buttons, and leather belts. Because of these fashions, people knew that punks belonged to a subculture.

Activity B | Read the sentences below and fill in the blanks with one of the verbs provided. Decide if each verb should be in the present tense or the past tense. Discuss your answer with a partner or small group.

be	believe	express	seem	think

1. In general, I _____ that young people can easily find a variety of subcultural groups today.

2. In the 1950s, there _____ to be a lot of pressure on children to match their identity with their family's expectations.

3. I _____ that the Internet has a huge influence on how people see themselves.

4. In yesterday's lecture, Professor Smith _____ doubt that subcultures were simply a refusal of mainstream culture.

5. There _____ a lot of evidence that people can have more than just one identity.

Reporting Verbs

Reporting verbs are used to introduce the ideas of other people in your writing. There are many reporting verbs, including *say, claim, think, believe, report, argue, assert, conclude,* and *maintain.*

Singh (2013) thinks gender roles are often reinforced by popular culture.

Professor Li believes that identity can be influenced by popular television shows.

Some sociologists claim that there are fewer subcultures than in the past.

In general, we use the past tense of reporting verbs to introduce the opinions held by others in the past.

Before her 2013 study, Professor Idris believed that the acquisition of language was a key moment in identity development.

After interviewing several people, Dr. Yamada concluded that more research into gender identity was needed.

Activity C | Dr. Scott Henderson from Brock University talked about the following ideas in the article "Misunderstood Subcultures" (Greenwood, 2015). Fill in the blanks with one of the reporting verbs below. Use the past tense of the reporting verb in each sentence. Note that the reporting verbs may fit correctly into more than one sentence.

argue	assert	believe	state

1. Dr. Henderson _____ that people usually focus on what is easy to see about a subculture, and they may misunderstand what they see.

2. Dr. Henderson _____ that we live in a visual culture, and we may judge things immediately based on what we see.

3. Dr. Henderson _____ that the average person may base what he or she thinks about a subculture just on external images.

4. Dr. Henderson _____ that subcultures are more complex than what is seen in external images.

Activity D | Choose one of the paragraphs you have written for this unit. Answer the following questions about your paragraph. Share your answers with a partner and discuss how each of you could improve the sentences in your paragraphs.

1. What verb tense is the most used in this paragraph?
2. Are there any other verb tenses used?
3. Are the verb tenses and forms used correctly?
4. If not, which tense do you think the verbs should be in?

Understanding a Writing Assignment

One of the first steps in the writing process is to understand the assignment. When you receive a writing assignment, ask yourself the following questions to make sure you understand how to complete it, and discuss any questions you might have with your instructor. Once you are clear about the assignment—its purpose, its format, and its reader or audience—you can then organize your time.

Think about the topic

- What topic am I writing about?

Think about the format

- What type of writing is it (for example, description, definition, explanation, or opinion)?
- How many words/pages should I write?
- What examples of previous writing assignments might be helpful?

Think about the process

- When is the assignment due?
- How much time will I need?
- When should I begin?
- How should I start my assignment?
- What do I need to submit with my writing?

UNIT OUTCOME

Writing Assignment: Opinion Paragraph

Write an opinion paragraph of 200 to 300 words on a topic related to identity or subculture. (Your instructor may give you an alternative length.) You may write on a topic based on your Unit Inquiry Question, develop another topic of your choosing connected to identity, or choose one of the following topics:

- Why does identity change over time?
- What is the most important factor in creating someone's identity?
- How does social media affect a person's identity?

Use the skills you have developed in this unit to complete the assignment. Follow the steps set out below to practise each of your newly acquired skills to write a well-developed paragraph.

1. **Brainstorm**: Use a listing brainstorm to come up with ideas related to your topic.

2. **Find information**: Find some information to support your main ideas. For example, you may choose to use information related to identity that you have read about in this unit.

3. **Compose a topic sentence**: Develop a focused topic sentence that states an opinion and includes a topic and a controlling idea.

4. **Outline:** Fill in the outline below to plan the first draft of your paragraph. You may make changes to the outline as necessary.

Topic Sentence

Focused topic sentence that states your opinion (topic + controlling idea):

Main Body (Supporting Ideas)

Supporting idea 1 (reasons and evidence):

Detail 1 (facts, examples, statistics, etc.):

Detail 2 (facts, examples, statistics, etc.):

Supporting idea 2 (reasons and evidence):

Detail 1 (facts, examples, statistics, etc.):

Detail 2 (facts, examples, statistics, etc.):

Supporting idea 3 (reasons and evidence):

Detail 1 (facts, examples, statistics, etc.):

Detail 2 (facts, examples, statistics, etc.):

Concluding Sentence

Concluding sentence restating the topic and controlling idea:

5. **Write a first draft:** Use your outline to write the first draft of your paragraph. Do not worry too much about spelling or grammar in the first draft. Try to get your ideas down on paper.

6. **Self-check**: Review the first draft of your paragraph for the following and revise as needed:

   - Review the organization of your supporting ideas. Make sure that you have good reasons and evidence for your opinion within ORE structure.

   - Remember to include evidence such as facts, examples, and statistics.

7. **Ask for a peer review**: Exchange the revised version of your first draft with a partner. Use the Evaluation Rubric below and on the next page to assess your partner's paragraph and provide suggestions to improve it. Consider your partner's feedback carefully and use it to make changes to your paragraph.

8. **Edit**: Edit your paragraph for the following:

   - Verb tenses: Check your verb tenses to ensure that you have used the present and the past tense appropriately.

   - Vocabulary: Check that you have used some of the AWL and mid-frequency vocabulary from this unit in your paragraph.

   - Transitions: Check that you have used transition words and phrases and concluding connectors appropriately. If you haven't used any transitions, think about adding some where needed.

9. **Write a final draft**: Write a final draft of your paragraph, making any changes you think will improve it. If possible, leave some time between drafts.

10. **Proofread**: Check the final draft of your paragraph for any small errors you may have missed. In particular, look for spelling errors, typos, and punctuation mistakes. If you used information from an outside source, double-check your in-text citations and your References list to make sure they are formatted properly.

Evaluation: Opinion Paragraph Rubric

Use the following checklist to evaluate your paragraph. In which areas do you need to improve most?

E = **Emerging**: frequent difficulty using unit skills; needs a lot more work
D = **Developing**: some difficulty using unit skills; some improvement still required
S = **Satisfactory**: able to use unit skills most of the time; meets average expectations for this level
O = **Outstanding**: exceptional use of unit skills; exceeds expectations for this level

Skill	E	D	S	O
The paragraph has a clear opinion that is not a simple statement of fact.				
Words and phrases for expressing opinions are used where appropriate.				

Content is organized logically using ORE structure, so readers can easily follow the writer's thinking.				
Transition words and phrases are used correctly and where appropriate, but they are not overused.				
There is good use of high-frequency vocabulary, with some lower frequency vocabulary choices.				
AWL and mid-frequency vocabulary items from this unit are used when appropriate and with few mistakes.				
If necessary, ideas and words from outside sources, such as websites, are accurately marked for the reader using reporting verbs.				
If required, APA-style in-text citations and a References list have been used.				
The paragraph is written in an academic style with a topic sentence, supporting sentences, and a concluding sentence.				
The topic sentence has a topic and controlling idea that show a clear opinion.				
The concluding sentence restates the main idea of the paragraph.				
Writing shows a good level of idea development and detail, with effectively organized supporting ideas.				
The present and past tenses have been used appropriately and with few errors.				

Unit Review

Activity A | What do you know now that you did not know before about identity or subcultures? Discuss with a partner or small group.

Activity B | Look back at the Unit Inquiry Question you developed at the start of this unit and discuss it with a partner or small group. Then share your answers with the class. Use the following questions to guide you.

1. What information did you find in this unit that helped you answer your question?
2. How would you answer your question now?

Activity C | Use the following checklist to review what you have learned throughout this unit. First decide which 10 skills you think are most important—circle the number beside each of these 10 skills. If you learned a skill in this unit that isn't listed on page 37, write it in the blank row at the end of the checklist. Then put a check mark in the box beside those points you feel you have learned. Be prepared to discuss your choices with the class.

Self-Assessment Checklist

☐	1. I can talk about identity and subcultures based on what I have read in this unit.
☐	2. I can develop an inquiry question.
☐	3. I can use ORE structure to organize a paragraph that includes an opinion, reasons, and evidence.
☐	4. I can use transition words and phrases to connect ideas in my writing.
☐	5. I can organize my vocabulary learning based on how frequently words are used in English. For example, I know to focus on higher frequency vocabulary first.
☐	6. I can use the AWL and mid-frequency vocabulary from this unit in my writing.
☐	7. I can distinguish fact from opinion.
☐	8. I can use the listing technique to brainstorm ideas for my writing.
☐	9. I can write a formal outline that shows the relationships between my ideas.
☐	10. I can evaluate the reliability of information from websites.
☐	11. I can use APA-style in-text citations and references for books and websites
☐	12. I can avoid plagiarism by understanding expectations related to academic integrity.
☐	13. I can write an effective topic sentence that expresses an opinion and includes a topic and a controlling idea.
☐	14. I can write an effective concluding sentence that restates the main idea of a paragraph.
☐	15. I can develop supporting ideas related to my topic.
☐	16. I can write a paragraph using simple present and simple past verbs appropriately.
☐	17. I can take the time to understand a writing assignment before I start.
☐	18. I can write an effective opinion paragraph.
☐	19.

Activity D | Put a check mark in the box beside the vocabulary items from this unit that you feel you can now use with confidence in your writing. Make a plan to practise the words that you still need to learn.

Vocabulary Checklist

☐ affect (v.) AWL		☐ generation (n.) AWL	
☐ aspect (n.) AWL		☐ identity (n.) AWL	
☐ belief (n.) 3000		☐ individual (adj.) AWL	
☐ crisis (n.) 3000		☐ inspire (v.) 3000	
☐ culture (n.) AWL		☐ jewellery (n.) 4000	
☐ dominant (adj.) AWL		☐ minority (n.) AWL	
☐ drawback (n.) 6000		☐ reflect (v.) 3000	
☐ dye (v.) 5000		☐ translate (v.) 3000	

UNIT 2

Environmental Sciences

Environmental Sustainability

EXPLORING IDEAS

Introduction

With 7 percent of the Earth's land surface, Canada possesses just about 7 percent of the world's renewable freshwater. Second only to Americans in their demands, Canadians use about 1650 cubic metres of freshwater per capita each year, more than double the average European rate.

Activity A | Discuss the following questions with a partner or small group.

1. Other than for agriculture, what are some common uses of water in your country?
2. Other than water, what are two valuable natural resources?
3. Are important resources, such as water and food, shared equally throughout the world? Explain.
4. How could governments make sure that enough of the world's resources are available for people's use now and in the future?
5. Do you think that the picture at the top of the page shows a responsible use of water? Why or why not?

Activity B | A Frayer model is a graphic organizer you can use to define a new word or concept. This model has four categories: definition, facts, examples, and non-examples. Use the ideas listed to define *sustainability*. Read each idea and decide in which category it fits best in the Frayer model below (Figure 2.1). Add in two more real-life examples and non-examples of your own. Share your Frayer model with a classmate and discuss how you define *sustainability*.

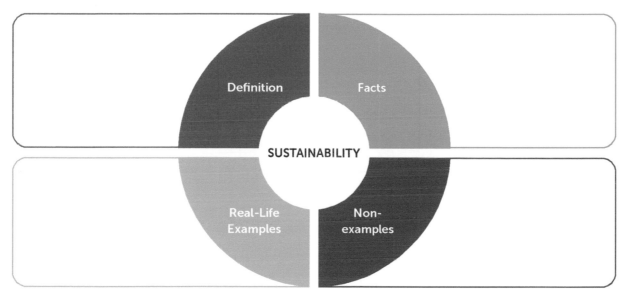

FIGURE 2.1 Frayer model

Ideas		
• the use of natural products and energy in a way that does not harm the environment	• 80 percent of a university's carbon footprint is from students and staff • forget to recycle or reuse paper	• save on household heating by lowering the temperature at home • do not turn lights on when leaving home in winter

Activity C | With a partner, review the examples of sustainable activities that you added to the Frayer model in Activity B. Discuss what you think are the most important ways that students could help their school campuses be a little more environmentally friendly.

Fostering Inquiry

Exploring Cause and Effect

Cause-and-effect inquiry questions often ask *why* or *how* something happens (cause) or *what* happens *when* (effect). For example, to explore the topic of reducing energy use in the home, you might ask, *How can people reduce their household energy use?* (cause question) or you might ask, *What happens when people reduce their household energy use?* (effect question). The flowchart on page 42 shows how the same topic can be explored as a cause or as an effect, depending on how you choose to analyze it.

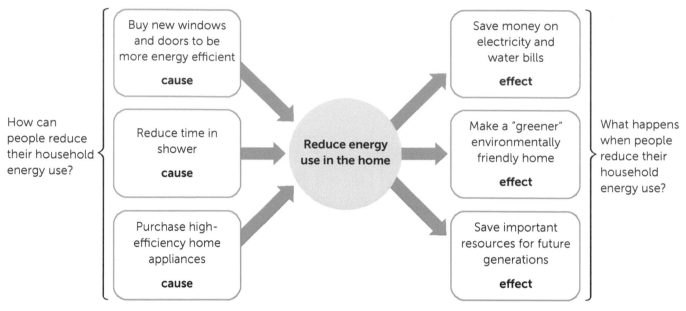

How can people reduce their household energy use?

Buy new windows and doors to be more energy efficient

cause

Reduce time in shower

cause

Purchase high-efficiency home appliances

cause

Reduce energy use in the home

Save money on electricity and water bills

effect

Make a "greener" environmentally friendly home

effect

Save important resources for future generations

effect

What happens when people reduce their household energy use?

FIGURE 2.2 Cause-and-effect flow chart

As you explore causes and effects, ask yourself the following:

1. Does the causal relationship actually exist? That is, does one thing actually cause another to happen, or is it just a coincidence? Does the relationship happen by chance?
2. Is the cause a major or a minor one?
3. Is the effect a short-term or a long-term one?

Activity A | What do you want to know more about in relation to the topic of environmental sustainability? For example:

- *How do everyday human activities affect the environment?*
- *What will happen when more people become concerned about global sustainability?*
- *How does greener local living help make the whole world greener?*

1. Write two or three questions you are curious about related to environmental sustainability.
2. When you are finished, compare your questions with a partner or small group.
3. Choose one question to guide you as you work through this unit. It does not have to be the same question as your partner or group. Your question may change as you learn more about your topic.
4. Write your inquiry question in the space provided. Look back at this question as you work through the unit. This is your Unit Inquiry Question.

My Unit Inquiry Question:

_____

_____

_____

_____

Activity B | Writing Task: Freewriting | Write for at least five minutes on the topic of your Unit Inquiry Question. Do not stop writing during this time. After five minutes, read what you have written and circle two or three ideas that you would like to explore further.

Structure

Cause-and-Effect Paragraph

Exploring causes and effects is one way to analyze a topic for your reader. Often, a cause-and-effect structure is used because it can explain the reasons behind an event (the cause) or the results or outcomes of an event (the effect).

Activity A | Read the cause-and-effect paragraph below, then answer the following questions with a partner or small group.

Green Universities

Universities play a key role in helping students learn about the environment. Bridgestock (2012) argues that students gain more than simply knowledge at university. In fact, they also develop values that will shape the rest of their lives. As a result, it is important for universities to provide environmental education. In addition to what they learn in the classroom, students can also get involved in environmentally friendly activities on campus. They could save energy and recycle used goods. Another reason for universities to take action is the fact that many staff and students spend most of their time on campus, and having that many people spend that much time in one place can lead to positive change if an effort is made. Bridgestock (2012) believes that university students do care about being "green." Student concern has led universities to create places for recycling and for donating unwanted goods. When universities work to reduce consumption, they contribute to environmental sustainability. In this way, universities can build environmentally friendly campuses.

Reference

Bridgestock, L. (2012, March 9). Green universities. *Top Universities*. Retrieved from http://www.topuniversities.com/student-info/choosing-university/green-universities

1. What two causes are mentioned in the paragraph?
2. What two effects are mentioned in the paragraph?
3. What words or phrases help you to recognize either the causes or the effects?

Focusing on cause or effect

Read the two related sentences below.

> These days, people have higher incomes. (cause)
>
> There is a demand for more products and services. (effect)

These sentences can be combined in two ways to focus the reader's attention on either the cause or the effect. Notice how this is done.

> People have higher incomes these days, and so there is a demand for more products and services.
>
> The demand for more products and services results from people having higher incomes.

The red words in the example sentences are used to express either cause or effect.

Language Tip

Expressing Cause and Effect

Specific words and phrases can show the cause-and-effect relationships that you want to explain to your reader. The chart below gives some examples of these common words and phrases, along with example sentences. The underlined part of the sentence expresses either cause or effect.

Causes		
because	1.	Because cities are rapidly expanding outward, less and less land is available to grow food.
when	2.	When polar ice melts in Canada's north, the water level in the Atlantic Ocean rises.
because of	3.	Because of the importance of climate change, there are many international conferences held to promote sustainability.
due to	4.	Due to the importance of water as an important global resource, Canada must play a role in water resource management.

Effects		
can result in	5.	Providing students with courses about sustainability can result in universities playing a vital role in protecting the environment.
lead to	6.	Recent student environmental activism has led to the university creating places for recycling and for donating unwanted goods.

Activity C | In the cause-and-effect sentence below, identify both the cause and the effect.

Universities play a vital role in protecting the environment, and so it is necessary for them to provide students with courses about sustainability.

1. Rewrite the sentence to emphasize the cause.

    _____

    _____

    _____

2. Rewrite the sentence to emphasize the effect.

    _____

    _____

    _____

Activity D | Read the short paragraph below about urbanization. Based on the ideas in the paragraph, write three sentences showing cause-and-effect relationships. One sentence should emphasize the cause, and two sentences should emphasize the effect. An example showing cause is given. Try using words and phrases from the *Language Tip* to write your sentences.

Impacts on Land

Much of the world's population is undergoing urbanization, the movement of people from rural areas to cities. In the United States, many people work in the cities but move into suburban areas around the cities. This suburban sprawl leads to traffic jams, inadequate infrastructure, and the reduction of land for farms and wildlife habitat. Meanwhile, housing within cities becomes more costly, more dense, and more difficult to find.

Source: Heithaus, M., & Arms, K. (2013). *Environmental science.* Boston, MA: Houghton Mifflin Harcourt.

Causes:

1. Rapid urbanization results in crowded living conditions in cities around the world.

2. _____

Effects:

3. _____

4. _____

Activity E | Share the sentences you just wrote with a partner. Identify the causes and the effects in your partner's sentences. Review the words or phrases used to express cause or effect. Are they used correctly?

Activity F | Revisit your Unit Inquiry Question on page 42. Now that you have learned more about your topic, you may have a better idea of how to answer your question, or you may consider revising it. Use the following questions to guide you in assessing your Unit Inquiry Question.

- What information have you learned that will help you answer your Unit Inquiry Question?
- What information do you still need to answer your question?
- Do you want to change your question in any way?

ACADEMIC READING

Vocabulary

Vocabulary Skill: Building Vocabulary by Learning Words with Related Meanings

Repeating words too often can make your writing boring for your reader. You can use different, but related, words to add variety. This will make your writing more academic and more interesting to the reader.

Learning words with related meanings is also an effective way to build your vocabulary. The more connections you can make between words, the faster you will be able to recall, and eventually remember, those words. The chart below shows five ways that words can be categorized in relation to one another.

Related By	Example
1. root word	environment/environmentalist/environmental
2. opposition (antonym)	future/past; successful/unsuccessful; water/land
3. similarity (synonym)	inhabitants/residents
4. inclusion (listing the parts or giving examples)	pollution → air pollution (e.g., CO_2), water pollution (e.g., chemicals), and land pollution (e.g., garbage)
5. common association	farm → farmer, livestock, land, crops

Activity A | Part of the paragraph on page 47 has been marked to show how words related in meaning can be used effectively. Read the paragraph and notice that the underlined words relate to *education* and the words in boxed relate to the *environment*.

Discuss the relationships between these words. Use the chart on page 46 to help you explain the relationships.

For example: The words *universities* and *students* are related by *inclusion* because the idea of *university* includes the idea of *students*.

Green Universities

Universities play a key role in educating students about the environment. Bridgestock (2012) argues that students gain more than simply knowledge at university. In fact, they also develop values that will shape the rest of their lives. As a result, it is important for universities to provide environmental education. In addition to what they learn in the classroom, students can also get involved in environmentally friendly activities on campus. They could save energy and recycle used goods.

Vocabulary Preview: The Academic Word List

Activity B | Scan the academic reading "Global Sustainability and Prosperity" on pages 51–52 for the words listed below. Place a check (✓) beside words that you know, a question mark (?) beside words you may have learned, but are still not sure about, and an ✗ beside words that are new to you. Try to guess the meaning of any unfamiliar words from the context of the sentence in the academic reading.

achieve	impact	resource
capacity	issue	technique
erosion	perspective	

In the chart that follows, pick the definition that most closely matches the meaning of the word in the reading.

AWL Word	Definitions
1. achieve (v.)	a. succeed in reaching a goal b. cause something to happen
2. capacity (n.)	a. the amount or number of things that something can hold b. the ability to understand or to do something
3. erosion (n.)	a. the process by which wind or rain gradually destroys the land b. the process that makes something weak over time
4. impact (n.)	a. the force caused when one object hits another b. the powerful effect that something has on somebody/something

5. issue (n.)	a. one of a series of magazine articles
	b. a problem or a concern that many people care about
6. perspective (n.)	a. a point of view on a topic
	b. the depth in a work of art, such as in a drawing or painting
7. resource (n.)	a. the supply of something that a country, a company, or a person has
	b. the support to help someone reach a goal
8. technique (n.)	a. a particular way of doing something that requires special skills
	b. the way in which something is generally done

Vocabulary Preview: Mid-frequency Vocabulary

Activity C | The mid-frequency words in the chart below appear in the unit's reading "Global Sustainability and Prosperity." Read each sentence and decide which part of speech the bolded word is, then choose the best synonym for the word. The first one is done for you as an example.

Words and Example Sentence	Synonym Choices
1. **ideal** (_adj._) = _perfect_ Some experts have claimed that the Earth's carrying capacity for humans, or the **ideal** number of humans on Earth, is about one billion.	large important ~~perfect~~ popular
2. **massive** (_____) = _____ In order to feed growing populations, **massive** commercial farms grow crops to sell in other parts of the world.	
3. **prosperity** (_____) = _____ We often think of **prosperity** in terms of economics, but we also prosper by living healthy lives in healthy environments.	analysis goal growth success
4. **objectives** (_____) = _____ Canada's sustainable development **objectives** will be achieved if Canadians commit to the idea that sustainability will make the country's future bright.	

Activity D | The mid-frequency words bolded in the four example sentences on page 49 appear in some form in the unit's academic reading, "Global Sustainability and Prosperity." Read the sentences to help you choose the definition of each bolded word and write the meaning of the word on the line. For each word, give some other related words: synonyms, associated phrases, or opposites. Use an English dictionary to help you find the related words.

Definitions

- related to the emotional or mental part of a person, rather than the physical
- plants, living creatures, and the physical environment of a particular area
- ~~travel between work and home~~
- a substance that is needed to keep a living thing alive and to help it grow

1. In cities, workers **commute** daily by bus, streetcar, train, or subway.

    commute (v.)

    Definition: _____ travel between work and home _____

    Related words—associated phrases: _____ trip, ride, journey, carpool _____

2. The **ecosystem** on many islands is easy to damage because it is often unique. For example, tourists can be dangerous for the animals, birds, and plants on the Galapagos Islands.

    ecosystem (n.)

    Definition: _____

    Related words—synonyms: _____

3. Taking care of one's **spiritual** health is as important as taking care of the physical body.

    spiritual (adj.)

    Definition: _____

    Related words—opposites: _____

4. Soil that is continuously used for farming loses **nutrients** and eventually cannot be used to grow anything.

    nutrient (n.)

    Definition: _____

    Related—synonyms: _____

Reading

The reading "Global Sustainability and Prosperity" on pages 51–52 contains a series of excerpts from *Living in a Globalizing World*, a social studies textbook that introduces Canadian secondary students to global issues. The reading describes the rapid growth of the world's population and its impact on how people access and use natural resources.

Activity A | A T-chart is a graphic organizer that shows different sides of a topic. Read the following sentences and think about how each idea connects to the topic of *rapid population growth*. Decide whether each idea expresses a cause or an effect of rapid population growth. The first two ideas have been added to the chart for you. Share your answers in a small group and decide together if each cause is major or minor and if each effect is short- or long-term.

a. ~~A rapidly growing population uses resources faster.~~
b. ~~Everyone has the right to have children.~~
c. The food trade between countries expands.
d. More and more money is needed by families to spend on food and homes.
e. Better health education and better health care are available for women.
f. The world's population is expected to reach nine billion between 2025 and 2040.
g. Agricultural production must increase to provide food for the world's growing population.

Cause (major/minor)	Topic	Effect (short- or long-term)
(b) Everyone has the right to have children. (minor cause)	rapid population growth	(a) A rapidly growing population uses resources faster. (short-term effect)

Activity B | Before reading "Global Sustainability and Prosperity", mark the following statements as true (T) or false (F), based on your current understanding of urbanization. As you read the text, think about whether your answers are correct. Paragraph numbers have been provided to help you check your answers after you are done reading.

1. _____ More people are moving to cities now than at any other time in human history. (2)

2. _____ Less and less land is available to grow food because of urbanization. (3)

3. _____ Sustainability concerns only future generations. (4)

4. _____ The Earth's natural resources can support 10 billion people. (6)

5. _____ The world food trade should increase to create more opportunities for prosperity. (7)

6. _____ Agribusiness needs to grow so that farmers can provide more food for people. (8, 9)

Activity C | Read the textbook excerpt on pages 51–52 and look specifically for details that explain the causes or the effects of globalization, urbanization, or intensive farming. Underline or highlight any of these details and make a brief note in the margin of the text to help you recall the idea later.

READING

Global Sustainability and Prosperity

1   Sustainability and **prosperity** are two important issues related to globalization and the environment. The state of the natural environment forces us to ask tough questions about sustainability. We often think of prosperity in terms of economics, but we also prosper by living healthy lives in healthy environments.

Sustainability and Urbanization

2   One of the biggest changes worldwide in the last century has been urbanization, or the growth of cities. More people live in cities now than at any other time in history. The growth of cities affects the environment, the economy, and people within the cities, but it also has strong effects on those who do not live in cities.

FIGURE 2.3   Canada's sustainable development objectives

*Each **objective** shown in the diagram must be **achieved** in order for the others to succeed.*

3   When people live together in high concentrations, local land is not available to grow food. Food has to be brought into a city to feed the residents. There is also nowhere to put the waste that is generated by the large population. Waste needs to be transported out of the city. Public transit[1] may cut down on car traffic, but traffic in and out of the city may increase, especially if people are **commuting** from surrounding suburbs. Air quality may be affected as a result of increased highway traffic.

4   When we look at sustainability, prosperity, and globalization, we are often dealing with sustainable development. There are many different definitions of sustainable development, because there are multiple **perspectives** on the idea. The definition that is quoted most often is the UN's definition, which is "development that meets the needs of the present without compromising[2] the ability of future generations to meet their own needs." When sustainable development is successful, sustainability and prosperity are in balance.

Sustainability as a Global Issue

5   Living in a globalizing world has made it easier for many people to have "more" of everything— more contact with other parts of the world, more opportunities for trade, more goods available to consume. Yet not all people have "more." The situation is sustainable and prosperous only if there is enough for everyone. As people who live in a more developed country, Canadians consume many more **resources** than people in less developed countries.

Sustainability and Population

6   Some experts have claimed that the Earth's carrying **capacity** for humans, or the **ideal** number of humans on Earth, is about one billion. In 2005, the

---

[1] the system of buses, trains, etc. that people use to travel from one place to another

[2] weakening or harming

population was already at about six billion, and it is expected to reach nine billion between 2025 and 2040.

7　There are many different perspectives on population and its effects on the environment. Some people believe that policy is required to curb[3] population growth. Others believe that everyone has a right to have children. There are religious and **spiritual issues** to be considered, too. Population growth is a complex issue, but it is an important one to think about as we examine sustainability and prosperity. Is population growth sustainable?

Food for All

8　Some people believe that we must increase farming and agriculture to provide food for the world's growing population. Many farmers practise sustainable farming **techniques** to keep the environment near their farms healthy. Scientists are constantly creating new, more environmentally friendly ways to water crops, fertilize[4] soil, and keep away insects. Not all farmers can or do use sustainable practices, however. Consider some of the **impacts** of farming on the environment:

- To clear land for farming, **ecosystems** are changed or destroyed.
- Chemical pesticides and fertilizers can affect soil, groundwater, and wildlife.
- Soil that is continuously used for farming loses **nutrients** and eventually cannot be used to grow anything.
- Irrigation, or watering of large crops, can cause water waste if it is not done carefully.
- Irrigation can also cause **erosion**, or the washing away of soil, so that it cannot be used to grow plants.

9　One of the biggest challenges in our globalizing world is that of large-scale agricultural business, or agribusiness. In order to feed growing populations, **massive** commercial farms grow crops to sell in markets in other parts of the world. These agribusinesses are often given money by governments that help them keep prices low.

Sustainability and Trade

10　One of Brazil's biggest exports is soya beans, which are sold in China. Since 1995, 1.7 million hectares[5] of Brazilian rainforest have been cleared for agriculture. Why is China not growing soya beans locally? Since 1995, China has converted six million hectares of arable[6] land into developed land by building roads, cities, housing, and factories. China now has less land available on which to farm, and a population of more than 1.3 billion to feed.

Source: Excerpted from Perry-Globa, P., Weeks, P., Zelinski, V., Yoshida, D., & Colyer, J. (2007). *Living in a globalizing world* (pp. 248–261). Don Mills, ON: Oxford University Press Canada.

---

[3] to control or limit something, especially something bad

[4] to add a substance to soil to make plants grow more successfully

[5] a unit for measuring an area of land; 10,000 square metres

[6] used or suitable for growing crops

Activity D | Discuss the following questions with a partner or small group.

1. What is sustainability?
2. How has globalization affected prosperity in different parts of the world?
3. Why have sustainability and sustainable development become global issues?
4. Are there any ideas discussed in the text that you do not quite understand? Discuss anything you are not sure about.

Activity E | Revisit your Unit Inquiry Question on page 42. Are there any ideas from the reading that will help you answer your question? Share your ideas with a partner or small group. At this point, you may consider revising your Unit Inquiry Question. Use the following questions to help you in assessing your question.

1. How does the information from this reading change your understanding of environmental sustainability?
2. Which ideas from the reading can be used to help answer your Unit Inquiry Question?
3. What additional questions do you have after finishing the reading?
4. Where could you find more information?

Activity F | Writing Task: Cause-and-Effect Paragraph | Write a short paragraph about urbanization in today's world. In your paragraph, explain why cities are growing and what happens to people and to the environment when cities grow very large. Before you write, use a T-chart, a Frayer model, or another brainstorming technique that you have learned, to help you come up with ideas to write about. Try to include five of the vocabulary words from this unit in your paragraph, but make sure the paragraph is written in your own words.

Activity G | Compare your paragraph to the sample paragraph in Appendix 2, then answer the questions that follow. Share your answers with a partner or a small group.

1. What is the main idea of the paragraph?
2. Does the paragraph focus on the causes or the effects of urbanization?
3. Does the paragraph give major or minor causes of urbanization?
4. Does the paragraph discuss long-term or short-term effects of urbanization? Why?
5. What cause or effect words or phrases do you see in the paragraph?
6. After reading the sample paragraph, is there anything you would like to revise in your paragraph?

Critical Thinking

Identifying Reasons and Examples

A writer includes reasons and examples to develop main ideas and to show the reader that there is support for these ideas. Reasons and examples essentially explain a writer's statements for the reader.

For example, if you say that sustainability is an important issue for students, you will need to support this statement with reasons and examples. When you give easy-to-understand reasons and clear examples, readers are more likely to believe you. Choose reasons that can be clearly explained by examples and be sure to use language that shows you are giving reasons (*because, so*) or giving examples (*such as, for example*). Keep in mind that too many reasons with no examples may not be very believable for the reader. Examples based on your personal experiences may not be the best choice as they are not general enough.

When structuring your paragraph, present the reasons first because they relate to general ideas.

One or more specific examples, based on facts or statistics, should follow each reason. Try to present two or three good reasons with concrete examples.

Statement	Reasons	Examples
Sustainability is becoming a more important issue for students . . .	because students have learned more about greener living.	Students take environmental education courses.
		Many on-campus activities promote greener choices.
	because they notice that on-campus resource use seems wasteful.	Lights are left on in many classrooms overnight.
		Often a large amount of paper used in courses.

PROCESS FUNDAMENTALS

Brainstorming and Outlining

Cube Brainstorm

A cube brainstorm is a way of arranging ideas that allows you to easily see different perspectives, or points of view. A cube has six sides, so when you do a cube brainstorm, you consider six perspectives. Each perspective has a question you ask yourself to start your brainstorming:

Don't worry about answering every question completely: the purpose of brainstorming is to start your ideas flowing.

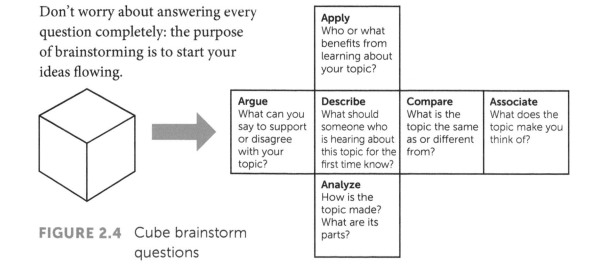

Apply
Who or what benefits from learning about your topic?

Argue
What can you say to support or disagree with your topic?

Describe
What should someone who is hearing about this topic for the first time know?

Compare
What is the topic the same as or different from?

Associate
What does the topic make you think of?

Analyze
How is the topic made? What are its parts?

FIGURE 2.4 Cube brainstorm questions

Activity A | Read the partially completed cube brainstorm below on the topic of recycling, then work in a small group to complete it. Each member of the group should choose one side of the cube and add at least two more ideas. Share your ideas as a group. A full-page unfolded cube is available for you to collect together and write down your group's ideas. Ask your instructor for a copy.

	Apply Recycling helps prevent waste.		
Argue Recycling is easy but only when you have time.	**Describe** Recycling is a way of reusing materials.	**Compare** Recyclables are NOT garbage.	**Associate** Recycling makes me think of other sustainable practices like reusing and reducing.
	Analyze Recycling is part of a bigger environmental program.		

Activity B | Reread the freewriting on your Unit Inquiry Question that you completed in Activity B on page 43. Choose one topic from your freewriting and complete a cube brainstorm on a separate page to expand your thinking around that topic.

Coordinating Ideas in an Outline

Coordinating ideas in an outline means arranging the ideas to show which ones belong together. In a well-coordinated outline, the relationship between ideas is easy to see: a more general or main point is at a higher level, while a supporting point is at a lower level.

Activity C | Figure 2.4 below is based on the sample paragraph found in Appendix 2. Read the outline, paying attention to its organization. Then discuss the following questions with a partner or small group.

1. What are the main points?
2. Are any facts or examples given?
3. How do you know that these are facts or examples?
4. Are the ideas in the outline equally developed?

I.   Topic: The cause and effects of urbanization

II.   Main point 1: People move to cities for opportunities.

    A.   Supporting point: Career or educational chances to improve

        1.   jobs, post-secondary education

    B.   Supporting point: People want to be successful.

III. Main point 2: Pollution and land loss are effects of urbanization.

    A.   Supporting point: Pollution changes the air quality.

        1.   The city grows hotter and smoggier.

    B.   Supporting point: New construction takes farmland away from growing food.

        1.   People eat food imported from outside the city.

FIGURE 2.4 Outline

Activity D | Use the following template to create a coordinated outline for a paragraph based on your Unit Inquiry Question. Add one or two supporting points for each of your main points.

I.   Topic: _____

II. Main point 1 (one important cause): _____

    A. Supporting point: _____

        1. _____

    B. Supporting point: _____

        1. _____

III. Main point 2 (two important effects): _____

    A. Supporting point: _____

        1. _____

    B. Supporting point: _____

        1. _____

IV. Concluding sentence: _____

Content Skill

Integrating Information from How-To Guides

How-to guides are often published by university or college student organizations, professors, or scientists. These guides present research from experts using easy-to-understand graphs, statistics, and short texts. How-to guides are written to inform the reader, so they provide useful general information on a topic.

Activity A | Read the excerpt below from a student guide to sustainable living. On a separate paper, take notes using the following headings. Remember that good note-taking means writing the ideas and information in your own words.

- purpose of the guide
- key topics
- facts/statistics

Green Guide

About This Guide

1   This guide has been created for the students, faculty, and personnel of the University of Waterloo looking to live more sustainable lifestyles. These suggestions aim not only to help in preserving the natural environment, but also to promote healthier and more economical[7] living. It is hoped that this guide will build awareness of on-campus and community resources available to both staff and students.

Showers and Toilet Use

2   In Canada, showers, baths, and toilet flushing account for 65 percent of water use inside the house. Reduce the number of showers you take or the length of time you're in the shower (consider turning the shower off while soaping up). You can also put a one-litre bottle filled with water and some sand, gravel,[8] or dirt into the toilet tank to reduce water usage for each flush.

Turn off Your Taps

3   There are many instances where you can avoid leaving the tap running. For example, rinse fruit

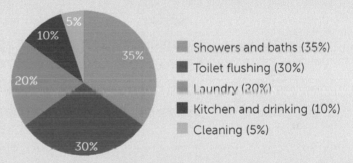

FIGURE 2.5 Water use in the home

and vegetables in a bowl of water, thaw[9] meats in the fridge overnight or in a bath of cold water, and wash dishes by filling one sink with wash water and the other with rinse water. Be wary[10] of leaking taps[11] or continuously running toilets, which can waste up to 200,000 litres of water in a year!

Source: Brum, C. (2014). *Green guide* (pp. 1, 5) Retrieved from https://uwaterloo.ca/sustainability/sites/ca.sustainability/files/uploads/files/sci-green-guide-2014-fall-web-40141.pdf

---

[7] using no more of something than is necessary

[8] small stones, often used to make the surface of paths and roads

[9] to let frozen food become soft or liquid

[10] careful when dealing with somebody/something because you think that there may be a problem

[11] a device for controlling the flow of water from a pipe into a bathtub or sink

Activity B | You need to evaluate all the information you read to see if it is reliable and useful for your writing assignment. Work in a small group to evaluate the information from the *Green Guide*. You may need to find the *Green Guide* online. Use the web address given in the blue box below. Together, answer the evaluation questions and share your results with the class.

1. Is the writer part of a college, a university, or the government?
2. Who is the intended reader of this guide?
3. Does the writer use outside sources to support the information in the guide?
4. Are the sources of the information (the references) listed in the guide?
5. Could you use the ideas and information from the guide in a writing assignment?

Reference Skill

Citing How-To Guides in APA Style

Most online how-to guides will be in the form of a web page or a PDF report. The *Green Guide* discussed in the previous activity is a downloadable PDF report. The bibliographic information for the document is set out below.

Author	Christian Brum
Organization	Sustainable Campus Initiative (University of Waterloo)
Report title	Green Guide
Date of publication	September 2014
Web address	https://uwaterloo.ca/sustainability/sites/ca.sustainability/files/uploads/files/sci-green-guide-2014-fall-web-40141.pdf

If you include any ideas, words, or statistics from an outside source in your writing assignment, you will need to write in-text citations and a References list. Here are examples of APA-style in-text citations and a references entry.

	APA Style
In-text citation	With a reporting expression: 1. According to the *Green Guide*, showers and baths account for the most water usage (35 percent) in the home (Brum, 2014). With a reporting verb: 2. Brum (2014) explains that showers and baths account for 35 percent of the water used in the home.
Reference entry	Brum, C. (2014, September). *Green guide*. Waterloo, ON: Sustainable Campus Initiative (University of Waterloo). Retrieved from https://uwaterloo.ca/sustainability/sites/ca.sustainability/files/uploads/files/sci-green-guide-2014-fall-web-40141.pdf

Activity A | The ideas below are from the *Green Guide*, of which you read and evaluated a few paragraphs in Activity B on page 58. Write complete sentences about students and sustainable activities and include an in-text citation in each sentence. For sentences 1 to 5, use the words and phrases given. Then write two more sentences with your own ideas and in-text citations. Follow the example in-text citations in the chart on page 58. For help with reporting verbs, see Unit 1, page 32. The first sentence has been written for you as an example.

1. According to the *Green Guide* / students / eat less meat / save money / save animals

   According to the Green Guide, students who eat less meat can save money and animals (Brum, 2014).

2. As the *Green Guide* points out / students / wash clothes / cold water / save energy

   _____

   _____

3. Brum / thinks / students / reuse items / reduce waste

   _____

   _____

4. According to / Brum / students / use scrap paper / make notes, jot down to-do lists, and work through homework problems.

   _____

   _____

5. Brum / encourages / students / be a little greener / join sustainability activities on campus

   _____

   _____

6. Your idea:

   _____

   _____

7. Your idea:

   _____

   _____

Managing Notes and Integrating Quotations

When you read a text for ideas to write about, you should keep detailed and organized notes. Note-taking has two main benefits: you can avoid accidental plagiarism and you can easily find the information later, when you begin writing. Using note cards or a note-taking worksheet are common ways to take notes. Ask your instructor if there is a specific note-taking method that you should follow.

Make sure you do the following when you take notes on a source of information:

- ✓ Copy down all the necessary bibliographic information accurately.
- ✓ Make it as easy as possible for you to find the information again.
- ✓ Write key or important phrases in your own words.
- ✓ Include a direct quotation only if the author says something in a specific way that you cannot rephrase.
- ✓ Write the page number where the quotation can be found.

- ✓ Use quotation marks if you copy a phrase or sentence from the original text.

Quotation marks show that the words are directly taken from the original text and have not been changed in any way. If you use a quotation, you must provide a page number in your APA-style in-text citation, as demonstrated below.

Brum (2014) explains that by promising to act in greener ways, universities and students can "help humanity overcome the challenges of environmental sustainability" (p. 1). This means that local actions can help everyone on Earth as well as the environment.

Brum, C. (2014, September). *Green guide*. Waterloo, ON: Sustainable Campus Initiative (University of Waterloo). Retrieved from https://uwaterloo.ca/sustainability/sites/ca.sustainability/files/uploads/files/sci-green-guide-2014-fall-web-40141.pdf

Format and Organization Skill

Organizing Cause-and-Effect Paragraphs

In cause-and-effect writing, you explain to the reader the cause-and-effect connections that you have found. However, you do not need to discuss all the causes and all the effects. If you write a short paragraph, you will most likely focus on either the most important cause or the most general effects.

- A focus-on-the-cause paragraph explains the most likely or significant cause and a few of the most important effects.
- A focus-on-the-effect paragraph explains a general effect and a few of the most important causes.

Figure 2.6 shows two possible ways to organize a cause-and-effect paragraph. Both formats help the reader to see the focus of your paragraph as well as your understanding of both the causes and effects.

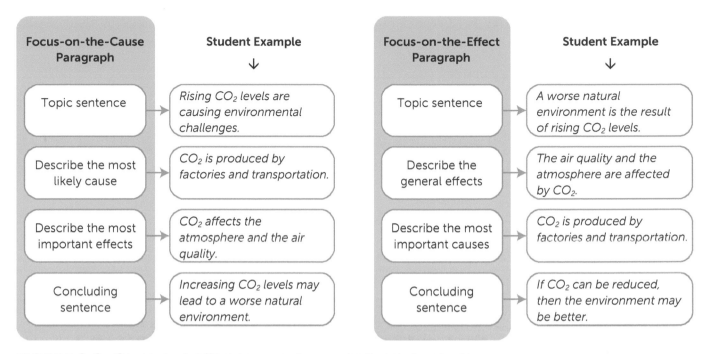

FIGURE 2.6 Cause-and-effect paragraph organizational structures

Activity A | Read the paragraph below. The topic sentence, one cause, and one effect in the paragraph have been identified for you. Can you find the other causes and effects the writer describes? Underline any causes and double underline any effects. Check your answers with a partner. Have you underlined the same or different sentences? Review Figure 2.6 and decide if the paragraph is organized to focus on the causes or on the effects. How do you know?

Rooftop Farms: The Future of Green Cities

Rooftop green spaces or farms may become more and more common in cities in the future. Rooftop farming is growing because these urban gardens are attractive. They make urban spaces more beautiful, and they can save people money. More and more people who work and live in the city want to create rooftop gardens to make their homes more relaxing and beautiful. Another reason why people create rooftop farms is that eating local has become more attractive. Eating local food costs less money and causes less pollution from transportation. Rooftop farms seem to provide great value for city residents. Working on these rooftop farms leads to more connection between people. For example, in apartment buildings, people who may not even know each other join together to create and maintain their urban garden. Sometimes, companies in offices with rooftop gardens allow employees to use their breaks to water or to weed. Another beneficial effect of urban gardens may be economic. If more fruits and vegetables are produced than needed, these could be sold at urban farmers' markets. As well, no long-distance transportation is required, so the food is both cheaper to buy and fresher to eat. In short, it seems that city farms will continue to grow if residents continue to be committed to leading green lives.

Activity B | Create a rough outline for a cause-and-effect paragraph that answers your Unit Inquiry Question. Follow the steps below to help you.

Before you write your outline

- Discuss with a partner any new ideas you have learned about that might help you answer your inquiry question.
- Decide if your paragraph will focus on the causes or the effects.
- Create a flowchart similar to Figure 2.6.

Write your outline

- Create an outline based your flowchart.

After you write your outline

- Make sure your outline is well coordinated (see page 55).
- Share your completed outline with another student.
- Ask your peer reader to give you two suggestions to improve your outline.

Topic Skill

Writing Cause-and-Effect Topic Sentences

Cause-and-effect paragraphs begin with a topic sentence, which has three parts:

- the topic—the subject you are writing about;
- the controlling idea—the main idea you are writing about; and
- words and phrases that show the reader the focus of the paragraph, either on the cause or the effect.

Examples

1. Topic sentence showing a cause focus:

    Generally speaking, global warming causes the sea levels to rise.

    topic   +   *causes*   +   **controlling idea**

2. Topic sentence showing an effect focus:

    Generally speaking, global warming has resulted in rising sea levels.

    topic   +   *has resulted in* + **controlling idea**

Activity A | In each of the topic sentences in the chart on the next page, which words show a cause-and-effect relationship? Complete the chart, then work with a small group to analyze each topic sentence and decide if it emphasizes cause or effect.

Topic Sentence	Main Topic	Controlling Idea	Words that Show Cause or Effect
1. Poverty likely still exists today because of the unequal distribution of resources in society.	poverty	unequal resource distribution	
2. Not caring about water use may lead to water shortages in many countries.	water shortages	careless water use	
3. The natural environment is affected in important ways by many human activities.	environment	human activities	
4. Due to widespread use of disposable water bottles, there is an alarming mass of plastic in our world's oceans.	plastic in oceans	widespread use of water bottles	

Activity B | Look at the two possible topic sentences for a cause-and-effect paragraph below. Find any words that signal cause or effect. Discuss with a partner whether each topic sentence emphasizes the cause or the effect.

1. In places that lack community water infrastructure, the water is unsafe because the local water supply may be used not only for drinking and washing, but also for disposing of sewage.
2. Rapidly growing populations might result in unsafe water in many communities.

Activity C | Writing Task: Topic Sentence for Unit Inquiry Question | Look back at the rough outline you created in Activity B on page 62. Based on the ideas in that outline, write a cause or effect topic sentence for your Unit Inquiry Question. First, decide on the focus for your topic sentence. Then write a topic sentence that clearly shows your focus. When you are finished, evaluate your topic sentence using the following questions.

- Does your topic sentence have a clear topic and a specific controlling idea?
- Does your topic sentence show if you are exploring a cause or an effect?

Conclusion Skill

Predicting

In a cause-and-effect paragraph, the concluding sentence may simply state a fact or general truth for the reader to focus on, as in the example below. Notice that the simple present tense is used.

When universities and students collaborate to reduce consumption, they contribute to protecting the environment.

Very often, the concluding sentence includes a prediction. This prediction is based on what the writer thinks might happen. The language used for these predictions shows how confident the writer is in the prediction. Notice how the verb form used can make the prediction more or less certain.

Fact/General Truth ↓	When universities and students collaborate to reduce consumption, they contribute to protecting the environment.
More Certain Prediction ↓	Once universities and students collaborate to reduce consumption, they will contribute to protecting the environment.
Less Certain Prediction	If universities and students collaborate to reduce consumption, they might contribute to protecting the environment.

Activity A | Read the following paragraph. Notice how the writer makes a prediction in the final sentence. Using the information and examples above, decide if the writer is more or less certain about the prediction. How do you know?

In general, many students think that the sustainable use of resources is extremely important. That is the reason why many universities support sustainable campus activities. However, the university's actions are not enough. Students should also take responsibility to be more green. Once student-led activities become common, then students and educational institutions will really be acting together to support sustainability.

Activity B | Read the topic sentences below. Identify the topic and the controlling idea. Write a concluding sentence that matches the main idea in each of topic sentence. In your concluding sentence, be sure to clearly show how certain your prediction is.

1. One reason why people move to cities is that the cities seem to offer better living conditions.

   Topic: _____

   Controlling idea: _____

   Concluding sentence: _____

   _____

   _____

   _____

2. The environment seems to be affected in important ways by everyday human activities.

Topic: _____

Controlling idea: _____

Concluding sentence: _____

_____

_____

_____

Activity C | Writing Task: Concluding Sentence for Unit Inquiry Question | Reread the topic sentence you wrote for your Unit Inquiry Question in Activity C on page 63. Think about what might happen and make a prediction for your reader. Decide how strongly you feel about your prediction, then write a concluding sentence.

WRITING FUNDAMENTALS

Composition Skill

Staying on Topic

Here are some common concerns that students have about writing paragraphs. Do you have similar challenges?

- I often include too many main ideas in my paragraphs.
- I write very short paragraphs because I am not sure what idea to write about next.
- I sometimes feel as if I am restating the same idea over and over again.
- I'm not sure when I have written enough so that my reader will understand.

Well-organized paragraphs help the reader follow the ideas in your writing. Be sure to organize the ideas in a way that the reader expects: write paragraphs that begin with a topic sentence, continue with supporting sentences, and end with a concluding sentence.

Well-developed paragraphs help the reader understand your main idea. Be sure to give your reader enough details. If you give too few details, then the reader does not fully understand. If you give too many details, then the reader may not be able to find your main idea.

Use the following tips to improve idea development in your paragraph.

✓ Introduce the reader to your topic and controlling idea in the topic sentence.
✓ Write supporting sentences that contain more detailed ideas about the main idea.
✓ Be careful not to include any ideas that are not directly related to your topic sentence.
✓ Link ideas using connecting words and phrases to help the reader move easily from idea to idea.
✓ Remind the reader of the main idea at the end of your paragraph.

Activity A | Read the following paragraph written by a student writer. Imagine that this writer has these five questions for you—the peer reader.

1. Is my topic sentence clear?
2. Do I have too many ideas?
3. Which is the main idea?
4. Are there any off-topic ideas? Explain.
5. Have I written enough? What might be missing?

Analyze the paragraph in order to answer these questions. Then compare your answers with a partner.

Top Tips for a Greener Home

Unplugging unused electronic devices is very important. The *Green Guide* states that "standby power accounts for up to 10% of average yearly household electricity use" (Brum, 2014, p. 3). Many students do not unplug their electronic devices because it bothers them. They do not know how inefficient it is. The amount of one person's wasted electricity does not seem that bad, but wasting electricity can add up. A little daily effort will greatly reduce electricity use. The *Green Guide* is very useful because it gives students many suggestions for sustainability. Many of these ideas are easy to carry out in everyday life, and they are also effective in reducing consumption.

Reference

Brum, C. (2014, September). *Green guide*. Retrieved from https://uwaterloo.ca/sustainability/sites/ca.sustainability/files/uploads/files/sci-green-guide-2014-fall-web-40141.pdf

---

Activity B | Your instructor will give you a marked-up copy of the paragraph you read in the previous activity. The paragraph has been marked up by the student's writing instructor to show which ideas the readers focus on when they are reading the paragraph. Marking up a text to show the chain of ideas in a paragraph helps the writer to more easily see which ideas flow well together and which ideas seem disconnected.

Work in pairs to review how the writing instructor marked up the paragraph's topic development. Decide if you wish to change your answers to the writer's questions in Activity A.

Sentence and Grammar Skill

Moving from Simple to Compound and Complex Sentences

Varying your sentence structure, or using different types of sentences in your writing, helps keep your reader engaged. Simple sentences can be effective in expressing the main idea of a paragraph, as in a topic sentence. However, longer sentences allow you to combine ideas. For example, supporting ideas are often written as compound or complex sentences.

Although the reader can sometimes guess the logical connection between ideas, it is better to show these connections clearly. By moving beyond simple sentences (to compound and complex sentences), you can begin to connect your ideas more clearly for your reader. To create complex sentences, it's important to understand that sentences are made up of two kinds of clauses: independent and dependent clauses.

Independent clause

An independent clause can be a sentence by itself. It has a subject and a verb (and sometimes more) and it expresses a complete thought. Every sentence must have an independent clause. Simple sentences and compound sentences are made up of independent clauses.

Simple sentences

1. Unplugging unused electronic devices can save money.
2. Unplugging devices and turning off the lights can save money.
3. Turning off the lights saves money and helps the environment.

Compound sentences

1. One person wasting electricity does not seem too bad, but many people wasting electricity can have significant consequences.
2. Reducing water use at home is easy to do, and many students should consider doing it.
3. Deforestation is increasing, yet many countries do little to save the forests.

Dependent clause

A dependent clause cannot stand by itself as a sentence. A complex sentence needs both a dependent clause and an independent clause.

The dependent clause in a complex sentence also has a subject and verb, but always includes some additional words. There are specific words that are used to introduce dependent clauses, including

- *who, whose, whom, which/that;*
- *because, after/before/once, if/unless, whereas/while;* and
- *that, if/whether.*

In the following sentences, the dependent clause (introduced by one of the words in the list above) is in red.

Complex sentences

1. Students who do not unplug their electronic devices pay more for their energy use.
2. If being green helps the environment, then students should be a little green.
3. Many students wonder whether or not sustainability is achievable on campus.

Activity A | Choose one of the paragraphs you have written for this unit. Review the tips for sentence variety below, then discuss your paragraph with a partner. Together, come up with two suggestions about how you could improve the sentence variety in your paragraph.

Tips for sentence variety

- Begin and end your paragraph with simple sentences.
- Highlight any ideas that you want to stand out for the reader with simple or compound sentences.
- In compound sentences, use *but* to show a change in thought; use *so* to show a result.
- Complex sentences express more complex logical connections. Use *because* to show reason, use *if* to show condition, or use *while* to show that actions occur at the same time or to show contrast.
- Begin your sentences in different ways with different sentence structures, but do not write too many complex sentences in a row. Add a simple sentence between the complex sentences when you wish to make the reader notice an important point.

Activity B | Use the suggestions from your partner in Activity A to decide which sentences to rewrite in your paragraph. Then combine or rewrite these sentences, paying attention to sentence variety. When you are finished, ask a partner to check the sentence structure and the use of connectors in your sentences. Revise your sentences as needed to correct them.

Learning Strategy

Helping Yourself Become an Academic Writer

How did you learn how to write a birthday greeting in your first language?

- ☐ I asked someone better at writing than I am to write the birthday message for me.
- ☐ I practised writing the message on a separate sheet, then wrote a good copy on the card.
- ☐ I studied the message on an old birthday card I had, then I wrote a new message on a new card.
- ☐ I tried to write the message myself with no help, but I also asked someone who was better at writing than me to check it.

Learning to write in an academic way is not very different than learning to write a message on a birthday card. You might study an example model, practise writing, and then ask a more experienced writer to help. Learning how to write a new kind of text requires the right kind of practice. Working through this textbook, you can help yourself become a better academic writer by actively learning about how to write in an academic style.

Observe Writing

- Notice how the paragraphs you study are organized.
- Notice whether the writer expresses ideas in a more formal or a more personal way.
- Notice whether or not the language is simple and clear.

Study Writing

- Preview the unit's key outcomes to see what you already can do.
- Decide what you really need to learn in the unit.
- Learn from others by taking advantage of the peer check opportunities throughout this book.
- Ask when you're not sure about any of the writing tasks.

Practise Writing

- Challenge yourself to produce your best writing with your best thinking.
- Experiment with new techniques for brainstorming or drafting.
- Ask for specific feedback on your writing; let your peer readers and instructor help you improve.

UNIT OUTCOME

Writing Assignment: Cause-and-Effect Paragraph

Write a cause-and-effect paragraph of 200 to 300 words on a topic related to the environment or environmental sustainability. (Your instructor may give you an alternative length.) You may write on a topic based on your Unit Inquiry Question, develop another topic of your choosing connected to the environment, or choose one of the following topics:

- What happens when universities create green campuses?
- What happens when students act in environmentally friendly ways?
- How can local green actions by individuals help make the environment better?

Use the skills you have developed in this unit to complete the assignment. Follow the steps set out below to practise each of your newly acquired skills and write a well-developed paragraph.

1. **Brainstorm**: Use a cube brainstorm to come up with ideas related to your topic.

2. **Find information**: Find some information to support your main ideas. For example, you may choose to use information related to the environment that you have read about in this unit.

3. **Compose a topic sentence**: Develop a focused cause or effect topic sentence that includes a topic and a controlling idea.

4. **Outline**: Fill in the outline below to plan the first draft of your paragraph. You may make changes to the outline as necessary.

Topic Sentence	Focused topic sentence that introduces the controlling idea (the main cause or the main effect to be discussed)
Main Body (Supporting Ideas)	Supporting detail 1 Describe the most likely cause (in a focus-on-the-cause paragraph): OR Describe the general effect (in a focus-on-the-effect paragraph):

Main Body (Supporting Ideas)

Supporting detail 2:
Describe the most important effects (in a focus-on-the-cause paragraph):
OR
Describe the most likely causes (in a focus-on-the-effect paragraph):

Concluding Sentence

Concluding sentence that makes a prediction:

5. **Write a first draft**: Use your outline to write the first draft of your paragraph. Do not worry too much about spelling or grammar in the first draft. Try to get your ideas down on paper.

6. **Self-check**: Review the first draft of your paragraph for the following and revise as needed.

   - Organization: Make sure that you have organized your main and supporting points according to the type of paragraph that you are writing, either a paragraph that focuses on the causes or effects.

   - Topic development: Make sure that you have added facts or examples to each of your supporting points to develop your main point.

   - Reporting verbs and expressions: Where you have included information from an outside source, make sure that the information is introduced using an appropriate reporting verb or expression.

7. **Ask for a peer review**: Exchange the revised version of your first draft with a partner. Use the Evaluation Rubric on page 72 to assess your partner's paragraph and provide suggestions to improve it. Consider your partner's feedback carefully and use it to make changes to your paragraph.

8. **Edit**: Edit your paragraph for the following:

   - Sentence structure: Make sure you have a variety of simple, compound, and complex sentences, and that each sentence is grammatically correct.

   - Vocabulary: Check that you have used some of the AWL and mid-frequency vocabulary from this unit in your paragraph.

   - Transitions: Check that you have used cause-and-effect words and phrases to signal any logical connections to your reader.

9. **Write a final draft**: Write a final draft of your paragraph, making any changes you think will improve it. If possible, leave some time between drafts.

10. **Proofread**: Check the final draft of your paragraph for any small errors you may have missed. In particular, look for spelling errors, typos, and punctuation mistakes. If you used information from an outside source, double-check your in-text citations and your References list to make sure they are formatted properly.

Evaluation: Cause-and-Effect Paragraph Rubric

Use the following checklist to evaluate your paragraph. In which areas do you need to improve most?

E = **Emerging**: frequent difficulty using unit skills; needs a lot more work
D = **Developing**: some difficulty using unit skills; some improvement still required
S = **Satisfactory**: able to use unit skills most of the time; meets average expectations for this level
O = **Outstanding**: exceptional use of unit skills; exceeds expectations for this level

Skill	E	D	S	O
The paragraph is organized to focus on either causes or effects of something.				
Content is organized logically with a clear topic sentence, supporting sentences, and a concluding sentence, so the reader can easily follow the writer's thinking.				
Words and phrases showing cause-and-effect relationships are used correctly and where appropriate.				
Writing shows a good level of idea development and does not go off topic.				
The paragraph includes vocabulary items with related meanings.				
AWL and mid-frequency vocabulary items from this unit are used where appropriate and with few mistakes.				
The topic sentence includes a topic and controlling idea, and clearly shows whether the paragraph will focus on causes or effects.				
The concluding sentence brings a satisfying close to the paragraph with a prediction logically related to the topic.				
A variety of simple, compound, and complex sentences are used correctly.				
Ideas and words from outside sources are clearly marked for the reader using reporting verbs and/or quotation marks.				
If required, APA-style in-text citations and References list have been included.				

Unit Review

Activity A | What do you know now that you did not know before about the environment or environmental sustainability? Discuss with a partner or small group.

Activity B | Look back at the Unit Inquiry Question you developed at the start of this unit and discuss it with a partner or small group. Then share your answers with the class. Use the following questions to guide you.

1. What information did you find in this unit that helped you answer your question?
2. How would you answer your question now?

Activity C | Use the following checklist to review what you have learned throughout this unit. First decide which 10 skills you think are most important—circle the number beside each of these 10 skills. If you learned a skill in this unit that isn't listed below, write it in the blank row at the end of the checklist. Then put a check mark in the box beside those points you feel you have learned. Be prepared to discuss your choices with the class.

Self-Assessment Checklist
☐ 1. I can talk about various causes and effects related to the environment and environmental sustainability based on what I have read in this unit.
☐ 2. I can develop an inquiry question to explore causes and effects.
☐ 3. I can use cause-and-effect words and phrases to connect ideas in my writing.
☐ 4. I can expand my vocabulary by learning words related by meaning.
☐ 5. I can use the AWL and mid-frequency vocabulary from this unit in my writing.
☐ 6. I can provide reasons and examples to support the main ideas in my writing.
☐ 7. I can use a Frayer model or a cube brainstorm to come up with ideas to write about.
☐ 8. I can write a well-coordinated outline.
☐ 9. I can take notes effectively when reading outside sources, and I can integrate quotations from these sources into my writing without committing plagiarism.
☐ 10. I can write clear topic sentences that refer to causes or effects.
☐ 11. I can write effective concluding sentences that make a prediction.

☐	12. I can edit a paragraph to include a variety of grammatically correct simple, compound, and complex sentences.
☐	13. I can write an effective cause-and-effect paragraph.
☐	14.

Activity D | Put a check mark in the box beside the vocabulary items from this unit that you feel confident using in your writing. Make a plan to practise the words that you still need to learn.

Vocabulary Checklist

☐ achieve (v.) (AWL)		☐ massive (adj.) (2000)	
☐ capacity (n.) (AWL)		☐ nutrient (n.) (5000)	
☐ commute (v.) (4000)		☐ objective (n.) (3000)	
☐ ecosystem (n.) (6000)		☐ perspective (n.) (AWL)	
☐ erosion (n.) (AWL)		☐ prosperity (n.) (3000)	
☐ ideal (adj.) (3000)		☐ resource (n.) (AWL)	
☐ impact (n.) (AWL)		☐ spiritual (adj.) (2000)	
☐ issue (n.) (AWL)		☐ technique (n.) (AWL)	

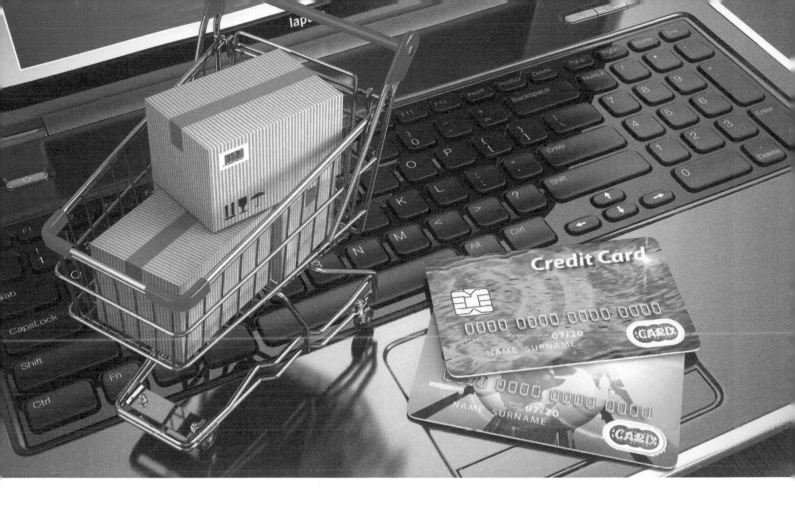

UNIT 3

Business Studies

Marketing and Consumers

EXPLORING IDEAS

Introduction

The Hudson's Bay department store in downtown Winnipeg, Manitoba

Activity A | Discuss the following questions with a partner or small group.

1. What are some of your favourite brands and products? Why do you like them?
2. *Marketing* is a business term that refers to how a company advertises, displays, and sells its products. How is your favourite brand or product marketed?
3. What Canadian brands do you know? Make a list of famous Canadian brands. Which ones are marketed the most effectively? Explain.
4. What is the role of social media, including Facebook and Twitter, in the marketing process?
5. How much does marketing influence the way you buy?
6. Have you ever shopped at Hudson's Bay (or The Bay), pictured above? If so, how was it the same as or different from another department store you are familiar with? If not, compare your favourite department store with the favourite department store of another person in your group.

Activity B | Compare two products or companies that you think are different from each other using the T-chart below. For each product or company, include as much information as you can. You might compare two different smart phone brands, two different types of technology, or two different grocery stores. Identify as many differences as possible.

Product or Company 1:	Product or Company 2:

Activity C | Review the chart that you filled in for Activity B. What are the biggest differences between the two products or companies that you compared? Discuss your ideas with a partner or small group. Then report your opinions to the class.

Fostering Inquiry

Making Comparisons

An interesting form of inquiry involves comparing two different things, people, places, processes, or events. Usually, the things you are comparing should be important to other people. Your goal is to find and discuss significant similarities or differences.

The things you are comparing are called the *subjects of comparison*. Compare-and-contrast inquiry questions can help you learn more about what is the same or different between two subjects of comparison. Through the process of inquiry, you explore how the subjects of comparison are the same or different.

For example, if you analyze the similarities or differences between two products such as smart phones, you might compare price, size, or colour. Alternatively, you might look at who the phones are designed for, how these phones are marketed, and where these phones are successful. The things you compare between the two subjects are called the *points of comparison*.

Activity A | What do you want to know more about in relation to the topic of marketing and consumer behaviour? For example:

- *What marketing strategies work for different generations?*
- *How are online and in-store shopping experiences similar or different?*
- *What are the advantages of online advertising compared to traditional print advertising?*

1. Write two or three questions you are curious about related to marketing and consumer behaviour.

2. When you are finished, compare your questions with a partner or small group.

3. Choose one question to guide you as you work through this unit. It does not have to be the same question as your partner or group. Your question may change as you learn more about your topic.

4. Write your inquiry question in the space provided. Look back at this question as you work through this unit. This is your Unit Inquiry Question.

My Unit Inquiry Question:

_____

_____

_____

Activity B | Writing Task: Freewriting | Write for at least five minutes on the topic of your Unit Inquiry Question. Do not stop writing during this time. After five minutes, read what you have written and circle two or three ideas that you would like to explore further.

Structure

Compare-and-Contrast Paragraph

Making comparisons is a useful way to analyze a topic. Usually, a compare-and-contrast paragraph focuses on either the similarities or the differences between two subjects of analysis. A practical way to organize a compare-and contrast paragraph is to examine the same set of points of comparison for both subjects of analysis. In a shorter paragraph, you may only have one, two, or three common points of comparison.

Consider the following brief outline for a paragraph on the marketing strategies of two fast-food restaurants with two subjects of analysis and three points of comparison. Note that the first part of the paragraph focuses on McDonald's, and it includes information on TV advertising, contests, and websites. The second part of the paragraph focuses on Tim Hortons, and the points of comparison are in the same order as for McDonald's. This type of compare-and-contrast organization is called block format.

Topic: Differences in the marketing strategies for McDonald's and Tim Hortons
    Subject of analysis 1: McDonald's
        Point of comparison 1: TV Advertising
        Point of comparison 2: Contests
        Point of comparison 3: Websites
    Subject of analysis 2: Tim Hortons
        Point of comparison 1: TV Advertising
        Point of comparison 2: Contests
        Point of comparison 3: Websites

In this unit you are going to focus on compare-and-contrast paragraphs. The compare-and-contrast structure is also useful for different types of academic writing such as writing an introduction to a debate, writing part of a report that looks at different options, or writing the results section of a research study.

Activity A | Read the following compare-and-contrast paragraph to learn more about product packaging and its effect on existing and new customers. Answer the questions that follow with a partner or small group.

Attractive and Informative Food Packaging

Packaging is an important part of how food processing companies communicate with both repeat and new customers. For all customers, food packaging needs to be attractive. Bright and attractive packaging helps repeat customers easily find and buy the products they like. For example, some people like only one type of soft drink. Nowadays there are many different brands of soft drink in the grocery store. However, if customers can quickly recognize a brand by its packaging, they are more likely to buy it. Similarly, attractive packaging is important for marketing to new customers too. Attractive packaging can encourage new customers to try a product. Bright colours and bold logos are noticeable. As a result, customers might be encouraged to try something new. A good example is frozen vegetables. A company can choose a colour no other brand is using on its package. This new colour can draw customers' attention to the frozen vegetables. In addition to being attractive, packaging should also be informative. From time to time, existing customers will want to know more about what they are buying. Lately, many people are becoming more interested in healthy eating. They may start to check product labels for nutritional information. For example, a customer might think they should stop buying their favourite brand of cookies. However, a quick look at the packaging might show them it is okay to eat just one or two. Likewise, the information found on food packaging is also important for new customers. For example, the words *new* and *improved* on a package might encourage someone to try something for the first time. New customers might also be encouraged to try something if they see that it is a good value. Using wording such as "300 grams for the price of 200 grams" or "coupon enclosed" are good ways to gain new customers. In short, communicating with customers through attractive and informative packaging helps food companies keep their existing customers and gain new ones.

1. What is the main idea of this paragraph?
2. What are the subjects of analysis?
3. What are the points of comparison?
4. What words and phrases help you determine that a comparison is being made in this paragraph?
5. What do you notice about the first and last sentences?

Compare-and-Contrast Connectors

When writing about similarities and differences, you can use a variety of words and phrases to help readers understand your analysis. The table below lists some words and phrases that show similarity or difference. Note the grammar and punctuation used in the example sentences.

Words and Phrases for Comparing (Showing Similarity)	
likewise	The price of a product is important. Likewise, the design can influence a customer's purchasing decision.
similarly	McDonald's advertises on television. Similarly, Tim Hortons uses television advertising to reach customers.
in the same way	Price is a good way to attract a new customer. In the same way, design is important to catch a new customer's eye.
Words and Phrases for Contrasting (Showing Difference)	
on the other hand	Customers want a low price for products. On the other hand, companies want high profits.
in contrast	Price is a good way to attract new customers. In contrast, design is less important for attracting new customers.
however	Low-fat products are becoming more popular with customers. However, low-salt products are no longer in high demand.

Activity B | Look at the pictures of a physical hardware store and a website landing page for another hardware business. What similarities and differences do you see between shopping in a physical Canadian Tire store and shopping at the online store for DIY Hardware? If you are not familiar with Canadian Tire, you can write about a physical store and an online store that you do know. Write about the similarities and differences using the compare-and-contrast connectors listed on the next page. Two example sentences have been provided for you.

1. **Likewise:** _____

_____

2. **Similarly:** The physical Canadian Tire store has a large logo on the side of the building. <u>Similarly</u>, the DIY Hardware website has a big logo that is easy to see.

3. **In the same way:** _____

_____

4. **On the other hand:** _____

5. **In contrast:** _____

_____

6. **However:** In the Hudson's Bay department store in downtown Vancouver, customers can try on clothes before they buy them. <u>However</u>, on the Hudson's Bay website, customers can only click on the pictures and guess how the clothes will fit.

Activity C | Share your sentences with a partner. Discuss how your ideas were similar or different. Then review the compare-and-contrast words and phrases that each of you used. Do these words correctly show similarities or differences? Has the correct punctuation been used?

Activity D | What ideas have you developed so far in relation to your Unit Inquiry Question? Based on the ideas in your freewriting brainstorm on page 78, as well as any new ideas you have come up with, write three sentences for each of your subjects of analysis. Connect your sentences with an appropriate compare-and-contrast connector. An example (based on the inquiry question *What are the main marketing tools for McDonald's and Tim Hortons?*) has been provided.

Subject of Analysis 1:	Connector	Subject of Analysis 2
McDonald's uses an annual Monopoly contest to encourage customers to purchase menu items by offering prizes.	Similarly,	Tim Hortons also has an annual contest, Roll Up the Rim to Win, that rewards customers with prizes.

Activity E | Writing Task: Compare-and-Contrast Paragraph | Using the ideas you wrote about in the previous activity, write a short compare-and-contrast paragraph. In the first part of your paragraph, include information related to your points of comparison for your first subject of analysis. In the second part of your paragraph, include information related to your points of comparison for your second subject of analysis. Use appropriate words and phrases to show comparison and contrast in your paragraph. The *Language Tip* box below contains additional words and phrases to help you.

Activity F | Exchange your compare-and-contrast paragraph with a partner. Read your partner's paragraph and answer the following questions.

1. What is the main idea of this paragraph?
2. What is the first subject of analysis? What is the second subject of analysis?
3. What points of comparison are explored for the two subjects of analysis? Are the points of comparison discussed in the same order for both subjects of analysis?
4. Does the paragraph include appropriate words and phrases to show comparison and contrast?
5. Do the first and last sentences help readers understand the main idea of the paragraph?

Language Tip

Showing Comparison and Contrast

When writing about similarities and differences, you can use a variety of words and phrases to help readers understand your analysis. In addition to the connectors introduced on page 80, you can use the words and phrases in the chart below to express similarities or differences. Consider using a variety of compare-and-contrast words and phrases in your own writing.

Words and Phrases for Comparing (Showing Similarity)	
and . . . too	McDonald's tries to keep prices low to attract customers, and Tim Hortons uses this strategy too.
and so does	McDonald's has many locations in shopping mall food courts, and so does Tim Hortons.
just as	McDonald's sells many different types of coffee drinks, just as Tim Hortons does.
both . . . and	Both McDonald's and Tim Hortons do a lot of television advertising as part of their marketing strategies.

Words and Phrases for Contrasting (Showing Difference)	
different from	The price that younger customers are willing to pay is sometimes different from what older customers will pay.
while	While the price of a smart watch is important for the younger generation, the features are more important for older customers.
whereas	Younger customers seem to adapt to new technology very easily, whereas older customers may take more time to become used to the same technology.
but	Technology users who are physically active might prefer a smart watch, but less active people might prefer a smart phone.

Activity G | Revisit your Unit Inquiry Question on page 78. Now that you have learned more about your topic, you may have a better idea of how to answer your question, or you may consider revising it. Use the following questions to guide you in assessing your Unit Inquiry Question.

- What information have you learned that will help you answer your Unit Inquiry Question?
- What information do you still need to answer your question?
- Do you want to change your question in any way?

ACADEMIC READING

Vocabulary

Vocabulary Skill: Understanding Word Forms and Suffixes

Knowing a word involves more than just knowing its definition. Other important information, such as its part of speech and its related word forms, is important to learn too. Knowing related word forms helps you to use new words more accurately.

Adding a suffix to a root word creates new words within a word family (words related by form). The suffix does not change the meaning of the root word. Notice how suffixes added to the word *compete* change the part of speech of the newly formed word.

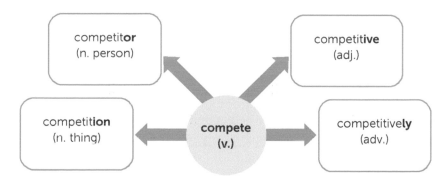

competit**or**
(n. person)

competit**ive**
(adj.)

competit**ion**
(n. thing)

compete
(v.)

competitive**ly**
(adv.)

Activity A | The chart below shows word families with examples of the four parts of speech. Complete the chart with any missing words. Use an English dictionary to find the words you are not sure about. Discuss your answers in a small group.

Noun	Verb	Adjective	Adverb
competition competitor	compete	competitive	competitively
	connect		
		informative	
market marketing marketers			
	recommend		
			successfully

Activity B | Discuss the questions below with a partner.

1. Which word families in the chart in Activity A follow a similar pattern to the *compete* word family?
2. Do you know any other word families with a similar pattern?
3. Which word families from the chart have a different pattern than the *compete* word family?

Vocabulary Preview: The Academic Word List

Activity C | The eight AWL words below appear in the unit's reading, "E-Commerce Basics," on pages 88–89. Study the definition(s) of each word. Then write each AWL word in one of the eight blanks to complete the paragraph on page 85 the list of definitions. You may need to change the form of the word. Use a dictionary to check that your word forms are correct.

communication (n.): the activity of expressing ideas or giving people information; the way of sending information, especially telephones, radios, computers
ensure (v.): to make sure that something happens or is definite
media (n.): the main ways that people receive information and entertainment; the companies involved in television, radio, and the Internet

network (n.): several computers or devices that are connected together

potential (adj.): having or showing the possibility of developing into something in the future

promote (v.): to help sell a product or service, or to make it more popular

retain (v.): to keep something, to continue to have something

strategy (n.): a plan of action to achieve a goal

Advertising in Schools

Companies often target future consumers early on in life. Sometimes, marketers try to _____ with children even when they are at school. Marketers use different _____ to do this, including using online magazines, social media _____, and product giveaways. However, many educational experts, parents, and teachers oppose companies that _____ their products to children in schools. They feel that advertising in schools may _____ change schools from places for education into places of business. Recently, a group of concerned parents succeeded in removing soft drink advertising from schools. The _____ have reported that seven out of ten Canadians feel that consumer advertising has no place in schools. For these Canadians, a school's goal is to _____ that children learn skills and knowledge necessary for success in life. Although companies need to work hard to attract and _____ customers, most Canadians do not agree with advertising to children in schools.

Vocabulary Preview: Mid-frequency Vocabulary

Activity D | The eight mid-frequency words in red in the sentences below appear in the unit's reading, "E-Commerce Basics" on pages 88–89. Read the sentences to help you determine the correct definition of each word. Then match the word and its definition.

Sentence	Definition
_____ 1. The software for the web enables users to see text, pictures, video, and animation and hear sound.	a. attracted to something or feeling a sense of involvement in it
_____ 2. Once customers have shopped, the website may prompt them to continue shopping by suggesting other products of interest.	b. make somebody decide to do something
_____ 3. Businesses need more strategies to retain their customers and persuade them to consider their products.	c. object or piece of equipment that has been designed to do a particular job
_____ 4. All a consumer needs to shop online is an Internet-enabled device, an Internet connection and software, and a credit card.	d. faithful to somebody/ something

Sentence		Definition	
_____ 5.	Sometimes businesses hire a social media expert to microblog and sometimes they contract the work out to a variety of loyal customers.	e.	the selling of goods to the public, usually though shops/ stores, but sometimes online
_____ 6.	Selling products to consumers over the Internet is called e-tailing, from the words *electronic retailing*.	f.	make somebody do something by giving them good reasons for doing it
_____ 7.	The volume of purchases by consumers has grown a great deal since Internet shopping first started in the mid-1990s and continues to grow at a very fast pace.	g.	make it possible for someone to do something
_____ 8.	Today, customers expect to be as engaged on a website as they would be strolling through a bricks-and-mortar store.	h.	speed at which something moves

Reading

The reading "E-Commerce Basics" on pages 88–89 contains excerpts from a chapter on information technology and social media in *Marketing Dynamics* (Canadian Edition), a textbook that introduces students to basic concepts in marketing. The reading describes e-commerce and explains what e-marketing strategies companies use to promote their products.

Activity A | Compare the in-store retail and the e-retail (e-tail) experience. With a partner, discuss how in-store and online shopping are similar or different. Use the key points of comparison listed below to help you think about what is similar and what is different.

Key Points of Comparison

- **shopping experience** (atmosphere/feeling, convenience, brand selection, quality)
- **customer service** (easy to purchase, exchange, or return products)
- **marketing** (promotions/sales, new/repeat customers)
- **pricing** (company costs, customer prices)

Add the best ideas from your discussion to the Venn diagram on page 87. The unshaded sections in the Venn diagram show the differences between e-tail and in-store retail. The shaded section, where the circles come together, shows the ways in which e-tail and in-store retail are similar. Your completed Venn diagram should clearly show important similarities or differences between in-store and online shopping experiences. For more information on using Venn diagrams, see the *Brainstorming and Outlining* section in this unit on page 91.

When you are finished, compare your Venn diagram with another group. Do you have similar or different diagrams? Are there any ideas that you would like to add to your own Venn diagram?

Activity B | Before reading "E-Commerce Basics", mark the following statements as true (T) or false (F) based on your current understanding of e-commerce. As you read the text, think about whether your answers are correct. Paragraph numbers have been provided to help you check your answers after you are done reading.

1. _____ E-commerce has developed as a result of a change in customer shopping preferences. (2)

2. _____ In an online store, customers want to be able to do the same things that they can in a physical store. (4)

3. _____ Online shopping should be as interesting as in-store shopping. (5)

4. _____ To communicate with customers about products, companies should use pop-up advertising. (6)

5. _____ Social media give information about customer preferences to companies. (9)

6. _____ Communicating with customers using social media (e.g., Facebook, Twitter) is effective. (10)

Activity C | Read the following text and compare the writer's ideas with what you already know about online shopping. When you find a new idea about e-commerce and online shopping, underline or highlight it.

READING

E-Commerce Basics

1   The Internet and the world wide web are changing how companies do business. E-commerce (short for *electronic commerce*) refers to business activities conducted via[1] the Internet. Business activities include buying, selling, **promoting**, product research, competition research, and customer service.

2   E-commerce is possible because of the Internet and the world wide web. The Internet is a computer-based **communications network**. The word *Internet* comes from the words *interconnected networks*. The Internet is a powerful means of communication because it connects millions of computers around the world. Computers from individuals, businesses, organizations, and governments are all connected. The Internet was developed in the 1950s as a research and military tool. Now it is used by all types of people in all walks of life, almost everywhere. The world wide web (the web) is the network of information sources that is available over the Internet. The web was developed in 1993. The web is part of the Internet. The software for the web **enables** users to see text, pictures, video, and animation[2] and hear sound. Online is the condition of being connected to the Internet or being available on the Internet. For example, online shopping is shopping that is done over the web.

3   Today, consumers can buy almost anything over the Internet. Just enter the name of the item you would like to buy into a search engine. The search engine will generate a list of websites where you can buy that item. Selling products to consumers over the Internet is called e-tailing, from the words *electronic retailing*. Companies that sell to consumers online are often referred to as e-tailers. E-tailing is also called online retailing. All a consumer needs to shop online

is an Internet-enabled **device**, an Internet connection and software, and a credit card.

4   In order for e-tailing to be successful, customers have to be able to easily do the things they do in a bricks-and-mortar store.[3] Businesses that sell products online want to **ensure** that customers are able to look at and select products, can receive product promotions, will return to purchase other products, can get help if they need it, and can pay for the products and return them if they need to.

Promotions and Social Media

5   Today, customers expect to be as **engaged** on a website as they would be strolling[4] through a bricks-and-mortar store. As a result, businesses need more **strategies** to **retain** their customers and **persuade** them to consider their products. One of these strategies is e-marketing. E-marketing is marketing using computer technology, including websites, email, and mobile phones. You may wonder why a business would need e-marketing if it already has a website, but a website is just a platform for reaching the customer through e-marketing.

6   On the website, the business may invite customers to sign up for weekly emails that promote products of interest. Usually, customers can select which products they would like to hear about by checking a box. These emails can also be directed to a customer's mobile phone. This kind of e-marketing is known as opt-in[5] marketing because the customer agrees to it, unlike pop-up ads that suddenly appear on the website. Marketers have learned that many customers prefer opt-in marketing.

7   Once customers have shopped, the website may **prompt** them to continue shopping by suggesting other products of interest. These products are chosen according to the characteristics of the products the

---

[1] by means of a particular person, system, etc.

[2] the process of making films/movies, videos, and computer games in which drawings or models of people and animals seem to move

[3] businesses with buildings that customers go to; a physical store

[4] walking in a slow, relaxed way

[5] choosing to be part of a system or an agreement

customer has already bought or viewed. Although it is possible to recommend products in person, the Internet allows businesses to suggest more products more quickly, based on more shopping preferences than one salesperson could ever suggest in person.

8   Many businesses with websites also have an accompanying Facebook page and Twitter account. Social **media** help businesses reach out to customers in a personal way and create a sense of community around a brand. Within these communities, customers can share their experiences using different products and connect with others who have had similar experiences.

9   Social media are also an excellent way for businesses to gather additional research about customer needs and wants. On a Facebook page, for example, a business can pose[6] a question to customers or conduct a survey. Many businesses run regular online contests that they announce on Facebook or Twitter keeping customers engaged with the business brand and its products.

10   Sometimes businesses pay bloggers to write about their products. They may send free samples in return for a positive review, hoping that many **potential**

customers will read the blog[7] post and try their product. The microblogging site Twitter is useful for updating customers about product developments and events, such as contests, gift ideas, and store openings. Microblogging is a short, immediate form of blogging— usually about 20 to 25 words. Sometimes businesses hire a social media expert to microblog and sometimes they contract the work out to a variety of **loyal** customers.

Future of E-tailing

11   The volume of purchases by consumers has grown a great deal since Internet shopping first started in the mid-1990s and continues to grow at a very fast **pace**. E-commerce has also created jobs and lowered expenses for businesses and consumers. Websites enable businesses to offer better customer service and information, even if they do not sell products online. Today consumers expect that every respectable business will have a website that at least provides information.

Source: Gregoriou, G., Pegis, J., Clark, B., Sobel, J., & Gendall Basteri, C. (2013). *Marketing dynamics* (Canadian ed., pp. 121–130). Don Mills, ON: Oxford University Press Canada.

---

[6] ask a question, especially one that needs serious thought

[7] a website where a person writes regularly about recent events or topics that interest them, usually with photos and links to other websites that they find interesting

Activity D | Discuss the following questions with a partner or small group.

1. What is e-commerce?
2. What is the first step to buying something over the Internet? Describe the process.
3. What role do social media play in online shopping?
4. What kinds of products do you buy over the Internet? Why do you make these purchases online instead of in a bricks-and-mortar store?
5. In your opinion, what are the major differences between shopping online and shopping in person?
6. What do you know now about e-commerce that you did not know before? Did you find any new information?
7. Are there any ideas discussed in the text that you do not quite understand? Discuss anything you are not sure about.

Activity E | Revisit your Unit Inquiry Question on page 78. Are there any ideas from the reading that will help you answer your question? Share your ideas with a partner or small group. At this point, you may consider revising your Unit Inquiry Question. Use the following questions to help you in assessing your question.

1. How does the information from this reading change your understanding of marketing and consumers?
2. Which ideas from the reading can be used to help answer your Unit Inquiry Question?
3. What additional questions do you have after finishing the reading?
4. Where could you find more information?

Activity F | Writing Task: Compare-and-Contrast Paragraph | Write a short paragraph describing the differences between shopping online and shopping in person. Before you write, brainstorm ideas related to the differences between online shopping and bricks-and-mortar shopping. Then choose two points of comparison to include in your paragraph. Try to include five of the vocabulary words from this unit, but make sure the paragraph is written in your own words.

Activity G | Compare your paragraph to the sample paragraph in Appendix 2, then answer the questions that follow. Share your answers with a partner or small group.

1. What is the main idea of the sample paragraph?
2. Does the sample paragraph focus on similarities or differences?
3. What are the subjects of analysis?
4. What are the points of comparison?
5. What compare-and-contrast connectors do you see in this paragraph?
6. How do the ideas in the sample paragraph compare to your ideas?
7. Did you use any compare-and-contrast connectors?
8. After reading the sample paragraph, is there anything you would revise in your paragraph?

Critical Thinking

Making Connections between Ideas and Information

Simply repeating information that you have heard or read is usually not enough for academic assignments—you will likely be asked to make connections to promote more careful thinking and deeper learning about a topic. Here are two important connections you could make:

- Connect what you know and what you need to know about a topic. This helps you decide

if you need to do more research, reading, or thinking to answer an inquiry question.

- Connect what two different writers think about a topic. This helps you decide if these writers have similar or different views on a topic. Then you can include these writers' opinions as support for your ideas in your writing.

The chart below shows how information that you get from different sources can be put together to more easily demonstrate connections.

Inquiry Question	Information from an Article about E-Marketing	Information from an Article about Wearable Technology	Connections
What marketing strategies work for different generations?	Older customers want information online on websites. Older customers are developing an interest in some social media (e.g., Facebook).	Younger customers receive information through social media. Younger customers want to be the first to know about new products.	Different: Older and younger customers have different ways of receiving information about products. Similar: Some types of social media may reach both older and younger customers.

PROCESS FUNDAMENTALS

Brainstorming and Outlining

Venn Diagrams

A Venn diagram, which you already used in a pre-reading activity (see page 87), is a graphic organizer that can help you brainstorm the relationships between two or more subjects of analysis. It consists of two or more interlocking circles. Each circle represents one subject of analysis. Similarities shared by the subjects of analysis are listed in the overlapping areas. Differences are listed in the areas that do not overlap. When you are finished brainstorming as many ideas as possible, you can see if there are more similarities or differences between your subjects of analysis. Thus, a Venn diagram helps you see how the subjects of analysis are similar and how they are different. You can also choose the best ideas in your Venn diagram and group these ideas into common points of comparison for both subjects of analysis.

The Venn diagram below shows the similarities and differences between online shopping and in-person shopping. Some possible common points of comparison include convenience, product information, and customer service.

Similarities and Differences between Shopping Online and Shopping in Person

Shopping Online

Shopping in Person

can stay home

shop any time

lots of pictures

can purchase from retailers all around the world

ship directly to your door

can't try on new clothes before you buy

have to wait for items to arrive

may have shipping costs

danger of shipping issues such as lost or damaged products

can read reviews of products online

detailed product information online

have to ship back products you don't want

purchases can be made instantly

easily buy and send gifts to people

can't use cash

risk of identity theft (e.g., credit card information)

no pressure from salespeople

save money on gas, parking, and transit

similar quality

familiar products

same brands

many companies have physical and online stores

pay with credit card

prices generally the same

same taxes

have to leave house

can touch (or smell) products

can try on clothes

limited space for stock

can take purchases home right away

no shipping costs

don't have to worry about products being lost during shipping

salespeople can answer questions and help

easy returns for products you don't want

only shop during store hours

may have to wait in line

some stores are cash only

safer payment transactions (less risk of identity theft)

support local businesses

Activity A | Brainstorm a list of the different types of advertising that companies use to convince customers to buy their products and services. Then create a Venn diagram in your notebook comparing and contrasting two kinds of advertising from your list. These two kinds of advertising are your subjects of analysis. For example, you could compare television advertising with newspaper advertising, social media advertising with product placement in movies, or junk mail (direct marketing) with spam. Write a title for your Venn diagram and label each of the circles with a subject of analysis. Fill each section of your Venn diagram with as many ideas as possible, then share your Venn diagram with a partner or small group and work together to think of more similarities and differences.

Activity B | Create a Venn diagram in your notebook to brainstorm ideas related to your Unit Inquiry Question. Think of as many similarities and differences as possible for your subjects of analysis. When you are finished, think about whether you want to focus more on similarities or differences in your writing. Also look for common points of comparison for the two subjects of analysis. Share your subjects of analysis and your points of comparison with a partner or small group.

Parallel Ideas in an Outline

Parallelism in an outline refers to the use of grammatically similar language in the headings and sub-headings. Using parallel language to describe the main and supporting points in your outline helps ensure that each of the points is equally developed in your outline. A parallel structure also makes the outline easier to follow when you are moving through the writing process.

The block format outline below is for a paragraph exploring the differences between marketing to gain new customers and to keep existing ones. Notice how the main ideas (information related to the subjects of analysis) and the supporting details (information related to the points of comparison) are written using the same grammatical patterns. Both of the main ideas, *marketing* and *retaining*, are gerunds and the supporting details, *social media, direct mail, customer surveys,* and *loyalty rewards programs*, are nouns.

I.   **Topic**: Different marketing strategies for new and existing customers
II. **Subject of analysis**: Gaining new customers
    A. **Point of comparison 1**: Online marketing
        1. Social media (Facebook & Twitter)
    B. **Pont of comparison 2**: Rewards
        2. Direct mail (free samples in the mail)
III. **Subject of analysis**: Retaining existing customers
    A. **Point of comparison 1**: Online marketing
        1. Customer surveys
    B. **Point of comparison 2**: Rewards
        2. Loyalty rewards programs

Activity C | Read the block format outline on the next page. It is based on differing marketing strategies for online businesses and bricks-and-mortar companies. Identify the main ideas, the supporting ideas, and the details. Rewrite the underlined words and phrases so that the main ideas, supporting ideas, and details are grammatically parallel.

I.   **Topic: Differing marketing strategies for online businesses and bricks-and-mortar companies**

II. **Subject of analysis**: <u>Businesses that are online</u>

    A. **Point of comparison 1**: Advertising

        1. <u>Having a strong presence on social media</u>

        2. Targeted web advertising

    B. **Point of comparison 2**: Direct communication

        1. Online newsletters

        2. <u>Sending emails with coupons and offers</u>

III. **Subject of analysis**: Bricks-and-mortar companies

    A. **Point of comparison 1**: <u>Different ways of advertising</u>

        1. Television and radio advertising

        2. <u>Having a lot of billboards and posters</u>

    B. **Point of comparison 2**: <u>Communicating directly with customers</u>

        1. Paper newsletter; flyers; direct mail

        2. Telemarketing

Activity D | Create an outline for a compare-and-contrast paragraph based on the Venn diagram you created for your Unit Inquiry Question in Activity B on page 93. Use the template for a block format outline below to help you as you create your outline. You can add more points of comparison and supporting details to your outline if required. Remember to keep the items in your outline parallel.

I.   Topic:

II. Subject of analysis 1:

    A. Point of comparison 1:

        1. Supporting detail:

        2. Supporting detail:

    B. Point of comparison 2:

        1. Supporting detail:

        2. Supporting detail:

III. Subject of analysis 2:

    A. Point of comparison 1:

        1. Supporting detail:

        2. Supporting detail:

    B. Point of comparison 2:

        1. Supporting detail:

        2. Supporting detail:

Content Skill

Integrating Information from Charts and Diagrams

Statistics are often included in academic writing because they are useful as evidence to support a writer's main ideas. Statistics also help make a writer's statements more believable. In a compare-and-contrast paragraph, not all points of comparison need to include statistics. However, a writer may choose to include statistics that are surprising or interesting. Charts and diagrams can be a good source of statistics. Learning to read a chart or diagram to find the most important statistics is a valuable skill.

Activity A | Look over the infographic below from the Canadian Marketing Association. Then answer the questions that follow to identify the most important statistics and general information about consumer behaviour in Canada.

FIGURE 3.1   How do shoppers in Canada behave?

1. How many Canadians visit a big-box store at least once a week?
2. What is the most popular category of items purchased at big-box stores?
3. What is the least popular category of items purchased at big-box stores?
4. What percentage of people bought baby products at a big-box store?
5. What percentage of consumers visit independent retailers at least a few times a week?
6. Which type of business is most likely to be recommended by customers on social media?

Activity B | An Industry Canada survey asked Canadians to list the items or services that they researched and bought online. Look over the survey results in the bar chart below. Then select two surprising statistics and share your answers with a partner.

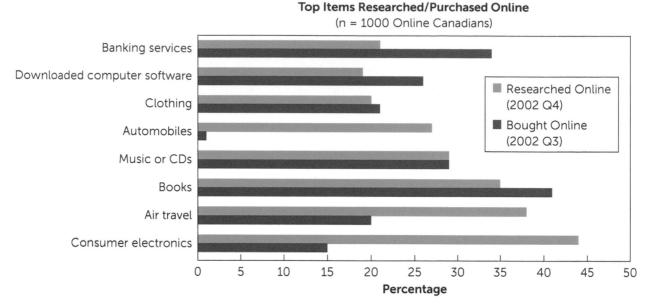

Top Items Researched/Purchased Online
(n = 1000 Online Canadians)

FIGURE 3.2   Industry Canada survey results

Activity C | Based on the bar graph in the previous activity, write sentences for each of the following products to compare or contrast the percentage of consumers who researched them online and the percentage of consumers who purchased them online. Use compare-and-contrast connectors where appropriate.

1. Banking services: Almost 35 percent of consumers bought banking services online. On the other hand, only slightly more than 20 percent of consumers researched these services online.

2. Clothing: The numbers of consumers who bought clothing online and the number of consumers who purchased clothing online was about the same at 20 percent.

3. Automobiles:

4. Music or CDs:

5. Books:

6. Air travel:

7. Consumer electronics:

Activity D | Writing Task: Compare-and-Contrast Paragraph |
Write a short paragraph comparing consumer behaviour in Canada with that in another country that you are familiar with. Include statistics from the infographic in Activity A on page 95 or the bar graph in Activity B on page 96 to support the main idea in your paragraph. You may also find some information online about consumer behaviour in the other country you are writing about.

When you are finished, share your paragraph with a partner and underline the statistics used to support the main idea. Do the statistics provide effective evidence to support your partner's topic statement? If not, suggest one or two ways that your partner could improve the use of statistics in the paragraph.

Reference Skill

Citing Information from Charts and Diagrams Using APA Style

As discussed earlier, charts and diagrams often contain good information for academic writing. When using statistics or facts from a chart or a diagram, you must include an in-text citation and an entry for a References list. Here is the bibliographic information for the infographic shown on page 95.

Author	no author
Figure title	How Do Shoppers in Canada Behave?
Type of figure	infographic
Organization	Canadian Marketing Association
Web page title	Marketing Facts—What You Need to Know Now
Date published	December 2014
Web address	http://www.the-cma.org/resource/bookstore/marketing-facts-2015

If you wish to include any statistics from the infographic "How Do Shoppers in Canada Behave?" in your writing, you will need to include in-text citations and References list including full bibliographical details. See the examples below showing the in-text citation and References entry for the infographic written in APA style.

	APA Style
In-text citation	The Canadian Marketing Association (2014) shows that 40 percent of Canadian shoppers visit big-box stores every week.
	About 40 percent of Canadians visit big-box stores every week (Canadian Marketing Association, 2014).
References entry	Canadian Marketing Association. (2014). How do Canadian shoppers behave online? [Infographic]. Retrieved from http://www.the-cma.org/resource/bookstore/marketing-facts-2015

Activity A | Review the sentences you wrote for Activity C on page 96 comparing and contrasting the percentage of consumers who researched products online and the percentage of consumers who purchased products online. Using the bibliographical information in the chart below, add in-text citations and a References entry in APA style for any statistics in your sentences.

Author	no author
Title	Top Items Researched/Purchased Online
Type of figure	chart
Organization	Ipsos-Reid
Report title	*Canadian Inter@ctive Reid Report, fourth quarter*
Date published	2002

Preventing Plagiarism

Understanding and Following Citation Styles Carefully

Following a citation style is important. Accurate citations connect your creative work with the work of other writers. Citations also show that you put care and attention into your assignment.

Different disciplines use different citation styles. For example, APA is generally used in the social sciences, whereas MLA is used in the liberal arts and humanities. It is important to find out which citation style is commonly used in your discipline, and more importantly, which style your instructor wants you to use in your assignments. This textbook presents information on APA style; the next book in the series, *Academic Inquiry 3*, provides information on and practice with both APA and MLA styles. Other styles you may see include the Chicago style (used in history and economics), IEEE style (used by electrical and electronics engineers), and the Vancouver system (used in science and medicine).

Knowing what to reference, when to reference, and how to reference outside sources is important in academic writing. You can apply this understanding to all your academic assignments.

Referencing Checklist

✓ Include citations next to each idea that is from an outside source.
✓ Clearly identify the name and year of the source in your reference.
✓ Include all the necessary bibliographical details accurately in the References list.
✓ Accurately format entries in the References list to help readers to find the sources.
✓ Include references only for sources that you read and cited.
✓ Be consistent with the style you use for in-text citations and References list.
✓ Use your library's website to help with formatting citations you are not sure about.

Format and Organization Skill

Organizing with Point-by-Point Format

In a compare-and-contrast writing assignment, there is generally no required number of points of comparison; however, you do need to have enough points of comparison to ensure that you have sufficiently analyzed and discussed the topic for your reader.

So far in this unit, you have been using block format to organize your writing. In block format, the points of comparison are gathered together for each subject of analysis, and they are written about in a block. You write all your ideas related to the first subject of analysis, and then you write all your ideas related to the second subject of analysis.

Point-by-point format puts the focus on the points of comparison. A point-by-point format is sometimes preferred for compare-and-contrast writing because it not only helps the reader see the important connections, but also helps you more fully analyze your topic. In point-by-point format, you write about each point of comparison separately, giving information about both subjects of analysis related to each of those points. Consider the point-by-point format illustrated in Figure 3.3.

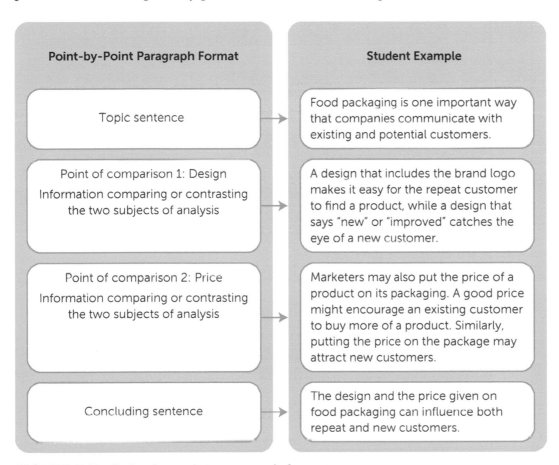

FIGURE 3.3 Point-by-point paragraph format

Activity A | Read the following paragraph, then answer the questions with a partner or small group.

Differences between Dot-Coms and Bricks-and-Mortar Businesses

Because of the differences in the way they do business, dot-coms still have a number of drawbacks compared to traditional bricks-and-mortar companies. First of all, the place of business is different. Dot-coms are companies that do not have physical buildings or stores for customers to visit. They exist only on the Internet, and they do their business through a website. As a result, it can be hard to speak to someone in person if you need help returning an item or have questions about a product. In contrast, bricks-and-mortar companies traditionally serve their customers from buildings or stores. Because there is a real store to visit, customers can look at the products they want to buy. For example, someone visiting a shoe store can try on a pair of shoes and decide right away if they fit before they buy them. Another difference is related to what these companies sell. Dot-coms often focus on items that can easily be shipped to customers, such as books, music, and other hard goods. On the other hand, traditional bricks-and-mortar stores can sell items that can't easily be shipped, such as fresh groceries like milk or fruit and vegetables. Whereas books are nice to have, fresh groceries and vegetables are necessary items. Finally, how these companies use the Internet is also different. Dot-coms depend on their websites to sell their goods and services online. They may also send customers emails and use social media. Different from dot-coms, traditional bricks-and-mortar stores are not dependent on their websites to sell products. Instead, they can use their websites to provide information along with useful coupons and promotions to bring customers into the physical locations. All in all, dot-coms, as compared to traditional physical businesses, still have some drawbacks related to where they do business, what they sell, and how they use the Internet.

1. What are the two subjects of analysis?
2. Does this paragraph focus more on similarities or differences?
3. What are the three points of comparison?
4. What are some of the supporting details the author uses for the points of comparison?
5. Does the author show a preference for one of the subjects of analysis over the other?

Activity B | Review the block format outline that you created for your Unit Inquiry Question in Activity D on page 94. Now, revise your outline so that it follows point-by-point format. Use the template on page 101 for a point-by-point outline to help you. You can add more points of comparison and supporting details to your outline if required.

Before you begin to revise your outline, ask yourself the questions below to help you organize the points logically in your outline.

1. What subjects of analysis are you exploring?
2. What are the main points of comparison?
3. What supporting details are compared or contrasted?
4. Are there any more details that you should add to the outline?

I. **Topic:**
II. **Point of comparison 1:**
   A. **Subject of analysis 1:**
      1. **Supporting detail:**
      2. **Supporting detail:**
   B. **Subject of analysis 2:**
      1. **Supporting detail:**
      2. **Supporting detail:**
III. **Point of comparison 2:**
   A. **Subject of analysis 1:**
      1. **Supporting detail:**
      2. **Supporting detail:**
   B. **Subject of analysis 2:**
      1. **Supporting detail:**
      2. **Supporting detail:**

Topic Skill

Writing Compare-and-Contrast Topic Sentences

A compare-and-contrast topic sentence serves two purposes. First, the topic sentence clearly states the subjects of analysis (topic). Next, a topic sentence indicates the focus (on similarities or on differences) and what the points of comparison are for the subjects of analysis. The focus and the points of comparison make up the controlling idea.

Activity A | In the example topic sentences below, underline the subjects of analysis and double underline the words that tell you whether the writer is focusing on similarities or differences. Then identify the points of comparison with a wavy line. The first one has been done for you as an example.

1. As consumers, Generation Y and Baby Boomers are similar in two important ways related to how they pay for purchases.

2. Generation Y is different from the Baby Boomer generation in the ways they receive information about products.

3. Online and traditional businesses have different approaches to promoting their products.

4. The methods of communicating with customers about products can be similar for online and traditional businesses.

Activity B | Identify the main idea in each set of sentences below and write an appropriate topic sentence. Be sure that your topic sentence clearly shows the topic (subjects of analysis) and the controlling idea (focus on similarities or differences with reference to the points of comparison).

1. Topic sentence: _____

    _____

    A dot-com has no building that customers can physically visit. A dot-com is a business that conducts all its sales and most of its promotion online. However, a bricks-and-mortar business is a business that serves customers from a building or store.

2. Topic sentence: _____

    _____

    Dot-coms focus on using the Internet for their business. For example, Amazon sells books, music, and other goods online. Although it has very few physical stores where customers can go to see and buy the books and other goods, customers can find a lot of information about their products on the website. Similar to dot-coms, many bricks-and-mortar businesses have created websites. These businesses now also do some of their sales and marketing on the Internet. For example, Canadian Tire is a bricks-and-mortar business with a website through which they sell sporting equipment, household tools, and other goods.

Activity C | Writing Task: Topic Sentence for Unit Inquiry Question | Look back at the brainstorming you did in Activity B on page 93 and the outline you created in Activity D on page 94, for your Unit Inquiry Question. Write a compare-and-contrast topic sentence that contains both a topic and a controlling idea in response to your Unit Inquiry Question. Compare your topic sentence with a partner and evaluate each other's sentences to make sure that they compare or contrast the subjects of analysis. Then evaluate how well your partner uses compare-and-contrast words, phrases, and connectors. Use the feedback guide in the *Learning Strategy* feature on page 109 to help you give suggestions to your partner.

Conclusion Skill

Recommending

In a compare-and-contrast paragraph, the concluding sentence can be used to make a recommendation to readers. The recommendation you make is based on what you think is important for the reader to think about or to do. You can make a strong, medium, or weak recommendation. The strength of your recommendation depends on the importance of your topic. It also depends on your audience. If your recommendation is too weak, readers might not think about it or do anything. If your recommendation is too strong, readers might become offended, especially if you have not provided a strong enough argument in your paragraph.

When you make a recommendation, use the same words that you would use to give advice. Choose your recommendation language carefully because you wish the reader to consider your recommendation.

Some example words and phrases to make a recommendation are set out below.

A very strong recommendation

- modal verbs and phrases: *had better/need to/have to/must*
- expressions: *it is essential/it is necessary*

A strong recommendation

- modal verbs and phrases: *should/ought to*
- expressions: *it is recommended/it is advisable*

A weaker recommendation

- modal verbs: *could/might/may*
- expressions: *it appears important/it might be better*

Activity A | Read the following paragraph. Notice that the final sentence is an example of a writer's recommendation. What kind of recommendation do you think the writer makes? Very strong, strong, or weaker?

New and Repeat Customers: Different Motivations

The motivation to buy a product is very different for new and repeat customers. New customers may buy a product on impulse (suddenly, without stopping to consider it carefully). They might do this for two reasons: they are influenced by advertising, or they strongly believe that this product satisfies their needs. In contrast, a repeat customer may not buy the same product on impulse. Repeat customers are more likely to buy the same product based on their previous experience with it. There are many different approaches to marketing and it is useful to consider the audience when developing a marketing strategy. Effective marketers should remember that existing and potential buyers often have different motivations.

Activity B | Write concluding sentences that match the main idea in the topic sentences that follow. Be sure to recommend that your reader think about or do something.

1. Topic sentence: Generation Y is different from the Baby Boomer generation in the way that they receive information about products.

    Concluding sentence: _____

    _____

2. Product promotion is one marketing area in which online and traditional businesses might have different approaches.

Concluding sentence: _____

_____

Activity C | Writing Task: Recommendation Conclusion for Unit Inquiry Question | Review your point-by-point format outline for your Unit Inquiry Question in Activity D on page 100, along with the topic sentence you wrote in Activity C on page 102. What are the most important ideas you want the reader to remember? What do you want readers to think about or do after reading your answer to your Unit Inquiry Question? Write a concluding sentence for your paragraph that includes a recommendation.

WRITING FUNDAMENTALS

Composition Skill

Organizing Logical Connections between Ideas

Exploring the similarities and differences between things, people, and events involves four major steps.

Identifying the things/persons/events to be compared (i.e., the subjects of analysis)

Exploring how the subjects of analysis are the same or different

Deciding on the points of comparison between the subjects of analysis

Organizing the points of comparison into a logical order so that readers can also clearly see the connections

The last step, organizing the points of comparison into a logical order, means organizing your ideas in a way that the reader expects. Doing so promotes reader understanding.

For a compare-and-contrast paragraph, there are a number of ways to logically order your points of comparison. The chart on page 105 contains some suggestions and examples. Use the method that best suits the topic you are writing about.

Organizational Method	Example
Chronological	Pepsi and Coke have both marketed their products differently throughout the 1980s, 1990s, and 2000s.
Spatial/geographic	The beautiful coasts, rich valleys, and stunning mountains that they share have led to British Columbia and Washington state developing similar tourist marketing campaigns.
Different parts in order	The Mazda Miata and the Fiat Spider are two sports cars with similar markets due to their powerful engines, sleek interiors, and streamlined exteriors.
Weakest point to strongest point (leave readers with the strongest point in mind)	Independent coffee shops are better than multinational chains because of their inviting atmospheres, homemade food, and artisan-style coffee.
Most familiar to least familiar (or vice versa)	Online stores can offer more customer satisfaction compared to traditional bricks-and-mortar stores due to their vast selection, competitive pricing, and free shipping policies.

Activity A | Organize the following 14 sentences into their most logical order from 1 to 14. In the original paragraph, the writer wanted to organize the points of comparison from the weakest point to the strongest point. When you are finished, share your answers with a partner along with what helped you to decide on the order the original writer used.

_____ A good example is the French's mustard logo.

_____ A simple logo can attract new customers and make them interested in a product.

_____ All in all, the information that new and existing customers see on food packaging is a necessary part of a product's marketing strategy.

_____ Finally, nutritional information is always needed by new and existing customers.

_____ First of all, the logo is an important part of a food product's packaging.

_____ For example, there is a picture of a hot dog on French's classic yellow prepared mustard squeeze bottle that suggests to both new and existing customers how the product can be used.

_____ For instance, both new and existing customers can easily read that one teaspoon of French's classic yellow mustard contains zero calories and zero grams of fat.

_____ It can also help existing customers by making the product easy to identify.

_____ New customers can be encouraged to try a product if they see that it is healthy for them.

_____ New customers can see how to use a product they might never have tried before, while existing customers can see new ideas for using a product.

_____ Secondly, colourful pictures on food packaging can attract customers.

_____ Similarly, existing customers may check from time to time to make sure they know what is in the food they are eating.

_____ The information provided on food packaging is important for both new and existing customers.

_____ This logo is a bright red flag with *French's* written in white.

Activity B | Writing Task: Compare-and-Contrast Paragraph |
With a partner or small group, brainstorm similarities and differences in the packaging of two products that you are familiar with. For example, you might compare the packaging for two different brands of chocolate bars or two different brands of potato chips. Then, based on three points of comparison, decide which packaging is more effective and why. Examples of points you might compare include the logos, pictures, colours, or nutritional information. On your own, write a short compare-and-contrast paragraph, remembering to organize your points of comparison in a logical order.

Activity C | Exchange your paragraph with a partner. Use the questions below to review your partner's paragraph, then share your answers with each other.

1. What are the points of comparison?
2. Are the points of comparison organized logically?
3. What organizational method do you think your partner used?
4. Is it clear which product packaging is more effective and why?

Activity D | Look back at the point-by-point outline you prepared for your Unit Inquiry Question on page 100. Discuss the organization of your points of comparison with a partner or small group. Use the questions below to guide your discussions. After you have shared some feedback, revise your outline to ensure the most logical organization of ideas.

1. What do you think the reader will generally know about your topic?
2. Why did you choose to write about your first point of comparison first?
3. What is the best way to organize your points of comparison? Why?

Sentence and Grammar Skill

Using Adverb Clauses

Form and meaning   Adverb clauses are dependent clauses that begin with words or phrases called subordinators. Subordinators can signal a variety of logical connections. The chart on page 107 contains some common subordinators you can use in your writing to express the following logical relationships: time, reason, contrast, condition, and purpose.

Logical Relationship	Subordinators	Example
Time	after before while as soon as when once as as long as	Once potential customers have read the nutritional information on a food's packaging, they can make an informed purchasing decision.
Reason	because as since	Clear nutritional information on food packaging is an important marketing tool because it can target new customers who are interested in healthy products.
Contrast	although while whereas	Although new customers might be attracted by a low price, existing customers might be more interested in receiving more product.
Condition	if unless when as long as	As long as the quality and value stay the same, a company can depend on retaining loyal customers.
Purpose	so that in order that	Some companies may lower their prices so that they can attract new customers.

Activity A | Fill in the blanks in the following sentences with the subordinator from the chart above that best matches the logical relationship between ideas.

1. _____ McDonald's introduced a new kind of coffee, Tim Hortons made their dark roast even darker.

2. Online stores should have free shipping _____ high shipping costs can hurt sales.

3. _____ buying clothes online can be convenient, many people prefer to shop in bricks-and-mortar stores because they can try things on.

4. _____ online bookstores offer free shipping, it is easy for them to compete with traditional bookstores.

5. Companies put nutritional information on their food products _____ customers can make informed purchasing choices.

Function   Writers often use complex sentences with adverb clauses to express precise logical connections between ideas in sentences, to make their writing seem more academic, and to improve the flow of sentences.

Activity B | Read the paragraph below and discuss the questions that follow with a partner.

New Wearables: The Race to Reach Customers

[1]New wearable technologies are arriving every day on the market. [2]Younger customers are very interested in learning about these products. [3]They want to stay informed. [4]These millennial customers have money to spend. [5]They are often the first to buy new wearable technology products. [6]They subscribe to social media. [7]They can stay informed about these new products. [8]A new product arrives. [9]Companies spread the news quickly with advertising on social media. [10]Many companies want to be the first to reach their customers with the new product updates.

---

1. Are the logical connections between the writer's ideas easy to understand?
2. Do the sentences flow well together?
3. Which sentences could be combined as complex sentences using subordinates to create adverb clauses?

Activity C | Edit the paragraph "New Wearables: The Race to Reach Customers" to improve the sentence flow and to make the logical connections between ideas clearer to the reader. Follow the editing instructions below to create adverb clauses. The first edit has been done for you as an example.

1. Combine sentences 2 and 3. Make a complex sentence showing a relationship of reason.

   Since younger customers are very interested in learning about these products, they want to stay informed.

2. Combine sentences 4 and 5. Make a complex sentence showing a relationship of reason.

   _____

   _____

3. Combine sentences 6 and 7. Make a complex sentence showing a relationship of purpose.

   _____

   _____

4. Combine sentences 8 and 9. Make a complex sentence showing a relationship of time.

   _____

   _____

Activity D | Choose one of the paragraphs you have previously written for this unit, such as the compare-and-contrast paragraph you wrote in Activity B on page 106. Mark all the adverb clauses. Have the subordinators been used correctly? Four common errors using adverb clauses are listed below to help you find mistakes. If you do not have any adverb clauses, consider adding or combing your ideas to add some of the subordinators from the chart on page 107.

1. Having two logical connectors in a sentence:
   * ✗ **Because** wearable technology is popular, **so** younger people buy it.
   * ✓ **Because** wearable technology is popular, younger people buy it.

2. Using unclear subordinators:
   * ✗ **While** companies contact customers, they use social media.
   * ✓ **When** companies contact customers, they use social media.

3. Confusing prepositional phrases with subordinators:
   * ✗ **Despite** smart watches cost more, they are becoming popular.
   * ✓ **Although** smart watches cost more, they are becoming popular.

4. Creating new subordinators:
   * ✗ **Even** this year's Fitbit models are not yet available, these wearables are expected to be popular.
   * ✓ **Even though** this year's Fitbit models are not yet available, these wearables are expected to be popular.

Learning Strategy

Giving and Receiving Feedback

To help you develop your revising skills, you will often be asked to give and to receive feedback. Giving and receiving feedback helps you learn to write for an audience.

Reading and commenting on someone else's writing can sometimes be uncomfortable. When giving feedback, your role is to be a critical reader and not an evaluator. For example, you do not have to comment on grammar, format, or mechanics. Instead, concentrate on ideas such as the organization and the connections between ideas.

Some of the feedback that you receive may be conflicting. In this case, ask questions to your peer reader or your instructor. Also, remain open-minded about the feedback that you receive because your readers may not see your writing in the same way as you do. Note the feedback that you think will most help you produce better quality writing in future assignments. Use the feedback guide below to help you:

Feedback Guide

1. Tell your partner something positive about her or his paragraph.

   The topic sentence is very clear to me and you remembered to write a concluding sentence. Good work!

2. Suggest ways that your partner could improve the topic development.

   Maybe you need more specific details or an example to support the idea about . . .

   I think the part about . . . should go before/after . . .

   I don't quite understand what you mean here. Could you add another idea?

3. Say what the best part of your partner's writing is.

   Overall, the way that you use transition words and phrases is effective. I had no difficulty following your ideas.

   Generally speaking, you clearly show the connections between ideas by correctly using compare-and-contrast connectors. I think the reader can clearly see which ideas you think are similar or different.

UNIT OUTCOME

Writing Assignment: Compare-and-Contrast Paragraph

Write a compare-and-contrast paragraph of 200 to 300 words on a topic related to marketing and consumers. (Your instructor may give you an alternative length.) Use at least two key points of comparison in your paragraph. You may write on a topic based on your Unit Inquiry Question, develop another topic of your choosing connected to marketing, or choose one of the following questions:

- How do different generations of consumers relate to technology?
- How are online retailers similar to or different from traditional bricks-and-mortar retailers?
- How does the type of marketing strategy depend on the type of product?

Use the skills you have developed in this unit to complete the assignment. Follow the steps set out below to practise each of your newly acquired skills to write a well-developed paragraph.

1. **Brainstorm**: Use a Venn diagram to come up with ideas related to similarities and differences between your subjects of analysis.

2. **Find information**: Find some information to support your main ideas. Include information from the unit readings in your paragraph if appropriate.

3. **Compose a topic sentence**: Develop a focused compare-and-contrast topic sentence that includes a topic and a controlling idea.

4. **Outline**: Fill in the point-by-point outline on page 111 to plan the first draft of your paragraph. You may make changes to the outline as necessary.

Topic Sentence

Focused topic sentence that states your subjects of analysis and your points of comparison:

Main Body (Points of Comparison 1 and 2)

Subject of analysis 1:
Supporting detail 1:

Supporting detail 2:

Subject of analysis 2:
Supporting detail 1:

Supporting detail 2:

Subject of analysis 1:
Supporting detail 1:

Supporting detail 2:

Subject of analysis 2:
Supporting detail 1:

Supporting detail 2:

Concluding Sentence

Concluding sentence that includes a recommendation:

5. **Write a first draft**: Use your outline to write the first draft of your paragraph. Do not worry too much about spelling or grammar in the first draft. Try to get your ideas down on paper.

6. **Self-check**: Review the first draft of your paragraph for the following and revise as needed:

   • Point-by-point format. Make sure that your points of comparison are significant and interesting to your readers.

   • Logical connections between ideas: Make sure that you have organized your points of comparison in the most logical order.

7. **Ask for a peer review**: Exchange the revised version of your first draft with a partner. Use the Evaluation Rubric below and on the next page to assess your partner's paragraph and provide suggestions to improve it. Consider your partner's feedback carefully and use it to make changes to your paragraph.

8. **Edit**: Edit your paragraph for the following:

   • Sentence structure: Check your adverb clauses to ensure that the logical relationships make sense and that the subordinators have been used correctly. If you do not have any adverb clauses, consider combining ideas to create some complex sentences.

   • Vocabulary: Check that you have used some of the AWL and mid-frequency vocabulary from this unit in your paragraph.

   • Transitions: Check that you have used compare-and-contrast connectors appropriately. If you haven't used any of these words or phrases, think about adding some where needed.

9. **Write a final draft**: Write a final draft of your paragraph, making any changes that you think will improve it. If possible, leave some time between drafts.

10. **Proofread**: Check the final draft of your paragraph for any small errors you may have missed. In particular, look for spelling errors, typos, and punctuation mistakes. If you used information from an outside source, double-check your in-text citations and your References list to make sure they are formatted properly.

Evaluation: Compare-and-Contrast Paragraph Rubric

Use the following checklist to evaluate your paragraph. In which areas do you need to improve most?

E = Emerging: frequent difficulty using unit skills; needs a lot more work
D = Developing: some difficulty using unit skills; some improvement still required
S = Satisfactory: able to use unit skills most of the time; meets average expectations for this level
O = Outstanding: exceptional use of unit skills; exceeds expectations for this level

Skill	E	D	S	O
The paragraph is organized in a point-by-point format with a focus on points of comparison or contrast.				
Content is organized logically with a clear compare-and-contrast topic sentence, supporting sentences, and concluding sentence so that the reader can easily follow the writer's thinking.				
Compare-and-contrast connectors are used throughout the writing and display variety.				

Where various word forms of a word family are used, suffixes are used correctly to create the right part of speech.			
AWL and mid-frequency vocabulary items from this unit are used where appropriate and with few mistakes.			
The topic sentence includes a topic and controlling idea, and clearly shows whether the paragraph will focus on comparing or contrasting.			
The concluding sentence brings a satisfying close to the paragraph with a strong, medium, or weak recommendation logically related to the topic.			
Adverb clauses are used appropriately to create complex sentences that show logical relationships between ideas.			
If required, APA-style in-text citations and References list have been included.			

Unit Review

Activity A | What do you know now that you did not know before about marketing and consumer behaviour? Discuss with a partner or small group.

Activity B | Look back at the Unit Inquiry Question you developed at the start of this unit and discuss it with a partner or small group. Then share your answers with the class. Use the following questions to guide you.

1. What information did you find in this unit that helped you answer your question?
2. How would you answer your question now?

Activity C | Use the following checklist to review what you have learned throughout this unit. First decide which 10 skills you think are most important—circle the number beside each of these 10 skills. If you learned a skill in this unit that isn't listed below, write it in the blank row at the end of the checklist. Then put a check mark in the box beside those points you feel you have learned. Be prepared to discuss your choices with the class.

Self-Assessment Checklist	
☐	1. I can talk about a number of different topics connected to marketing and consumer behaviour based on what I have read in this unit.
☐	2. I can develop my own inquiry question that illustrates a comparison between two different subjects of analysis.
☐	3. I can use compare-and-contrast words and phrases to connect ideas in my writing.
☐	4. I can select appropriate word forms to fit grammatically into my sentences, and use suffixes to change word forms when necessary.

☐	5. I can use the AWL and mid-frequency vocabulary from this unit in my writing.
☐	6. I can make logical connections between ideas and information I have read about to come to a deeper understanding of a topic.
☐	7. I can use Venn diagrams to illustrate and brainstorm similarities and differences.
☐	8. I can write an outline that is parallel in its organization.
☐	9. I can understand and follow citation styles carefully to avoid plagiarism.
☐	10. I can integrate information from charts and diagrams into my own writing.
☐	11. I can write compare-and-contrast topic sentences.
☐	12. I can write concluding sentences that recommend the reader think about or do something.
☐	13. I can use adverb clauses to provide variety in my writing.
☐	14. I can write an effective cause-and-effect paragraph.
☐	15.

Activity D | Put a check mark in the box beside the vocabulary items from this unit that you feel confident using in your writing. Make a plan to practise the words that you still need to learn.

Vocabulary Checklist

☐	communicate (n.) AWL		☐	pace (n.) 3000
☐	device (n.) 4000		☐	persuade (v.) 3000
☐	enable (v.) 2000		☐	potential (adj.) AWL
☐	engaged (adj.) 2000		☐	promote (v.) AWL
☐	ensure (v.) AWL		☐	prompt (v.) 3000
☐	loyal (adj.) 4000		☐	retail (n.) 3000
☐	media (pl. n.) AWL		☐	retain (v.) AWL
☐	network (n.) AWL		☐	strategy (n.) AWL

UNIT 4

International Education

Globalization and Cultural Adjustment

EXPLORING IDEAS

Introduction

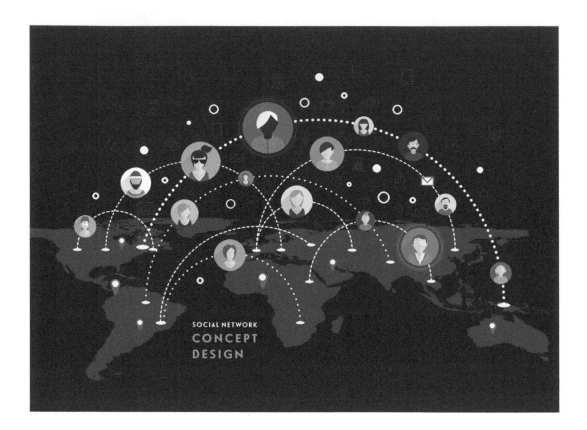

Activity A | Discuss the following questions with a partner or small group.

1. Consider the image at the top of the page. Why is it a suitable illustration of this unit's theme? What does it show?
2. Why do some students choose to go abroad for their higher education?
3. What are the world's most popular study destinations for international students?
4. How different are the post-secondary experiences of international and local students?
5. Apart from language challenges, what important kinds of challenges do international students face when they go abroad to study?
6. How can colleges and universities support international students during their studies abroad?

Activity B | Read the Friendship Chart in Figure 4.1 and the description that follows. These results are based on a survey of international students in Canada. In a small group, identify and discuss any surprising results from the chart.

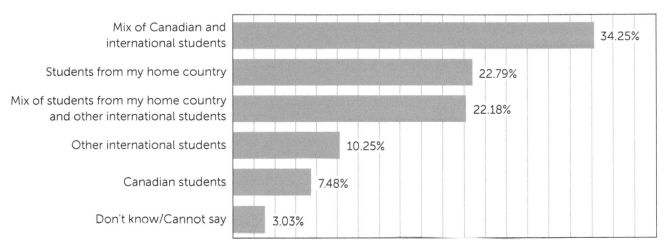

FIGURE 4.1 Friendship chart: Where are most of your friends in Canada from?

Approximately one-third of international students are friends primarily with a mixture of Canadian students and other international students. Fifty-five percent of students are friends primarily with other international students, including 23 percent who indicated they are friends primarily with students from their home country. Approximately 7 percent of students said they are friends primarily with Canadian students.

Activity C | Read and answer the two questions in the survey below about socializing, friendship, and meeting new people. Answer Yes or No for each question, and give a reason and an example to support your answer.

Share your answers with a partner, then work with your partner to create two more questions about socializing to add to the survey. If needed, ask your instructor for a survey sheet to write your questions on. Conduct your four-question survey with as many other students as you can in the class. Record your classmates' responses. Ask follow-up questions, such as *Why do you think that?* or *Can you give me an example?* Write their reasons and examples in the chart as needed.

Survey Questions and Responses	Answer	
	Yes	**No**
1. Do you find it easy to make friends with local students? Reason: Example:		
2. Do you participate in on-campus social activities? Reason: Example:		
3. Question: Reason: Example:		
4. Question: Reason: Example:		

Fostering Inquiry

Responding to Ideas and Information

Responding to ideas and information in an academic way is not very different than responding to films. When you see a film, you respond very naturally to the ideas and information that you see or hear. Most filmgoers respond immediately as they leave the cinema. See the two examples below of responses to the movie *Kung Fu Panda*—one is descriptive and one is analytical.

A descriptive response is something you might say when talking to friends. It describes how you feel.

I loved the movie. Po is an amazing panda. The animation is fantastic!!

An analytical response would be more like what you would write as part of a review for a film studies course. It explains what you think.

The film is set in a mountain valley similar to Sichuan Province. The location appears to be in China, but the main character, Po, in his actions and words, seems more like an American. Although the film mixes two countries and cultures, filmgoers all over the world will understand the most important theme of the film: friendship.

Activity A | What do you want to know more about in relation to the topic of international education? For example:

- *What are the main benefits of studying abroad?*
- *How do students adapt to a new academic culture?*
- *Why is friendship important when studying abroad?*

1. Write two or three questions you are curious about related to international education.
2. When you are finished, compare your questions with a partner or small group.
3. Choose one question to guide you as you work through this unit. It does not have to be the same question as your partner or group. Your question may change as you learn more about your topic.
4. Write your inquiry question in the space provided. Look back at this question as you work through this unit. This is your Unit Inquiry Question.

My Unit Inquiry Question:

_____

_____

_____

Activity B | Writing Task: Freewriting | Write for at least five minutes on the topic of your Unit Inquiry Question. Do not stop writing during this time. After five minutes, read what you have written and circle two or three ideas that you would like to explore further.

Structure

Summary-and-Response Paragraphs

The ability to write summary-and-response paragraphs is useful for different academic tasks: book or film reviews, course reading responses, and exam preparation notes, among others.

Summary Paragraph   Summarizing involves more than simply describing or repeating another person's ideas and words. In a summary paragraph, you use your own words to write about someone else's ideas, in a shorter and simpler way. Writing a summary paragraph shows that you have understood a text and that you can distinguish between the major and minor ideas expressed in it.

Response Paragraph   Giving a response is similar to expressing an opinion but there is one key difference between a response paragraph and an opinion paragraph. In an opinion paragraph, you express an opinion about a topic and support that opinion with reasons. In a response paragraph, you express new or different thinking about a topic and support your thinking with reference to ideas that you have heard or read. You are responding to someone else's ideas and opinions.

A response paragraph shows how your current thoughts about a topic are connected to what you have heard or read.

When you think about new ideas and information, consider what you already know about the topic or an idea related to the topic. Ask yourself the following questions to move your thinking from the level of opinion to the level of response.

1. Is the idea that I heard or read surprising to me in any way?
2. Is the idea that I heard or read the same as or different than what I already know or believe?
3. How have my ideas changed, or what new ideas do I now have based on what I've read or heard?
4. Are my new ideas justified? Can I support these ideas?

Activity A | Read the two paragraphs on page 120 about how students and universities can promote social contact between international and local students. The first paragraph is a summary of the main ideas in a report titled "The Integration Challenge: Connecting International Students with their Canadian Peers" and the second paragraph is a response to those ideas. When you have finished, discuss these questions with a partner or small group:

1. How many main ideas from the report are presented in the summary? What are these ideas?
2. What is the writer's main idea in the response paragraph? How do you know?

International Students and Social Experiences

Summary

When students feel connected to their instructors and classmates, successful learning happens. Knight-Grofe and Deacon (2015) surveyed international students to discover how schools can promote positive social experiences between international and Canadian students. Their report "The Integration Challenge: Connecting International Students with their Canadian Peers" informs schools about international student experiences and recommendations. In their report, Knight-Grofe and Deacon (2015) propose that student orientations start later in the first semester. More international students then have a chance to participate. As well, assignments that mix together Canadian and international students should be planned into courses. Doing this makes it easier for all students to get to know one another outside of class. According to Knight-Grofe and Deacon (2015), Canadian students should spend time learning about the different cultures and perspectives on today's internationalized campus. In short, Knight-Grofe and Deacon's report suggests ways that colleges and universities can promote international student integration into the campus community.

Response

Building social networks remains difficult for some international students, especially those students from a cultural background that is very different from the local culture. Knight-Grofe and Deacon (2015) explain that there may be cultural barriers which prevent some students from mixing with Canadian students. Generally, it is thought that some international students may need more time to adapt to the local way of life. Knight-Grofe and Deacon (2015) make important recommendations about effective ways to help international and local students connect socially. Community activities, such as volunteering, can help international students participate more in the local culture. Students who volunteer develop cross-cultural skills more quickly. I believe that students with these skills have a greater appreciation of the similarities and differences between cultures on campus. International students who connect to, and try to understand, the local culture seem to be more satisfied and more successful. Also, Morrison (2014) suggests that students need more than survival strategies—they need guidance from the university on how to navigate their new multi-cultural academic community. Once new international and local students discover effective intercultural resources from the university's student support services, then they will be able to succeed in their first year.

References

Knight-Grofe, J. & Deacon, L. (2015). CBIE Research in Brief #2 *The integration challenge: connecting international students with their Canadian peers.* [Report] Ottawa, ON: The Canadian Bureau for International Education.

Retrieved from http://cbie.ca/wp-content/uploads/2016/04/CBIE-Research-in-Brief-2-The-Integration-Challenge-EN.pdf

Morrison, I. (2014, January 13) *Study abroad challenges*. Canadian Bureau for International Education. Retrieved from https://web.archive.org/web/20140419040500/http://istudentcanada.ca/study-abroad-challenges/

Activity B | Review "International Students and Social Experiences" to decide if the following statements are true (T) or false (F). Compare your answers with a partner and discuss any differences. Then work together to rewrite the false statements to make them true.

The Summary Paragraph . . .	The Response Paragraph . . .
_____ 1. contains a description of the authors' (Knight-Grofe's and Deacon's) report.	_____ 10. begins with a clear topic sentence.
_____ 2. does not mention the authors' names or their ideas very often.	_____ 11. does not mention the authors' names or ideas.
_____ 3. provides many details about the authors' report.	_____ 12. uses opinion language.
_____ 4. includes quotations.	_____ 13. includes only the response writer's ideas.
_____ 5. includes the summary writer's own ideas.	_____ 14. has no concluding sentence.
_____ 6. has more words than the response.	_____ 15. uses summary statements to include the authors' ideas in the response.
_____ 7. presents the authors' main ideas in the same order as in the report.	
_____ 8. uses reporting verbs/expressions.	
_____ 9. has a concluding sentence.	

Language Tip

Writing Summary Statements

Because a summary paragraph should not include quotations, it is necessary to write summary statements to report another author's ideas. In writing a response paragraph, you often use summary statements as a way to include the author's ideas that you are responding to. Figure 4.2 on page 122 shows the differences between direct quotations, paraphrases, and summary statements. Notice how similar quotations and paraphrases are to one another.

As you can see in Figure 4.2 on the next page, a summary statement is the furthest from the words in the original text. A summary statement is more about expressing the main ideas presented in the original text than detailing the specific ideas or examples.

Though a summary statement is written entirely in your own words, it refers to another person's work, so this author (or authors) must be credited as the source of the ideas in the summary statement. This can be done in two different ways.

A summary statement can be written with an APA-style in-text citation at the end of the sentence. For example:

In recent years, more and more international students have come to Canada to study. (Humphries, Rauh, & McDine, 2013).

A summary statement can also be written using a simple citation style that includes author's last name + (year) + reporting verb + noun clause. For example:

Humphries, Rauh, and McDine (2013) explain that in recent years, more and more international students have come to Canada to study.

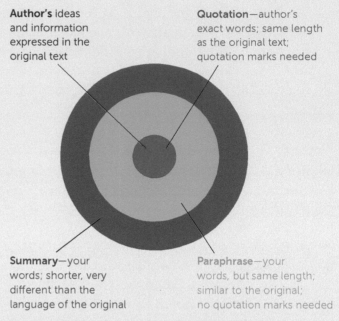

Author's ideas and information expressed in the original text

Quotation—author's exact words; same length as the original text; quotation marks needed

Summary—your words; shorter, very different than the language of the original

Paraphrase—your words, but same length; similar to the original; no quotation marks needed

FIGURE 4.2 Quotations, paraphrases, and summary statements

When writing a response statement to an opinion statement, start by asking yourself, *What do I think about the ideas in this statement?* and *What do the ideas in the statement make me think of?* Consider the following opinion statement:

Group work helps learning at university.

The chart below includes some brainstormed ideas (in response to the two questions above) and the response statements created from them.

Brainstormed Ideas	Response Statement
- get new ideas from other people - work faster because we can divide up tasks - have fun	Group work can improve learning because lots of new ideas can be created between people in a short amount of time. Group work is also a social time, and having fun doing assignments together will help keep students motivated.

Activity C | With a partner, read the following two opinion statements and ask yourselves, *What do we think about the ideas in this opinion statement?* and *What do the ideas in the statement make us think of?*

Communication in class discussions is a challenge.

Grades should be given for participating in class.

Brainstorm two or three ideas you have in response to each of the opinion statements. Then express your response in two or three sentences for each opinion.

Activity D | Exchange your response statements with another pair of students. Read their response statements and pick one to summarize. Use the *Language Tip* on page 121 to help you write a one-sentence summary of their response.

Here are two examples of one-sentence summaries (summary statements) based on two students' responses to the opinion statement *Group work helps students learn at university.*

> **Informal summary statement**: Kate and Yuki believe that group work is good for thinking and for socializing, both of which help students learn.

Notice first names and a reporting verb (*believe*) are used.

> **Formal summary statement**: Thepsuree and Nakamura (2018) believe that group work is good for thinking and for socializing, both of which help students learn.

Notice last names, the year, and a reporting verb (*believe*) are used.

Activity E | Revisit your Unit Inquiry Question on page 118. Now that you have learned more about your topic, you may have a better of idea of how to answer your question, or you may consider revising it. Use the following questions to guide you in assessing your Unit Inquiry Question.

- What information have you learned that will help you answer your Unit Inquiry Question?
- What information do you still need to answer your question?
- Do you want to change your question in any way?

ACADEMIC READING

Vocabulary

Vocabulary Skill: Understanding Word Forms and Prefixes

Learning how prefixes are used to change the meaning of words within a word family can help you build your vocabulary and improve word choice in your writing. Prefixes are letters added to the beginning of a word to make a new word. A prefix influences what a word means. By separating the prefix from the root word, you can sometimes understand the meaning better. For example, the prefix *dis* means *not*, which can help you understand the meaning of the words *disagree* and *distrust*.

dis + agree = not + agree

dis + trust = not + trust

Activity A | Review the common prefixes below. Then add examples of other words you already know that include each prefix. Three words are there to get you started.

Prefix	Meaning	Examples	Your Examples
re-	again	review (look again)	
im- in- un- il- ir-	not	impossible (not possible) inefficient (not efficient) unsurprising (not surprising) illegal (not legal) irresponsible (not responsible)	*irreplaceable, irrelevant, irregular*
dis-	not	disappear (not appear)	
mis-	bad or wrongly	misbehave (behave badly) mishear (hear wrongly)	

Activity B | Match each prefix in the chart below with its meaning from the list in the text box. Write the meaning in the second column, then write your own example of a word with this prefix in the last column. The first one has been done for you. If you need more information, check an English dictionary.

~~good~~	too much	in the middle of	too little
together	after	between	before

Prefix	Meaning	Examples	Your Example
1. bene-	*good*	benefit	*benevolent (=kind)*
2. co-		co-worker	
3. inter-		interaction	
4. over-		overuse	
5. under-		underpay	
6. pre-		pre-semester	
7. mid-		midday	
8. post-		post-quiz	

Vocabulary Preview: The Academic Word List

Activity C | The AWL words in red appear in the readings on pages 128–129. Read the example sentence for each word, then choose the synonym that most closely matches the meaning of the word in red. If you need more information about the words, check an English dictionary.

1. Effective student time-management strategies have a beneficial effect on grades.
   a. helpful
   b. harmful

2. Economic **circumstances** affect the ability of international students to study abroad.
   a. political
   b. financial

3. The Canadian Bureau for International Education **estimates** that the number of international students in Canada will grow by 10 percent over the next few years.
   a. costs
   b. guesses

4. Students who travel to other countries to study are **exposed** to new ways of thinking.
   a. experience
   b. reveal

5. On many campuses, exchange programs are the **norm** because many students wish to travel overseas to study.
   a. standard
   b. exception

6. Larger urban centres in Canada tend to be more culturally **diverse** than smaller cities. Many new Canadians often choose larger cities to settle in.
   a. different
   b. varied

7. Social **interactions** between international and local students are very important to build a campus-wide feeling of community.
   a. communication
   b. reaction

8. Universities in Canada actively **seek** to recruit international students.
   a. achieve
   b. look for

Vocabulary Preview: Mid-frequency Vocabulary

Activity D | The eight mid-frequency words in the left-hand column in the following chart appear in the readings on pages 128–129. They are grouped by part of speech. Study the definition of each word, then complete the paragraph on page 126 with the best word for each blank.

Noun	
majority	the largest part of a group of people or things
Adjective	
ample	enough or more than enough
optimistic	expecting good things to happen or something to be successful
vigilant	very careful to avoid danger or trouble
vital	necessary or essential for something to succeed or exist

Verb	
enrich	to improve the quality of something, often by adding something to it
navigate	to find the right way to deal with a difficult or complicated situation
Adverb	
abroad	in or to a foreign country

As the need for international communication grows, an increasing number of international students go _____ to study. Many students are attracted to Canada and other English-speaking countries to continue their education in order to _____ their marketable skills. Essentially, the _____ of these students feel that speaking more than one language will help them to _____ the complex job market in the future. Students are naturally _____ when they begin their studies in a new country. However, there can be challenges when moving from high school to college or university, and all students, both international and local, need to be _____ about improving their academic skills. Some authors have suggested that although students have _____ opportunities to communicate through speaking, they must also develop their reading and writing skills. These academic skills are _____ to student success because most academic tasks require students to do a great deal of reading and writing.

Reading

The readings on pages 128–129 are excerpted from two publications of the Canadian Bureau for International Education, an organization that has done research into international education in Canada for the past 25 years. The first excerpt is from a report that describes international education in Canada. The second excerpt describes challenges students might have.

Activity A | Read Figure 4.3, "Canada's Performance and Potential in International Education, 2015," on the next page then discuss the following questions with a partner or small group.

1. Which countries do most international students in Canada come from?
2. Why do international students choose to study in Canada?
3. Why do you think only 1 to 3 percent of Canadian students go abroad to study?
4. Do you think the number of international students in Canada will increase or decrease? Why?

FIGURE 4.3 Canada's performance and potential in international education, 2015

Activity B | Before doing the readings, mark the following statements as true (T) or false (F) based on your current understanding of international education. As you read the text, think about whether your answers are correct. Paragraph numbers have been provided to help you check your answers after you are done reading.

1. _____ Canada is one of the top 10 countries to receive international students. (Reading 1, para. 1)

2. _____ Canada's international student population has almost doubled since 2001. (Reading 1, para. 1)

3. _____ The number of students who go abroad to study will decrease by 2025. (Reading 1, para. 2)

4. _____ China's share of international students has seen a significant increase. (Reading 1, para. 3)

5. _____ International students help Canadian students develop more global attitudes. (Reading 1, para. 4)

6. _____ Language challenges are the greatest challenges when studying abroad. (Reading 2, paras. 3–5)

Activity C | Read the following excerpts and look specifically for ideas that could be used to help answer your Unit Inquiry Question later in the unit. Underline or highlight any potentially suitable ideas or details.

READING 1

A World of Learning: Canada's Performance and Potential in International Education

Summary: International Students

1   In 2011, Canada enrolled about 5 percent of internationally mobile students, making it the seventh most popular host country behind the US, UK, China, France, Germany, and Australia. Since 2001, the number of international students in Canada has increased by 94 percent to over 265,000 students at all levels. Canada's international student population comes from countries across the globe, but a few send far more students than others. The top five source countries remained unchanged between 2011 and 2012: China, India, Korea, Saudi Arabia, and the US, combined, continue to make up more than half of Canada's international students. These countries, among other high-growth countries such as Nigeria, Brazil, and Vietnam represent key international education markets that add to the cultural and social fabric of Canada and provide linkages for future business, research, and diplomatic partnerships.

International Students in Canada

2   In this age of rapid globalization and increasing interconnectedness, a growing number of students are **seeking** an international education. The Organisation for Economic Co-operation and Development (OECD) **estimates** that the global demand for international higher education is set to grow from nearly 4.1 million students in 2010 to 7.2 million students in 2025. The OECD reports that the **majority** (about 53 percent) of international students are from Asia with the largest number of students coming from China, India, and Korea (OECD, 2011, 2012, 2013).

3   While in 2011, Canada enrolled about 5 percent of all internationally mobile students, in seventh position, Australia, a country of similar size and population to Canada, received 6 percent of the international student market. China, which was not in the top eight host countries in 2001, is now in third position globally receiving 7 percent of the international student market (Project Atlas, 2012).

4   The impact of international students in Canada goes far beyond the **economic**. Students with education and experience from around the world contribute to the cultural and social fabric of Canada. While in Canada, they provide Canadian students with the opportunity to reflect on global perspectives in a classroom setting, and learn about **diverse** cultures through out-of-class **interactions**.

5   After graduation, if they choose to stay in Canada, they are highly desirable immigrants. With their international backgrounds coupled with Canadian education and fluency[1] in one or both of Canada's official languages, they have the potential to address employment shortages, and more than that, **enrich** our workforce, including maintaining contacts with networks at home or in other countries, all while understanding how Canada does business. Students who return to their home country or move to another

---

[1] the ability to speak or write a language, easily and well

country become unofficial ambassadors[2] for Canada, potential future collaborators on cross-border research and partners in business and diplomacy.[3]

6   International students in Canada are highly valued and highly **beneficial** to this country's

educational landscape,[4] and **vital** to the globalized educational institution of the future.

Source: Humphries, J., Rauh, K., & McDine, D. (2013). *A World of learning: Canada's performance and potential in international education* (pp. iv, 9). Ottawa, ON: The Canadian Bureau for International Education.

[2] a representative of a country
[3] managing relations between different countries

[4] everything you can see when you look across a large area of land; *educational landscape* refers to the whole educational system

READING 2

Study Abroad Challenges

1   International students have to cope with a variety of study **abroad** challenges. Culture shock, language barriers, institutional policies, and fear of the unknown are issues that international students deal with. A small amount of guidance, structure, and support can make for a smoother transition for both international students and their host institutions.

2   All international students will face, to some degree, the challenge of adapting to a new culture. Culture shock is experienced to some degree by almost every individual entering into a new environment, which has a history and well-established set of **norms** and expectations. Culture shock does not only occur when one travels to a foreign country. For those who do, however, there is a greater chance that culture shock will be more pronounced.

3   Upon arrival in Canada, international students tend to be **optimistic**. Their surroundings are novel[5] and exciting. As students begin their studies, however, pressure builds. They may **be exposed to** new methods of instruction and, of course, a new language. Many students struggle to **navigate** the government and institutional bureaucracies.[6] All the while, these students carry the expectations of family members back home. This pressure can be too much

for many students. They may face anxiety, depression, or any number of mental health–related issues.

4   It is important that during the first few months of a new school year, schools are **vigilant** to provide added support for international students. Simple tasks that most of us take for granted can be difficult for newcomers. Some students have unique dietary requirements. Many are unprepared for the cost of living in Canada. Others have never experienced winter. Students may also struggle with culturally ingrained[7] expectations such as formality or punctuality.[8] Spending some time to explain issues such as banking, shopping, transportation, weather, and general expectations can help international students adapt. It is also important to make students aware of student services available to them, such as counsellors, financial aid, and health care services.

5   Finally, students often arrive in Canada alone. In doing so, they may be leaving behind a network of family and community support. The adjustment to the individuality of Canadian society can be very difficult. For that reason, ensuring that students have **ample** opportunity to form relationships and communities will help students to better adjust to life in Canada.

Source: Morrison, I. (2014, January 13). Study abroad challenges. *iStudent Canada*. Retrieved from https://web.archive.org/web/20140419040500/http://istudentcanada.ca/study-abroad-challenges/

[5] new
[6] the system of official rules and ways of doing things

[7] firmly fixed or established and therefore difficult to change
[8] the fact or quality of being on time

Activity D | Discuss the following questions with a partner or small group.

1. What are the benefits for host countries when international students choose to study in those countries?
2. How can schools, colleges, and universities support international students?
3. Why do you think more and more students will choose to study abroad?
4. Are there any ideas discussed in the text that you do not quite understand? Discuss anything you are not sure about.

Activity E | Revisit your Unit Inquiry Question on page 118. Are there any ideas from the readings that will help you answer your question? Share your ideas with a partner or small group. At this point, you may consider revising your Unit Inquiry Question. Use the following questions to help you in assessing your question.

1. How does the information from these readings change your understanding of international education?
2. Which ideas from these readings can be used to help answer your Unit Inquiry Question?
3. What additional questions do you have after finishing the readings?
4. Where could you find more information?

Activity F | Writing Task: Response Paragraph | Reading 2, "Study Abroad Challenges," discusses some of the particular challenges international students may have while studying here in Canada. Write a short response paragraph about one idea that you found important in Reading 2. Before you write, brainstorm ideas using any of the techniques you have learned so far. Try to include five of the vocabulary words from this unit, but make sure that the paragraph is written in your own words.

Activity G | Compare your paragraph to the sample paragraph in Appendix 2, then answer the questions that follow. Share your answers with a partner or a small group.

1. What is the main topic of the paragraph?
2. How does the writer support the ideas in the paragraph?
3. Is there a concluding sentence? Does it include the main idea from the topic sentence?
4. After reading the sample paragraph, is there anything you would like to revise in your paragraph?

Activity H | Read the short text on page 131 by Susan Wu, an international student in Canada. Susan recommends different ways that international students can improve their communication skills. As you read, underline Susan's recommendations to other students. Do you think that international students will follow Susan's recommendations? Why or why not? Discuss your answers in a small group.

Living Abroad: How to stay positive and be social

By Susan Wu

Living and studying day-to-day in another language and culture is worth the effort even though every student faces challenges at some point—the language may not be very easy and the local customs may not be very familiar. Here, I'd like to share some advice about how we can maintain healthy attitudes and make the most of our intercultural experiences.

[1] Stay positive! When we're abroad, misunderstandings are normal and happen to everyone. We interpret what we see or hear based on our own background, and so our interpretations can sometimes be mistaken. We shouldn't feel down though, especially if we don't understand everything and everyone all the time. Not understanding is really a chance to learn, and learning is our main motivation for going abroad. We should try to learn as much as we can—the more we know, the easier it will be to adapt and the less strange everything will seem.

[2] Be social! At home, it's easy to find someone to chat with, but in a different country, it isn't. Because we're away from our social network, we'll have to make a greater effort to interact. Being able to break the ice with new people is a life skill we'll need, so think of it as practice now for the future. Although we might worry that we're not expressing ourselves clearly, we shouldn't let that fear stop us. Friendships with others will naturally develop if we can discover our common interests.

It's much easier to socialize with friends from our home country, but the more connections we have to the local community, the more successful we'll feel. My last recommendation for you is this: get involved! Don't study day and night. Instead, take some time to get to know local people by joining a club or a team on campus or volunteering in the community—in the end, you'll be glad you've made the most of your time and experiences abroad to grow as a person.

Critical Thinking

Recommending a Course of Action

Recommending what action should be taken is a useful skill for problem-solving in your academic and professional life. As well, in academic writing assignments, you often choose to make a recommendation to your reader in your concluding sentences. Before you make a recommendation, be sure to give yourself enough time to think about your recommendation so that you can recommend something that you believe in. To make a more meaningful recommendation to your reader, think about what might happen if the recommendation is not followed. If nothing negative would happen, try making a more meaningful recommendation. Consider the advice in the decision funnel on page 132 when deciding what recommendation to make.

Recommending Action—Guidelines

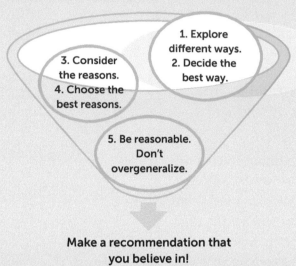

Make a recommendation that
you believe in!

DO

✓ Look at different ways of doing something and decide which way is the best.
✓ Think about how to convince your reader. What reasons could you use?
✓ Try to be believable and be specific.

DON'T

✗ Make overly general recommendations, such as:
  ✗ The government should do more to help international students to adapt.
  ✗ As we all know, international students should be more confident in their speaking abilities.

PROCESS FUNDAMENTALS

Brainstorming and Outlining

Idea Webs

An idea web, sometimes called a mind map or a concept map, is an effective way to brainstorm and record ideas.

- Idea webs creatively combine images and language.
- Idea webs closely match the way you think: your thinking moves easily in many directions.

> **topic ⟷ general ideas ⟷ more specific ideas ⟷ examples**

- Idea webs are excellent for collaborative writing assignments. Two or more people can easily brainstorm and contribute ideas.
- Idea webs help to create many ideas in a short time. All ideas are acceptable to begin with. When you are done brainstorming, you can evaluate and rank your ideas.

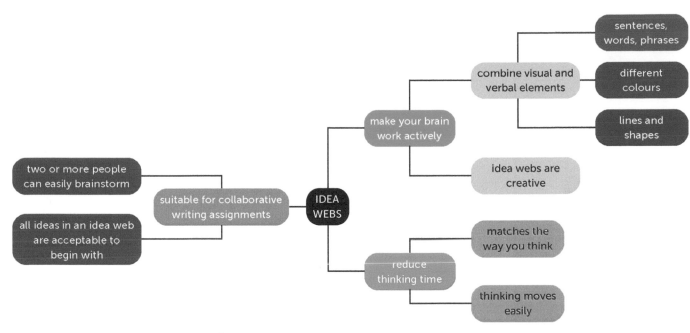

FIGURE 4.4 Brainstorming with idea webs

Creating an idea web is a skill that develops with practice. Do not worry about creating very colourful and artistic idea webs. Instead, begin with small idea webs and experiment as you become more confident. Remember that thinking about your topic and creating ideas are more important than what the final web looks like.

Activity A | With a partner, create an idea web on a separate paper for the inquiry question *How can international students start to feel at home in a new culture?* The idea web you build should explore various ideas about cultural adjustment. After you finish, present your idea web to another pair, and discuss the following questions.

1. What other more specific ideas or examples could be added?
2. How could you order your ideas before outlining?
3. Which idea should be first? Why?

Outline for Summary-and-Response Paragraphs

A summary-and-response writing assignment can be organized in two separate paragraphs.

- The first paragraph contains the introductory sentences and the summary.
- The second paragraph contains the response and the concluding sentences.

Figure 4.5 on page 134 shows the basic format for a two-paragraph summary-and-response assignment. This format is preferred because it presents the summary separately from the response, so it is easier for the reader to understand each of the two parts.

Summary-and-Response Two-Paragraph Organization	Information to Include in Each Section
Paragraph 1 Introduction and Summary	• 2 background sentences introducing the topic • a statement describing who the author is and what the author's purpose for writing is • 2 or 3 sentences summarizing the main ideas from the source text
Paragraph 2 Response and Concluding Sentences	• a topic sentence introducing your opinion about the topic • supporting point 1: explaining what the author thinks about the topic • supporting point 2: explaining what you think about the author's idea • the topic sentence rephrased • a concluding sentence recommending the reader do something or think more about something

FIGURE 4.5 Summary-and-response paragraphs

Activity B | Reread Susan Wu's blog post on page 131. Prepare your ideas to write a response to her recommendations. Create an idea web and share it with a partner. Discuss what you think would be the easiest ideas to write about in a response paragraph.

Activity C | Read the completed outline of an example response paragraph below. Notice how it is set up to follow the Paragraph 2 requirements in Figure 4.5.

Response to Susan Wu's Recommendations about Finding Friends

Topic: Finding Friends

Topic sentence: Participating in local activities helps students find friends and settle in.

Supporting point 1 (What does the writer, Susan Wu, think?):
International students should make changes in their lives. They could be more interactive with the local community to feel more at home and not so alone.

Supporting point 2 (What do you think about Susan Wu's ideas?):
Wu makes an excellent point about trying new activities with new people.
　–Studying abroad can be life changing.
　–Making new friends and sharing common interests have a positive influence on feeling connected.

Rephrased topic sentence: Changing behaviour is difficult, but positive changes to students' social lives do help students to really join in and feel at home.

Concluding sentence with recommendation:
Students do not need to feel alone. They should make new friendships and participate in new experiences. These are real ways to settle in to their new home-away-from-home.

Choose one main idea from the idea web you created in Activity B. Develop this idea to complete a response paragraph outline. Include the topic, topic sentence, supporting points, and concluding sentences (restatement of the topic sentence and recommendation). Ask your instructor for a full-page outline. Refer to the information in Figure 4.5 to help you decide which information to add to the blank outline.

Content Skill

Integrating Information from Reports

Reports are generally written by subject matter experts. Reports are useful because they provide detailed information on a topic. As well, reports often contain short summaries, so it is easier for you as a researcher to locate the report's main conclusions.

Activity A | The international student survey results in the graphic below are from a report by the Canadian Bureau for International Education. The survey asked international students how they felt about six statements on the topic of adjusting to life and making friends in Canada. The graphic shows how the students responded to the statements. For example, 45 percent of international students strongly agreed that Canada is a welcoming and tolerant society, but only 34 percent strongly agreed that Canadians are friendly when you get to know them.

Read the statements in the graphic below and decide how strongly you agree or disagree with each one. Share your answers in a small group, and discuss how your answers compare to the graph.

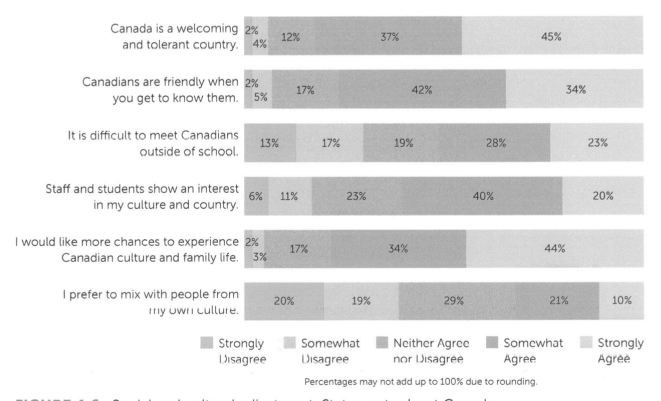

FIGURE 4.6 Social and cultural adjustment: Statements about Canada

Activity B | Below is a summary paragraph that reports the results of the student survey referenced on page 135. As you read the paragraph, underline the key ideas from the survey and make notes in the margin. Summarize any key ideas in one or two words in the margin. When you find a surprising idea, write a brief response in the margin. Experiment with using abbreviations (short forms of words) and symbols to indicate what you think (your response) about what you are reading.

Social and Cultural Adjustment: Statements about Canada

The graph above shows that the majority (82%) of international students agree that Canada is a welcoming and tolerant[9] society. While approximately half (51%) of respondents indicated that it is difficult to meet Canadians outside of school, 76% believe that Canadians are friendly when you get to know them, and 60% indicated that staff and students show an interest in their culture and country. The majority (78%) said that they would like more chances to experience Canadian culture and family life; however, approximately one-third (31%) agree that they prefer to mix with people from their own culture, roughly the same number (29%) are undecided, and 39% indicated that they prefer to mix with cultures other than their own.

———————————

[9] able to accept what other people say or do, even if you do not agree with it

Source: Humphries, J., Rauh, K., & McDine, D. (2013). *A world of learning: Canada's performance and potential in international education.* Ottawa, ON: The Canadian Bureau for International Education.

Activity C | Writing Task: Response Paragraph | Review your marginal notes from Activity B. Choose one main idea that you could respond to. Create a rough outline for a response paragraph (see Activity C on page 134), then write a short paragraph responding to the one main idea you chose Support the ideas in your paragraph using information from the summary paragraph above.

When you are finished, share your paragraph with a partner. Discuss the ideas in each other's response paragraphs, using the following questions to guide your discussion.

1. Which ideas or facts came from the original paragraph ("Social and Cultural Adjustment: Statements about Canada")?
2. Are there any ideas in your partner's paragraph that are new to you?
3. Are there any ideas in your partner's paragraph that are surprising to you in any way? How are these ideas surprising?
4. What do you know now about the topic of friendship between international and Canadians?

Work together to help each other credit the ideas of the report's authors. Refer to the *Language Tip* on page 121.

Activity D | Statistics Canada publishes reports that provide researchers with valuable data on Canada and Canadians. Skim the reading below, which is an excerpt from a Statistics Canada web page that summarizes a report titled *International Students Who Become Permanent Residents in Canada, 1990 to 2013*.

- Find the main ideas of the excerpt.
- Highlight the main ideas that you think should be included in a summary.
- Compare your highlighting with a partner. Have you highlighted similar or different ideas?
- Decide with your partner which ideas are the most important to include in a summary of this excerpt.

International Students Who Become Permanent Residents in Canada, 1990 to 2013

1 Twenty to twenty-seven percent of the international students who came to Canada to study during the 1990s and early 2000s obtained permanent resident status in the 10 years after receiving their first study permit.

2 Lu and Hou examine the changing characteristics of international students in Canada from 1990 to 2013, and their rate of transition into permanent resident status.[10]

The Number of International Students Rose Quickly in Recent Years

3 From 1990 to 1994, Canada admitted 158,000 international students, or an average of about 31,000 per year.

4 From 2005 to 2009, Canada admitted 340,000 international students, or an average of about 68,000 a year. In the four years from 2010 to 2013, Canada admitted 385,000 international students, or an average of about 96,000 a year.

5 Source country composition also changed. Most notably, the proportion[11] of international students from China or India increased from 6 percent in the early 1990s to 37 percent in the early 2010s.

International Students More Likely to Apply in the Economic Class

6 In the early 2000s, the selection process of immigrants changed as principal applicants[12] in the economic class received more points for being of prime working age, proficient[13] in English or French, having Canadian work experience, and having a university degree.

7 Correspondingly, international students became more likely to be admitted to Canada as principal applicants in the economic class. Those who landed also became more likely to have higher levels of educational attainment.[14]

8 For example, of the international students who became permanent residents within 10 years, 36 percent of those from the 1990 to 1994 cohort[15] had a university degree at the time they landed. In contrast, this was the case for 56 percent of those from the 2000 to 2004 cohort.

Source: Adapted from Statistics Canada. (2015, December 10). *Study: International students who become permanent residents in Canada, 1990 to 2013*. Retrieved from http://www.statcan.gc.ca/daily-quotidien/151210/dq151210c-eng.htm

---

[10] the legal position of a person, group, or country

[11] the relationship of one thing to another in size, amount, etc.

[12] a person who makes a formal request to do something

[13] able to do something well because of training or practice

[14] something that you achieved

[15] a group of people who share something in common

Activity E | Writing Task: Summary Paragraph | Review the main ideas that you highlighted in Activity D. Write a short summary paragraph of the reading, using the following checklist to help you draft your paragraph.

- ☐ I begin with a description of the reading text.
- ☐ I mention a shortened title of the reading (for example, "International Students") often enough to remind the reader that I am summarizing the main ideas of the author.
- ☐ I explain the reading's most important main ideas.
- ☐ I do not include any direct quotations from the original text.
- ☐ I do not include my own opinions about the ideas in the original text.
- ☐ I present the ideas in my summary in the same order as in the original text.
- ☐ I use reporting verbs/expressions to introduce any summary statements of ideas from the reading.
- ☐ I have a concluding sentence to end my summary paragraph.

Exchange paragraphs with a partner and give each other one or two suggestions about how to improve the other's paragraph.

Preventing Plagiarism

Integrating Summary Statements

"Accidental" plagiarism can happen if your summary statements are too similar to the author's words in the original text. Review the techniques below that will help you avoid plagiarism in your summary statements.

- ✓ Read and reread the original text until you are sure that you understand the meaning.
- ✓ Make brief notes in your own words on a separate paper while you read.
- ✓ Rephrase and reduce the original text. Do not copy directly from the original text.

- ✓ Write your summary statement from your notes, not from the original text.
- ✓ Compare the main idea from the original text to your summary statement.
- ✓ Be sure that you have not changed the author's meaning.
- ✓ Choose an appropriate reporting verb that expresses the author's meaning.
- ✓ Include an in-text citation as needed.

Reference Skill

Citing Reports in APA Style

Here is the bibliographic information for the report referenced earlier in this unit that discusses Canada's role in international education.

Authors	Jennifer Humphries, Karen Rauh, and David McDine
Organization	The Canadian Bureau for International Education
Title	A World of Learning: Canada's Performance and Potential in International Education
Date of publication	2013
Place of publication	Ottawa, Ontario
Web address	http://cbie.ca/wp-content/uploads/2016/04/Report_Research_Flagship_2013_EN.pdf

If you included any ideas or information from *A World of Learning: Canada's Performance and Potential in International Education* in your response paragraph in Activity C on page 136, you need to write both in-text citations and a reference entry in APA style.

The chart below shows how the in-text citations and the reference entry for this report are written in APA style.

	APA Style
In-text citations	1. Humphries, Rauh, and McDine (2013) report that a high number of international students (82%) find that Canada is friendly. 2. A high number of international students (82%) find that Canada is friendly (Humphries, Rauh, & McDine, 2013).
Reference entry	Humphries, J., Rauh, K., & McDine, D. (2013) *A world of learning: Canada's performance and potential in international education* [Report]. Ottawa, ON: The Canadian Bureau for International Education. Retrieved from http://cbie.ca/wp-content/uploads/2016/04/Report_Research_Flagship_2013_EN.pdf

Activity A | Read the summary on page 140 from a writer who has read Lu and Hou's full report. The writer has forgotten to write APA-style in-text citations and a References list. Use the bibliographic information from the chart below the summary to add in-text citations and an end-of-text entry for the ideas from Lu and Hou's report.

> Post-secondary education is now a common pathway to immigration for international students. The authors report that from 1990 the number of international students has more than tripled to 98,000 students per year in 2013. The study also reveals that students from Southeast Asia (India) and East Asia (China) are roughly one-third (37%) of Canada's international student population. These authors show that more international students now apply for permanent residence because they are desirable immigrants. These students have Canadian experience and education as well as language skills.
>
> Reference
>
> _____
>
> _____
>
> _____
>
> _____

Authors	Yuqian Lu and Feng Hou
Organization	Statistics Canada
Title	Insights on Canadian Society: International Students Who Become Permanent Residents in Canada
Date of publication	10 December 2015
Place of publication	Ottawa, Ontario
Web address	http://www.statcan.gc.ca/pub/75-006-x/2015001/article/14299-eng.pdf

Compare your in-text citations and end-of-text References entry to the examples in the chart on page 139. Did you use APA style correctly?

Then exchange your in-text citations and Reference entry with a partner and check to see if your partner's in-text citations and Reference entry correctly follow APA style.

Format and Organization Skill

Writing General-to-Specific Introductory Sentences

The introductory sentences in a summary paragraph can follow a general-to-specific pattern to bring the reader smoothly into the topic. The reader moves from a more general introduction of the topic to a more specific understanding.

Activity A | The following are introductory sentences describing international students and social networks. Read the paragraph and mark up the text in a way that makes sense to you, to help you follow the movement of ideas from general to specific.

Building International Student Social Networks

In Canada, the international student population is growing. Many universities now think about the challenges that international students face during their transition. These universities offer language and communication skills courses to support international students. However, building social networks remains difficult. Some students, especially students from a cultural background that is very different from the local culture, can find it difficult to make friends.

The chart below shows the function of each sentence above and how the sentences relate to one another.

Statement	Function
1. In Canada, the international student population is growing.	presents a general idea to introduce the topic of the summary
2. Many universities now think about the challenges that international students face during their transition.	presents a more specific idea
3. These universities offer language and communication skills courses to support international students.	presents another specific idea that flows from the first specific idea
4. However, building social networks remains difficult.	begins transition to introducing the problem

When you are finished reading the text and reviewing the chart, discuss the following questions with a partner.

1. What topic am I going to read about?
2. What does the writer want me to know about this topic?

Activity B | In addition to the introductory sentences, in a summary paragraph it is common to write one or two sentences that introduce the author, the title of the text, and the purpose of the text. Review the model summary in "International Students and Social Experiences" in Activity A on page 120. Notice how this introduction to the authors and their report is done. With a partner, discuss what sentences you could write to introduce a paragraph summary of Susan Wu's blog entry (see page 131).

Activity C | Writing Task: Introduction for Unit Inquiry Question |
Based on your thinking so far on the topic of international education, write an introduction (three to five sentences) for your answer to your Unit Inquiry Question. When you are finished, evaluate how well your introductory sentences pull the reader into your topic. Do the ideas flow well from a general understanding to a more specific understanding of your topic? Have you included a sentence that introduces the text that you are summarizing (if you have chosen one already)?

Topic Skill

Writing Topic Sentences for a Response Paragraph

A well-written topic sentence clearly states the topic to be discussed and the controlling idea. In a topic sentence for a response paragraph, the topic is the subject that you are writing about and the controlling idea is your main idea—the idea that you develop based on your reading and thinking about the topic. The topic sentence in a response paragraph often appears near the beginning of the paragraph; it usually follows a more general background sentence about the topic.

Read these first two sentences from a response paragraph about group work and learning.

> There is a lot of group work at university. Through group work, students can be more actively involved in their learning.

What is the topic of the paragraph? What is the writer's controlling idea? Compare your answers to the information in the chart below.

General background sentence	There is a lot of group work at university.
Topic (the subject of the paragraph)	group work
Controlling idea (the writer's main idea)	students can be more actively involved in their learning

Notice that the reader of this paragraph expects to read more about the controlling idea—how group work helps students be more active in their learning, not about the ideas in the general background sentence—how often students do group work.

Activity A | Read the first two sentences in a response paragraph about friendship between international and local students. As you read the topic sentence, underline the topic and double underline the controlling idea.

> International students should try to make friends with local students. Feeling connected to people from their host country helps international students adapt to their lives abroad.

In a small group, discuss the following questions.

1. Does the general background sentence introduce the topic?
2. What topic do you expect to read about in the response paragraph?
3. What is the writer's main idea?
4. Based on the reading you have done so far in this unit, do you think the writer's main idea is supportable? Are there facts to support the main idea?

Activity B | Sometimes the controlling idea in a topic sentence can be an answer to an inquiry question. Below are two inquiry questions related to international education. A general background sentence and a topic sentence are given for the first one. Write a general background sentence and a topic sentence for the second inquiry question. With a partner, evaluate your sentences using the questions in Activity A.

Inquiry question: How can international students make friends with local students?

[General sentence] Friendship can develop naturally when people share common interests. [Topic sentence] Participating in extracurricular activities that truly interest them helps international students make friends.

Inquiry question: How can universities and colleges provide the right kind of support to international students?

General sentence + Topic sentence:

_____

_____

Activity C | Writing Task: Topic Sentence for Unit Inquiry Question | Review your Unit Inquiry Question and write a general sentence and a topic sentence related to it. Evaluate your sentences by asking yourself the questions in Activity A. With a partner or small group, discuss how your sentences could be improved.

Conclusion Skill

Integrating an Expert Opinion

The concluding sentences at the end of a response paragraph have two important functions:

- to help refocus the reader on your main idea, which has already been expressed in your topic sentence—here you restate your main idea using different words; and
- to provide support for your main idea. This support can come from another writer who is an expert on the topic. This support from an expert makes your main idea more believable for the reader.

There are two possible ways to integrate support from another writer in your concluding sentences: include a quotation or make a summary statement. A summary statement may be preferred in academic writing because summarizing another person's ideas shows that you understand what you have read. Ask your instructor which approach is better for your writing course.

1. Use a quotation from another writer:
   - Use quotation marks and copy the writer's words exactly.
   - Do not quote more than one or two sentences.
   - Follow APA style: write an in-text citation including a page number.

2. Write a summary statement explaining an idea from another writer:
   - Express the writer's idea in your own words.
   - Do not change the original meaning.
   - Follow APA style: write an in-text citation with a reporting verb.

(See the *Language Tip* on page 121 for help writing summary statements.)

The sample text below includes a title, general sentence, topic sentence, and concluding sentences for a response paragraph.

Title: Improving International Student Communication

General sentence: Many international students will face language challenges when they study in a country where the local language is different than their first language.

Topic sentence: Building confidence by using the local language as much as possible in daily life is important for international student success.

_____

_____

_____

Concluding sentences: In short, it seems to be very important that students gain confidence in daily communication by increasing their opportunities to speak in out-of-class situations. By improving their daily communication skills, students can increase their feelings of success later.

To find the best place to add support from another writer in the concluding sentences, follow these steps:

1. Reread the topic sentence and underline the controlling idea in the topic sentence.
2. Reread the concluding sentences to find this same idea, expressed in different words, and highlight it.
3. Mark the spot in the text with a slash (/) between the sentence with the controlling idea restated and the last sentence. This is the best place to add support from another writer.

Now read the concluding sentences with a summary statement added. Notice that the writer has repeated the controlling idea, then added a summary statement referencing a published report to support that main idea.

> In short, it seems to be very important that students gain confidence in daily communication by increasing their opportunities to speak in out-of-class situations. In fact, Morrison (2014) argues that the simplest day-to-day tasks can be the most difficult, so focusing on daily communication is a good language learning habit. By improving their daily communication skills, students can increase their feelings of success later.

Notice how the summary statement referring to one of Morrison's ideas follows the simple citation style and includes a transition phrase (*in fact*), which connects the summary statement back to the previous sentence.

Activity A | Reread "Study Abroad Challenges" by Morrison (Reading 2 on page 129) and find any two ideas in the reading that could be used to support the following controlling idea.

> In short, it seems to be very important that students gain confidence in daily communication by increasing their opportunities to speak in out-of-class situations.

Share your two ideas with a partner, and choose the best two of the four ideas. Work together to write a summary statement using a simple citation style for each. (See the *Language Tip* on page 121 for help.) Don't forget to include a suitable transition word or phrase.

Summary statement 1 _____

_____

Summary statement 2 _____

_____

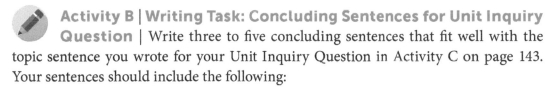 **Activity B | Writing Task: Concluding Sentences for Unit Inquiry Question** | Write three to five concluding sentences that fit well with the topic sentence you wrote for your Unit Inquiry Question in Activity C on page 143. Your sentences should include the following:

- two sentences to refocus the reader on the main idea;
- one summary statement of another writer's ideas (using any reading in this unit); and
- one sentence that makes a recommendation to your reader (see Unit 3, pages 102 103).

Exchange your concluding sentences with a partner. Evaluate each other's concluding sentences. Do the concluding sentences refocus the reader on the writer's main idea? How?

WRITING FUNDAMENTALS

Composition Skill

Paragraphing

Because it is important for you as a writer to consider your reader, you need to think about how you build your paragraphs in a way that makes it easy for the reader to understand your ideas. It is difficult to read one long text with no paragraph breaks. You should make it as easy as possible for the reader to see when you change main ideas by starting a new paragraph.

Activity A | Read the text below. This text would be better written as two paragraphs. Decide where you could separate the text and mark the spot.

Survival Strategies

International students sometimes develop "survival strategies" to manage their studies. Some students might avoid courses with writing assignments. Other students might rely too much on writing models. Some students might also rely on having other people check their writing assignments. It is clear that these students should evaluate the effectiveness of these strategies. They might see that these strategies will not lead to success over time. International students also find speaking to be difficult. Surprisingly, most difficulties seem to occur in day-to-day communication on and off campus. For example, students are concerned about expressing their ideas fluently. These students worry about talking with others in class and in daily life. In the end, many students might find that they can overcome most speaking challenges in time with focused practice.

Activity B | Discuss and answer the following questions with a partner.

1. Where would you divide the text in Activity A to make two paragraphs? Explain why you chose to end the first paragraph where you did.

   _____

   _____

   _____

   _____

2. What kind of transition word or phrase could be added to introduce the second paragraph? Would you show addition (*moreover, furthermore, another reason/idea is*)? Or would you show contrast (*however, in contrast*)? Write the first sentence of your second paragraph including your chosen transition word or phrase.

    _____

    _____

3. Rewrite the concluding sentence of the first paragraph to make a smooth transition to the second paragraph.

    _____

    _____

Sentence and Grammar Skill

Avoiding Sentence Fragments, Comma Splices, and Stringy Sentences

Three common sentence-level errors are sentence fragments, run-on sentences, and stringy sentences. These mistakes can happen to all writers when they do not proofread carefully enough.

Sentence Fragments   A sentence fragment is a mistake in sentence structure. There are two ways that sentence fragments can be created.

Possibility 1: The sentence is missing a main verb.

- ✗ English clearly important as the language of international business.
- ✓ English is clearly important as the language of international business.
- ✗ My essay how the future of English will look.
- ✓ My essay will examine how the future of English will look.

Possibility 2: The sentence has a dependent clause, but is missing an independent clause. (To review types of sentences, see Unit 2, pages 67–68.)

- ✗ Because Mandarin has the most speakers in the world.
- ✓ Because Mandarin has the most speakers in the world, it is an important language for Canadians to learn.
- ✗ Although English is an important language.
- ✓ Although English is an important language, it is not the only one.

Comma Splices   A comma splice is a mistake in the punctuation of a sentence.

- ✗ English won't dominate the world forever because people will begin to study more and more other languages, consequently, a multilingual generation will be created.
- ✓ English won't dominate the world forever because people will begin to study more and more other languages. Consequently, a multilingual generation will be created.

✗ Children learn English easily, because they do not have the shyness that adults have, children are able to learn languages faster.

✓ Children learn English easily. Because they do not have the shyness that adults have, children are able to learn languages faster.

Stringy Sentences   A stringy sentence contains too many ideas that are better written as two separate sentences.

✗ English is the language of globalization, and also the language of computers and the Internet and it is common in international business as well.

✓ English is the language of globalization. It is also the language of computers, the Internet, and international business.

✗ Globalization leads to the spread of English and more and more people, who speak different languages, go abroad to study.

✓ Globalization leads to the spread of English. More and more people, who speak different languages, go abroad to study.

Activity A | With a partner, identify the common sentence error in each group of words below, and explain the problem. The first one has been done for you as an example.

Sentence with Errors	Sentence Fragment	Comma Splice	Stringy Sentence
1. Not only international students in Canada, but also local students' success. Problem: ____ *no verb* ____	✓		
2. Because students find it difficult to express themselves accurately in their writing assignments. Problem: _____			
3. Many authors study the challenges faced by international students, their studies suggest some solutions that universities could use to help their students. Problem: _____			
4. Some authors make general conclusions about international students, but do not focus on the unique difficulties of each student, so it is not always easy to understand why some students face more challenges than others. Problem: _____			
5. Many international student blogs present ideas about how to support international students because they share successful student stories, and this might help students new to academic life in Canada. Problem: _____			

Activity B | With a partner or small group, read each of the sentence errors below and discuss different ways to correct them. As a group, decide on the best way to correct each sentence. Then correct the sentence and suggest how the writer could avoid this kind of mistake in the future. The first one is done for you.

1. **Incorrect**: Because students find it difficult to express themselves accurately in their writing assignments.

   Suggested correction: Because students find it difficult to express themselves accurately in their writing assignments, they may rely on some unhelpful survival strategies.

   Advice: Join the dependent clause to an independent clause

2. **Incorrect**: Not only international students in Canada, but also local students' success.

   Suggested correction: _____

   _____

   _____

   Advice: _____

   _____

3. **Incorrect**: Many authors study the challenges faced by international students, their studies suggest some solutions that universities could use to help their students.

   Suggested correction: _____

   _____

   _____

   Advice: _____

   _____

4. **Incorrect**: Many student life staff suggest that students make friends early on and at the start of the new school year is a good time because the majority of first-year students are looking for new friends and study partners.

   Suggested correction: _____

   _____

   _____

   Advice: _____

   _____

When you are finished, compare your suggested corrections with another group. Share your advice on how to correct these kinds of mistakes with the whole class.

Activity C | Choose one of the paragraphs you have written for this unit. Edit it for any sentence fragments, comma splices, or stringy sentences. Rewrite the paragraph to improve your sentences, then share your rewritten paragraph with a partner. Discuss the sentence corrections you made and explain why you made these corrections. Refer to the advice in Activity B to help you explain.

Learning Strategy

Participating in Group Work

Working with other students helps you develop skills that you will use in your academic and professional future. However, working together is not always easy. Students have different ideas about what makes good group work. Some students are enthusiastic and like to take charge; some students are more relaxed and prefer to let their partners organize the group's work. The following guidelines may help you with starting your group work and keeping your group working well together.

Before You Start

- ✓ Discuss how each of you understands the assignment that you must complete.
- ✓ Match your group members' responsibilities with their abilities and interests.

- ✓ Share responsibilities and duties equally between group members.
- ✓ Get to know your group members, including their interests and activities outside school.
- ✓ Share your contact information so that all group members can stay in touch.

While You Work

- ✓ Set a meeting schedule and try to stick to it.
- ✓ Be co-operative and flexible. Understand that sometimes plans can change.
- ✓ Be well prepared for group meetings.
- ✓ Encourage all group members to exchange ideas.
- ✓ Help one another, especially if one group member is having difficulties.

UNIT OUTCOME

Writing Assignment: Summary-and-Response Paragraphs

Write one summary paragraph of 100 to 150 words and one response paragraph of 125 to 175 words on a topic related to international education. (Your instructor may give you an alternative length.) You may write on a topic based on your Unit Inquiry Question, develop another topic of your choosing connected to international education, or choose one of the following topics:

- How can international students overcome academic challenges when abroad?
- How valuable is an international education in today's world?
- How does living in another country create a better understanding of one's own country?

Use the skills you have developed in this unit to complete the assignment. Follow the steps set out below to practise each of your newly acquired skills to write well-developed summary-and-response paragraphs.

1. **Brainstorm**: Use an idea web to come up with ideas related to your topic.

2. **Find information**: Find a text related to your topic that you can summarize and respond to. Then, if necessary, find some additional information to support the ideas in your response paragraph. You may include information from the unit readings if appropriate.

3. **Compose a topic sentence**: Develop a focused topic sentence, which includes a topic and a controlling idea, for each paragraph.

4. **Outline**: Fill in the outline below to plan the first draft of your paragraphs. You may make changes to the outline as necessary.

Summary Paragraph— (Introductory Sentences + Summary)

Topic sentence presenting the topic and controlling idea of the original text to be summarized:

Sentence that includes author's name, title of the piece of writing to be summarized, and the purpose of the original text:

Summary of the most important ideas from the original text:

Response Paragraph— (Response + Concluding Sentences)

Topic sentence presenting your topic and your controlling idea:

Presentation of the writer's view in the original text:

Response to the writer's views expressed in the original text:

Restatement of controlling idea:

Statement that includes support from an expert (or another author):

Prediction or recommendation related to the topic:

5. **Write a first draft**: Use your outline to write the first draft of your paragraphs. Do not worry too much about spelling or grammar in the first draft. Try to get your ideas down on paper.

6. **Self-check**: Review the first draft of your paragraphs for the following and revise as needed:

   - Organization: Make sure that you have organized your main points according to the type of paragraph that you are writing. In your summary paragraph, the main points should follow the same order as the original author's text.

   - Topic development: In your response, make sure that you have added a summary statement from another author to each of your supporting points to develop your main point.

7. **Ask for a peer review**: Exchange the revised version of your first draft with a partner. Use the Evaluation Rubric below and on the next page to assess your partner's paragraphs and provide suggestions to improve them. Consider your partner's feedback carefully and use it to make changes to your paragraphs.

8. **Edit**: Edit your paragraphs for the following:

   - Sentence structure: Check for any sentence fragments, comma splices, or stringy sentences. Correct any of these errors to ensure that all of your sentences are grammatically correct.

   - Vocabulary: Check that you have used some of the AWL and mid-frequency vocabulary from this unit in your paragraphs.

   - Quotations or summary statement: Check that you have correctly integrated the ideas from the original text into your writing, that you have not changed the original meaning, and that you have not plagiarized.

9. **Write a final draft**: Write a final draft of your paragraphs, making any changes you think will improve them. If possible, leave some time between drafts.

10. **Proofread**: Check the final draft of your paragraphs for any small errors you may have missed. In particular, look for spelling errors, typos, and punctuation mistakes. If you used information from an outside source, double-check your in-text citations and your References list to make sure they are formatted properly.

Evaluation: Summary-and-Response Paragraphs Rubric

Use the following checklist to evaluate your paragraphs. In which areas do you need to improve most?

E = **Emerging**: frequent difficulty using unit skills; needs a lot more work
D = **Developing**: some difficulty using unit skills; some improvement still required
S = **Satisfactory**: able to use unit skills most of the time; meets average expectations for this level
O = **Outstanding**: exceptional use of unit skills; exceeds expectations for this level

Skill	E	D	S	O
Paragraphs fit a summary-and-response format and include introductory sentences, a summary, a response, and concluding sentences.				
The content is logically organized with introductory sentences moving from the general to the specific, so that the reader can easily follow the writer's thinking.				
The writing shows a good level of idea development and detail.				
Paragraphing is appropriate.				
Transition words and phrases are used correctly and where appropriate, but they are not overused.				
Summary statements are accurately written using the simple citation style with reporting verbs.				
AWL and mid-frequency vocabulary items from this unit are used when appropriate and with few mistakes.				
There are no sentence fragments, comma splices, or stringy sentences in the paragraphs.				
Ideas and words from outside sources are clearly marked with reporting verbs and in-text citations.				
If required, APA-style in-text citations and a Reference list have been included.				

Unit Review

Activity A | What do you know now that you did not know before about international education? Discuss with a partner or small group.

Activity B | Look back at the Unit Inquiry Question you developed at the start of this unit and discuss it with a partner or small group. Then share your answers with the class. Use the following questions to guide you.

1. What information did you find in this unit that helped you answer your question?
2. How would you answer your question now?

Activity C | Use the following checklist to review what you have learned throughout this unit. First decide which 10 skills you think are most important—circle the number beside each of these 10 skills. If you learned a skill in this unit that isn't listed below, write it in the blank row at the end of the checklist. Then put a check mark in the box beside those points you feel you have learned. Be prepared to discuss your choices with the class.

Self-Assessment Checklist	
☐	1. I can discuss topics related to international education in a general, less personal way, based on what I have read in this unit.
☐	2. I can develop an inquiry question to explore and respond to new information and ideas.
☐	3. I can write clear and accurate summary statements using the simple citation style.

☐	4. I can use prefixes to create and understand new words within a word family.
☐	5. I can use the AWL and mid-frequency vocabulary from this unit in my writing.
☐	6. I can make logical recommendations related to the topic I am writing about.
☐	7. I can use an idea web to brainstorm ideas and illustrate the connections between general ideas, specific ideas, and examples.
☐	8. I can create an outline following a summary-and-response format.
☐	9. I can use information from a report to support my ideas.
☐	10. I can avoid plagiarism when I include summary statements in my writing.
☐	11. I can organize my introductory sentences in a way that moves the reader from the general to the specific.
☐	12. I can write a topic sentence that shows my response to the ideas that I have read.
☐	13. I can write a conclusion that integrates an expert opinion from an outside source.
☐	14. I can recognize and correct sentence fragments, comma splices, and stringy sentences.
☐	15. I can write two paragraphs to summarize a text and respond to the ideas expressed in it.
☐	16.

Activity D | Put a check mark in the box beside the vocabulary items from this unit that you feel confident using in your writing. Make a plan to practise the words that you still need to learn.

Vocabulary Checklist

☐	abroad (adv.) 3000		☐	interaction (n.) AWL
☐	ample (adj.) 5000		☐	majority (n.) 3000
☐	beneficial (adj.) AWL		☐	navigate (v.) 4000
☐	diverse (adj.) AWL		☐	norm (n.) AWL
☐	economic (adj.) AWL		☐	optimistic (adj.) 4000
☐	enrich (v.) 4000		☐	seek (v.) AWL
☐	estimate (v.) AWL		☐	vigilant (adj.) 5000
☐	be exposed to (v.) AWL		☐	vital (adj.) 3000

UNIT 5

Understanding Processes

Design

EXPLORING IDEAS

Introduction

Activity A | Discuss the following questions with a partner or in a small group.

1. What do designers do? Why is their job important?
2. Name something that you think has been well designed, such as a car or kitchen appliance. What makes it well designed?
3. Name something that you think has been poorly designed, such as a classroom or a cellphone. What makes it poorly designed?
4. Have you ever designed and built something? How did you do it?
5. What do you need to know before you design and build something?
6. Do you think the items in the pictures above are well designed for a student? Why or why not? How would you improve them?

Activity B | The design process shown in Figure 5.1 has six steps to help designers improve a product, service, or space. The six steps are listed out of order. Label the design process, putting the steps in the appropriate order. Then compare your answers with a partner or small group. The first step has been added to the illustration for you.

brainstorm and analyze	collect information	~~define the problem~~
develop solutions	improve on your design	present your ideas

Design Process

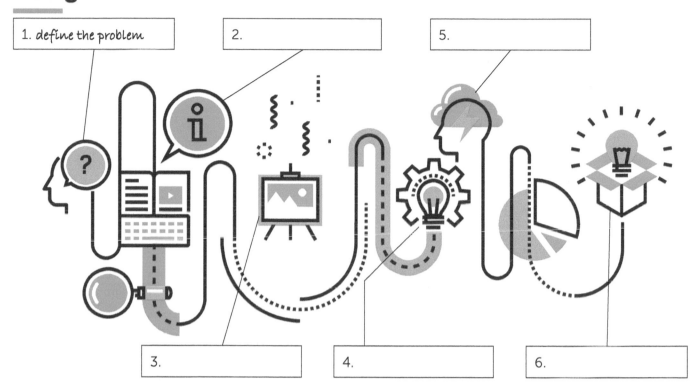

1. define the problem

2.

5.

3.

4.

6.

FIGURE 5.1   The design process

Activity C | What do you think about the design process illustrated in Activity B? Is it useful for people who want to design something? Choose a product, service, or space that you would like to design, such as a cellphone, computer repair service, or classroom. Then use the steps in the design process to talk about how you would design the product, service, or space you chose. The following questions will help guide you through the design process.

1. What is the problem with the product, service, or space that you are going to design?
2. Where could you gather information to help solve the problem?
3. How would you present and share your ideas, and to whom?
4. What could you do to improve the design of the product, service, or space?
5. How would you brainstorm and analyze your ideas?
6. What do you think is the solution to the problem you identified?

Discuss your ideas with a partner or small group. Then report your opinions to the class.

Fostering Inquiry

Analyzing a Process

When you ask questions about a process, you are looking for answers to explain how to do something or understand how something works or happens. These kinds of inquiry questions can explore two types of processes.

The first kind of process inquiry question looks at how to do something. The answer to this kind of question is often a set of instructions that gives you a better understanding of how to create something. For example, you might ask the question *How can students create their own bookshelves?* This type of analysis explains clearly and simply what steps to complete and the order in which to follow those steps.

The next kind of process inquiry question explores how something works or happens. In this case, the answer does not explain how to create something. Rather, it provides an understanding of a process. For example, you might ask the question *How do cellphones work*?

Activity A | What do you want to know more about in relation to the topic of design and the design process? For example:

- How can students build strong bookshelves out of inexpensive materials?
- What is the best way to create a company's website?
- How can a classroom be designed to be a better learning space?

1. Write two or three questions you are curious about related to design processes.
2. When you are finished, compare your questions with a partner or small group.
3. Choose one question to guide you as you work through this unit. It does not have to be the same question as your partner or group. Your question may change as you learn more about your topic.
4. Write your inquiry question in the space provided. Look back at it as you work through the unit. This is your Unit Inquiry Question.

My Unit Inquiry Question:

_____

_____

_____

Activity B | Writing Task: Freewriting | Write for at least five minutes on the topic of your Unit Inquiry Question. Do not stop writing during this time. After five minutes, read what you have written and circle two or three ideas that you would like to explore further.

Structure

Process Writing

Process writing is often used in the fields of science, technology, and engineering. It can involve a series of steps that show readers how to do something. This type of process writing is analytical, and it breaks the process down into specific steps. After reading this type of process paragraph or essay, readers should be able to carry out the process themselves. This writing is basically a set of instructions. For example, this type of process paragraph or essay might show readers how to send and receive entertaining text messages on an Android smart phone.

Process writing can also inform readers about how something happens. In this case, a process paragraph or essay is not a set of instructions. Rather, it helps readers understand how something works. This type of process writing is descriptive, and it explains the most important stages in a process. For example, this type of process paragraph or essay might inform readers about how thunder and lightning are created during a storm.

Activity A | With a partner or small group, consider this example of a paragraph on using a 3D printer to design and create new objects. Answer the questions that follow.

Creating Objects with a 3D Printer

Technology has given us the ability to create objects using a 3D printer by following just a few simple steps. To begin the process, you first have to design the object you want to print, generally by using a computer-aided design (CAD) software program. Once you have designed your object using the CAD software, you then input the design into the 3D printer. Next, you have to select the printing options you want to make sure that the texture and colour of plastic matches the design requirements. After everything is set up, you can begin printing. It can take a while for an object to print, so you will have to be patient. When the object has finished printing, light sanding or painting may be required to achieve the appropriate look. Finally, you will have a unique object that you designed yourself. In short, creating objects with a 3D printer can be a very rewarding experience that involves only a few easy-to-follow steps.

1. What process is being described in this paragraph?
2. Is the process mainly about how to do something or how something happens?
3. How many main steps are there in this process? What are they?
4. What words and phrases help you understand the steps in this process?
5. What do you notice about the first and last sentences?

Writing a Process Essay

Just like a process paragraph, a process essay can explain to readers how to do something or how something happens. A short process essay usually has an introduction, two or three main body paragraphs, and a conclusion. The main body paragraphs explain the steps in the process. Each paragraph can describe one major step, or each paragraph can contain a few similar and related steps grouped together. There should be no missing steps, and the steps should be presented in a logical order so that they are easy to understand. The essay should include enough details so that readers fully understand all the steps in the process. Each step might include the equipment needed, explanations of specialized terms, background information, or examples.

FIGURE 5.2
Four-paragraph
process essay with
two sets of steps

Figure 5.2 shows the structure of a process essay with two sets of steps. In your essay, you can adjust the number of sets of steps depending on the process you are describing. Some shorter essays might only have one set of steps, and some longer essays might have three sets of steps.

Activity B | The following essay is an example of process writing. Read the essay carefully, thinking about the role of each paragraph. Answer the questions that follow.

The Engineering Design Process: Finding Solutions to Problems

How do engineers solve complex design problems? The problem could be as simple as building a sidewalk or as complex as constructing a bridge across a wide lake. To solve a design problem, such as building a bridge, engineers follow the engineering design process. In Kelowna, British Columbia, for example, engineers followed that process to overcome the challenge of building a bridge across Okanagan Lake. Their creative solution was to build a floating bridge that is over 1000 metres long. An effective engineering design process contains some key steps related to preparing to solve a design problem, testing a possible prototype or model, and reflecting on the results of the test.

The first set of steps in the engineering design process is related to preparing to solve a design problem. To begin this process, engineers need to identify the design problem clearly. Generally, engineers need to know all of the details related to the problem as well as the major challenges involved. Once engineers have identified the problem, they can begin to research solutions. This research involves collecting information to solve the problem. They may check with experts, or they may check books, journals, and the Internet for solutions to similar types of problems. After the engineers have completed their research of possible solutions, they can then begin to brainstorm specific solutions to their own design problem. They should think of as many solutions as possible. In this step, it is most important to be creative and to think of many alternatives.

The second set of steps in the engineering design process is related to testing possible solutions to the design problem. First of all, engineers pick the best possible solution from the previous brainstorming step and develop plans to create that solution. There should be a logical reason for the chosen solution. As soon as the plans are created, they can build a sample model, or a prototype. A prototype is a fully functional model of the solution. After the prototype has been built, the engineers can then test the prototype to see if it works. In other words, the engineers will use the sample model and see what happens.

Finally, the last set of steps in the engineering design process is related to reflecting on the testing stage and deciding on the final design. However, engineers should first communicate the results of the testing stage. This communication might involve a public demonstration of the prototype or a written report about what happened when they tested the prototype. Next, engineers can reflect on the results of the testing and communication steps. They might have received feedback from people about the test or the information they shared. In the reflection step, engineers can think about their solution so far and any feedback they might have received. At this point, they can also think about how to improve their prototype. Then engineers can begin to redesign and rebuild the sample model based on what they have learned during the entire design process. At this stage, they may then go through the entire engineering design process again and again until they find the perfect solution to the problem. The process stops only once a satisfactory solution has been found.

To sum up, the engineering design process helps engineers develop solutions to design problems through a series of steps involving preparation, testing, and reflection. This type of process can lead to creative solutions for challenging problems, such as how to build a bridge across a wide body of water or design a smart phone that can be used underwater. It is important to remember that without following these steps, the best possible solution might never be found.

1. What is the main idea of this essay?
2. How many sets of steps are there?
3. How many steps are there in total? What are they?
4. What sorts of details does the author include to support the main steps?
5. What language helps you understand that this is an example of process writing?
6. What is the purpose of the last paragraph?

Activity C | Writing Task: Process Paragraph | Think about a process that you are familiar with. For example, you may think about something that you can build, or you may think about how something works. Write a short paragraph explaining how the process works. Include process connectors to help you explain the process. See the Language Tip on page 162 to help you.

Activity D | Exchange your process paragraph with a partner. Read your partner's paragraph and answer the following questions.

1. Does the paragraph describe a situation or problem for the reader? Where?
2. What question does the writer ask the reader?
3. Is the question interesting for the reader? Why?
4. Are the steps or stages in the process clear or unclear? How so?
5. Does the concluding sentence remind the reader of the importance of the process? How?
6. Are process connectors used correctly? Are there too many or too few?

Using Process Connectors

Process connectors can be used to signal the relationship between the steps in a process. Often process connectors appear at the start of a new sentence or step. Not every sentence will need a process connector and overusing them can make your writing seem unnatural and difficult to read. The chart below shows the functions of some common process connectors and how they are used in sentences.

Function	Connectors	Example
to give the purpose of the step or the process	generally, in order to, ordinarily	In order to solve a problem, engineers need to know all of the details related to the problem as well as the major challenges involved.
to introduce a step in the process	first, second, next, previously, finally	Next, the engineers can develop plans to create that solution.
to explain a step in more detail	to begin this process, furthermore	To begin this process, engineers need to identify the design problem clearly.
to describe the time order of two or more steps	before, prior to, after, subsequently, following, afterward, once, as soon as, when	Once engineers have identified the problem, they can begin to research solutions.
to describe two steps happening at the same time	simultaneously, at the same time, meanwhile	Workers built roads to the planned location of the new bridge. At the same time, other workers started to build the bridge over the water.
to explain why a step is important	especially, most important	In this step, it is most important to be creative and to think of many alternatives.

Activity E | Revisit your Unit Inquiry Question on page 158. Now that you have learned more about your topic, you may have a better idea of how to answer your question, or you may consider revising it. Use the following questions to guide you in assessing your Unit Inquiry Question.

- What new information have you learned that will help you answer your Unit Inquiry Question?
- What information do you still need to answer your question?
- Do you want to change your question in any way?

ACADEMIC READING

Vocabulary

Vocabulary Skill: Varying Vocabulary Using Synonyms

Adding variety to your vocabulary can help build interest for the reader. You can use synonyms, or words with similar meaning, to add variety. However, sometimes substituting one synonym for another can have the wrong effect. An inappropriate synonym can affect the tone of the writing or suggest an idea that the writer did not intend. Consider the following sentence.

Some designers see mistakes as learning opportunities.

The word *mistake* has a number of synonyms, including *error, blunder, gaffe, fault, miscalculation, boo-boo, snafu,* and *aberration.* However, each of these synonyms has a slightly different connotation, which refers to the tone of the word or the impression that it leaves on the reading. For example, some words have a more negative connotation than others. *Blunder* is much more negative than *error.* As well, some synonyms can sound childish or more informal than others. *Boo-boo* has a childish tone, and *gaffe* is much more informal than *miscalculation,* for example. While it takes time to learn the connotation of different synonyms, a good dictionary can often help.

Activity A | In the paragraph on page 164, the author repeats the word *build* and its related word forms too much. Rewrite the paragraph using synonyms for the word *build* to create interest and variety. Try to replace at least 10 instances of words from the *build* family. You may need to rephrase some of the sentences to fit the synonyms you choose.

A list of synonyms for the verb *build* (along with their definitions) has been provided to help you. You may use these synonyms, but you do not need to use all of them. You might also come up with some synonyms on your own. Finally, you may use the same synonym more than once in your writing.

Synonym for *Build*	Definition
construct (v.)	to build or make something such as a road, building, or machine
assemble (v.)	to fit together all the separate parts of something, for example a piece of furniture
erect (v.)	to build something upright
make (v.)	to create or prepare something by combining materials or putting parts together
set up (v.)	to put something together in a particular place
fabricate (v.)	to make or produce goods, equipment, etc. from various different materials
put up (v.)	to build something or place something somewhere
manufacture (v.)	to make goods in large quantities, using machinery
create (v.)	to make something happen or exist

Building a Floating Bridge Across Okanagan Lake

The floating bridge that connects Kelowna to West Kelowna over Okanagan Lake was **built** over a period of four years. The first step in **building** this bridge was to prepare the shore. Sections on each side of the lake were prepared to carry the weight of the bridge. Next, a dry dock was **built**. A dry dock is an area for **building** things that float. The dry dock was used to **build** concrete pontoons. A pontoon is an empty structure that floats. Workers **built** nine pontoons for the bridge. At the same, workers started to **build** new roads on each side of the lake. Soon, four pontoons were put in the water. Once the pontoons were in the water, workers started **building** the bridge over the pontoons. After part of the bridge deck was **built**, the rest of the pontoons were put in the water. Then the rest of the bridge deck was **built** over the pontoons. Workers then finished **building** all the roads leading up to the new bridge. Afterwards, workers completed **building** all the different parts of the bridge. Finally, the newly **built** bridge was ready for testing. The bridge was considered safe, and it was officially opened in 2008. All in all, the four-year process to **build** a floating bridge across Okanagan Lake was successful.

Vocabulary Preview: The Academic Word List

Activity B | Look at the AWL words and their definitions below. Then read the paragraph that follows on how to make jewellery. Match the words or phrases in bold from the paragraph with the AWL word that is closest in meaning.

assemble (v.): to fit together all the separate parts of something, for example, a piece of furniture

attach (v.): to fasten or join one thing to another

conceptual (adj.): related to abstract ideas

construction (n.): the process or method of building or making something, especially roads, buildings, bridges, etc.

funds (n.): an amount of money that has been saved or has been made available for a particular purpose

overall (adj.): in general; when you consider everything

principle (n.): a law, a rule, or a theory that something is based on

unique (adj.): very special or unusual

Making a leather bracelet can be inexpensive and fun, and the process is easy once you get the hang of it. The first step is to make an **abstract** decision about the type of bracelet you want to make. Once you know the design **points that must be done**, you can then identify the **money** required to buy the materials. After that, you can go to the craft store and buy the materials you need. Next comes the best part, which is the **building** of the bracelet. At this point, you are going to

join together the different pieces of leather. Then you can decorate the bracelet by **adding** beads or feathers onto the leather with glue. To conclude, if you follow this **general** process, you will have a **very different** piece of jewellery that was enjoyable to make.

Vocabulary Preview: Mid-frequency Vocabulary

Activity C | The mid-frequency words in red in the sentences below appear in the reading "Making Design Decisions," on pages 167–168. Read the sentences and match the words in red with the most appropriate definition.

Sentences	Definitions
_____ 1. Before we build our bookcase, we should sketch the design we are going to use.	a. concerned with beauty and art and the understanding of beautiful things
_____ 2. The designer's job was to find a softer sound to replace the harsh buzzing sounds of the alarm clock in the morning.	b. to make a quick drawing of somebody or something
_____ 3. My aesthetic decisions are what make my designs look different from everyone else's.	c. a piece of jewellery consisting of a chain, string of beads, etc. worn around the neck
_____ 4. She designed several stunning pieces of jewellery, including the expensive diamond and pearl necklace that everyone loved.	d. unpleasant to experience
_____ 5. The clothing designer struggled with the delicate details on the jacket he was creating.	e. a soft reddish-brown metal used for making electric wires, pipes, and coins
_____ 6. Jewellery designers will often use copper because this material is flexible and easy to work with.	f. the way a surface, substance, or piece of cloth feels when you touch it, for example how rough, smooth, hard, or soft it is
_____ 7. My sister is a designer who creates jewellery for teens. It is very popular with young people.	g. made or formed in a very careful and detailed way
_____ 8. The designer put a lot of thought into creating the cellphone case. For example, she even included a rough texture on the back so that it would be easy to hold.	h. people who are between 13 and 19 years old

Reading

The reading "Making Design Decisions" on pages 167–168 contains excerpts from *Technology: Engineering Our World*, a textbook that introduces Canadian secondary students to design concepts. The text contains design activities for students who are looking to expand their science, technology, engineering, and math (STEM) knowledge. The reading describes the principles of good design to create a quality product for consumers.

Activity A | Designers make decisions at many points in the design process. The cycle graphic below shows the steps in the design process, and beside it is a list of five types of decisions that designers might make. Work with a partner or small group to decide where in the process designers might make each of these types of decisions. Note that a decision may be made in more than one step in the process.

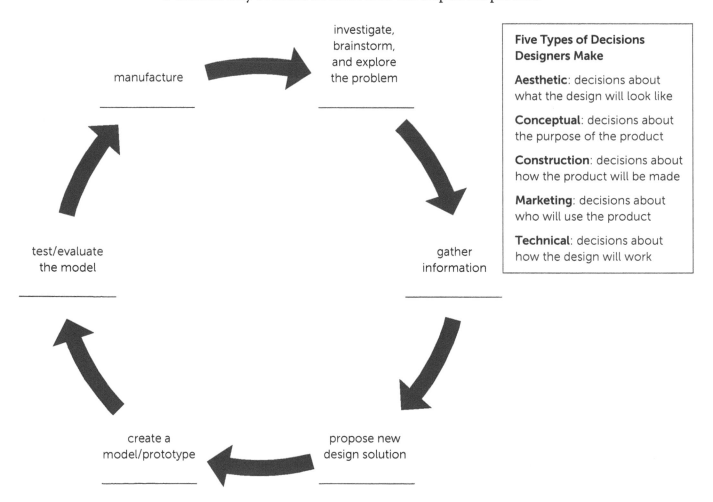

Activity B | Before reading "Making Design Decisions", mark the following statements as true (T) or false (F), based on your current understanding of design. As you read the text, think about whether your answers are correct. Paragraph numbers have been provided to help you check your answers after you are done reading.

1. _____ How things look, feel, taste, smell, and sound is important. (1)

2. _____ Most people notice line, shape and form, texture, and colour when they look at an object. (3)

3. _____ Design principles are strict rules that must be followed. (4)

4. _____ Aesthetic decisions relate to how the product will be made and assembled. (8)

5. _____ The five types of design decisions are highly interconnected. (10)

6. _____ All designs follow the exact same steps in the design process. (12)

Activity C | Read the following textbook excerpt and look for the five main types of decisions referred to in Activity A. As you read, highlight references to those decisions along with any details you think are important. When you are finished, compare your highlighting with a partner or small group.

READING

Making Design Decisions

1   All products appeal to our senses in some way. We buy clothing that looks good. We enjoy the smooth feel of the polished wooden arm of a chair. A meal on a plate must not only look attractive but also should taste and smell good. The sound of musical chimes[1] is preferable to the **harsh** sound of a door buzzer.

2   When you see something you like, ask yourself what it is you like about the product. Is it the colour? Is it the shape or form? Is it the **texture**? Does its texture remind you of the beauty of things found in nature?

3   Line, shape and form, texture, and colour are the four elements of design. They are what most people notice when they look at an object. When you examine any object, you will find that the elements of design have been combined to create a **unique** look.

4   Design **principles** do not provide hard and fast rules. They act only as a guide. You must make the actual design decisions. The five basic types of design decisions are **conceptual**, marketing, technical, constructional, and **aesthetic** decisions.

Conceptual Decisions

5   Conceptual design decisions have to do with the **overall** purpose of the design. What sort of product is needed? For example, what sort of product could students in your school make and sell to raise **funds** for a school trip? Should you design printed T-shirts, birthday cards, or jewellery? You ask a number of parents and friends which they might purchase and discover that jewellery is most popular. Choosing jewellery is a conceptual design decision.

Marketing Decisions

6   Who will use the product you are designing? Where and how will they use it? These questions will help you make marketing design decisions. Marketing decisions might also include where the product will be sold and the selling price. For example, you could decide to design jewellery for **teens**, a special friend, or a favourite aunt. You could design jewellery to give as presents, to sell in a trendy[2] boutique,[3] or to sell at a festival celebrating a special occasion.

---

[1] the ringing sound of a bell

[2] very fashionable

[3] a small shop/store that sells fashionable clothes or expensive gifts

Technical Decisions

7   Technical design decisions explain how the design will work. What individual pieces are required? What materials are best for each component? What size will you make the overall product and each component? What are the safety requirements? For example, you could decide to design jewellery using natural materials such as wood and feathers. You could decide to use an easily worked metal such as **copper**, or recycled materials such as bottle tops. If the jewellery uses electronics, will it contain lights or sound? How will the lights be controlled? What components are needed to make sound?

Construction Decisions

8   Decisions about how the product will be made and **assembled** are **construction** design decisions. What tools and techniques will you need to form small pieces of copper into the shape you have chosen? How will the individual pieces fit together? What joining techniques will you use? For example, how can you join the copper pieces to create a **necklace**? How could they be **attached** to a leather cord or metal chain?

Aesthetic Decisions

9   Aesthetic (artistic) decisions determine what the design will look like. What overall effect do you want? Will you make large, clunky[4] jewellery or small,

delicate jewellery? What shapes might a pendant[5] have? Will you use natural or geometric[6] shapes? What colours might you use? What textures could you use?

10   Although these five types of design decisions are described separately, they are highly interconnected. If you change one decision, you may have to change others. For example, suppose you decide to use a leather cord at first. Later you change your mind and decide to use a metal chain (technical design decision). This will affect how the decorative elements are attached (constructional design decision).

Solving a Design Problem

11   Designing and making a product requires the designer or engineer to use a number of skills. These skills include doing research, **sketching**, 3D modelling, and testing. The general process used to solve design problems is called a design process

12   Sometimes you will hear people talk about "the design process" as though the way in which you design a product is the same every time. This is not true. The steps a designer or engineer uses to produce a solution to a problem depend partly on the problem. For example, a dress designer works differently from an architect. The work of both is different from that of a graphic designer. However, all designers and engineers use some common steps and design process skills.

Source: Gradwell, J., & Welch, M. (2012). *Technology: Engineering our world.* (7th ed., pp. 33, 43, 58–59). Tinley Park, IL: Goodheart-Willcox.

---

[5] a piece of jewellery that you wear around your neck on a chain

[6] having regular shapes or lines

---

[4] heavy and awkward

Activity D | Discuss the following questions with a partner or small group.

1. What are the four elements of design that people notice most when they look at an object? Which element do you think is most important?

2. Describe each of the five basic types of design decisions in your own words. Which of these decisions do you think is the hardest to make?

3. What does it mean that the five basic design decisions are interconnected? What happens if you change one of your decisions?

4. How do the four elements of design and the five basic design decisions relate to an object, service, or space that you have created or built? Did you think about the four elements and the five decisions? Why or why not?

5. What do you know now about design that you did not know before?

6. Are there any ideas discussed in the text that you do not quite understand? Discuss anything you are not sure about.

Activity E | Revisit your Unit Inquiry Question on page 158. Are there any ideas from the reading that will help you answer your question? Share your ideas with a partner or small group. At this point, you may consider revising your Unit Inquiry Question. Use the following questions to help you in assessing your question.

1. How does the information from this reading change your understanding of design processes?

2. Which ideas from the reading can be used to help answer your Unit Inquiry Question?

3. What additional questions do you have after finishing the reading?

4. Where could you find more information?

Activity F | Writing Task: Process Paragraph | Write a short paragraph explaining what decisions are necessary during the design process. Before you write, brainstorm ideas related to the different types of decisions you need to make during the design process. In other words, what do you have to think about? When? Put these steps in order and write your paragraph in your own words. Include five of the vocabulary words from this unit in your paragraph.

Activity G | Compare your paragraph to the sample paragraph in Appendix 2, then answer the questions that follow. Share your answers with a partner or small group.

1. What is the main idea of the sample paragraph?

2. What steps are described in the sample paragraph?

3. What process connectors do you see in the sample paragraph?

4. How do the steps in the sample paragraph compare with the steps in your paragraph?

5. Did you use any process connectors? Are they used correctly?

6. After reading the sample paragraph, is there anything you would like to revise in your paragraph?

Identifying Assumptions

Sometimes writers might not provide any proof when they are making a statement because they think that what they are saying is true or obvious to readers. If a writer makes a statement based on personal beliefs or perceived facts, but does not support the point with evidence, the writer is making an assumption. A critical reader is able to identify a writer's assumptions in a text. Critical readers recognize assumptions based on the lack of evidence in the text. Consider the assumptions being made by the writing in the statements set out in the chart below.

Some assumptions are necessary in writing, but it is important to use only those that readers are likely to share. This means you need to think carefully about who your reader is and what your reader already knows about your topic. If you don't think that your readers will share the same assumptions you have, you should avoid making assumptions in your writing by providing evidence and proof to support what you are saying.

Statement	Assumption
Plain-looking products, even if they are very useful do not sell well.	Customers are more interested in how a product looks than its usefulness.
Customers should be involved in the testing phase of the design process.	Customer feedback would not be very useful during the other phases of the design process.
Focusing on aesthetics will lead to an increase in sales.	Product sales depend more on visual impressions than other factors.

PROCESS FUNDAMENTALS

Brainstorming and Outlining

Sticky Note Process Map

Making a sticky note process map can help with brainstorming ideas for a process writing assignment. To begin, think about each of the steps in your process and make a separate sticky note for each one. Using sticky notes helps you to organize the steps in your process before putting it to paper in a flowchart because the sticky notes allow you to rearrange the ideas as they are developing.

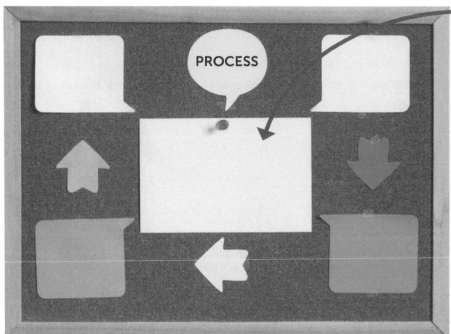

PROCESS

1. **Brainstorm** steps. Put each on a sticky note. On each note, **describe** the step simply.

2. **Discuss** and **decide** on the best order for your process:
   a. chronological (time-based) order
   b. order of importance

3. You will see connections between the steps. **Arrange** the sticky notes in that order.

4. Once you are satisfied, **number** the sticky notes.

5. **Add** arrows to show the flow.

FIGURE 5.3 Sticky note process map steps

Activity A | Think back to the product, service, or space you talked about designing in Activity C on page 157. What steps would you need to follow to design and create that product, service, or space? Create a sticky note process map that includes all of your steps. Arrange them in chronological order or order of importance. After you have finished, show your map to a partner and ask your partner to describe the process back to you. Revise any unclear steps or add in any missing steps.

Activity B | Use what you have learned about the topic of design so far to create a sticky note process map for your Unit Inquiry Question. Exchange your map with a partner and describe the process. Ask your partner for feedback using the questions below.

1. Is it clear what inquiry question I am trying to answer?
2. What are the main steps in my process?
3. Are there any steps that are missing or unclear?
4. Could the order of the steps in the process be improved in any way?

Process Essay Outline

An outline for a process essay has three basic parts.

1. The first part is the introduction, which introduces readers to the main ideas in the essay.
2. The next part contains the major steps in the process. There are no restrictions on how many paragraphs you have in this part of the essay, but generally there is one body paragraph for each major step or group of closely related steps (called stages). You can also add in supporting ideas, details, examples, and explanations for the steps in your process.

3. The last part of the outline contains the conclusion, which reminds the reader of the importance of the process and the main stages.

When you are including supporting ideas, details, examples, and explanations for the steps in your process, a multi-level format is preferred because it helps the reader follow the steps in the process. Figure 5.4 shows a multi-level outline and what to include in it.

Title/Inquiry Question: What decisions do designers have to make to create a great product?

I.   **Introduction**

    A.   <u>Opening statement</u>: Everyone has experienced the situation of trying to build something, only to find that it could not be assembled properly.

    B.   <u>Supporting information</u>: The design process is complicated.

    C.   <u>Main idea</u>: Involves six interconnected decisions to achieve a great product.

II. **Body paragraph (stage 1)**: Three initial steps to create a quality product

    A.   <u>Step 1</u>: Define the problem

       Supporting ideas/details/examples: Focus on the central problem.

    B.   <u>Step 2</u>: Research the problem

       Supporting ideas/details/examples: Investigate how others have dealt with similar problems.

    C.   <u>Step 3</u>: Develop a solution

       Supporting ideas/details/examples: Ask *how* questions to develop a solution.

III. **Body paragraph (stage 2)**: Three final steps to create a quality product

    A.   <u>Step 4</u>: Prototyping a solution

       Supporting ideas/details/examples: Observe how the prototype works in the design space.

    B.   <u>Step 5</u>: Testing a solution

       Supporting ideas/details/examples: Test using the intended users of the product.

    C.   <u>Step 6</u>: Improving the solution

       Supporting ideas/details/examples: Focus on the details of the prototype.

IV. **Conclusion**:

    A.   Achieving a quality product is dependent on the steps taken during the design process.

FIGURE 5.4   A multi-level outline for a process essay

Activity C | Look back at the sample process essay "The Engineering Design Process: Finding Solutions to Problems" on pages 160–161. Create a process essay outline by filling in the template below with key information from the essay.

Title: The Engineering Design Process: Finding Solutions to Problems

I.   **Introduction**:

    A. Opening question:

    B. Supporting information:

    C. Main idea:

II. **Body paragraph (stage 1)**:

    A. Step 1:

        Supporting ideas/details/examples:

    B. Step 2:

        Supporting ideas/details/examples:

    C. Step 3:

        Supporting ideas/details/examples:

III. **Body paragraph (stage 2)**:

    A. Step 4:

        Supporting ideas/details/examples:

    B. Step 5:

        Supporting ideas/details/examples:

    C. Step 6:

        Supporting ideas/details/examples:

IV. **Body paragraph (stage 3)**:

    A. Step 7:

        Supporting ideas/details/examples:

    B. Step 8:

        Supporting ideas/details/examples:

    C. Step 9:

        Supporting ideas/details/examples:

V.   **Conclusion**:

    A. Restated main idea:

    B. Reminder to readers:

Activity D | Create an outline for a process essay based on the sticky note process map you made for your Unit Inquiry Question in Activity B on page 171. Try to group your steps into two or three main stages. Use the template below to help you create your outline. You can add to or delete stages, steps, and supporting ideas as required.

Unit Inquiry Question: _____

I.   **Introduction**:

II. **Body paragraph (stage 1)**:

    A.   <u>Step</u>:

          Supporting ideas/details/examples:

    B.   <u>Step</u>:

          Supporting ideas/details/examples:

    C.   <u>Step</u>:

          Supporting ideas/details/examples:

III. **Body paragraph (stage 2)**:

    A.   <u>Step</u>:

          Supporting ideas/details/examples:

    B.   <u>Step</u>:

          Supporting ideas/details/examples:

    C.   <u>Step</u>:

          Supporting ideas/details/examples:

IV. **Conclusion**:

Content Skill

Integrating Information from Magazine Articles

Magazine articles can provide a writer with information to start learning about a topic. Some magazines will contain research, but most will have easy-to-understand information, diagrams, or graphs. Most magazines are written to inform readers and can provide useful information when starting your research. There are many indexes and databases at your library that can be used to help find magazine articles on your topic.

If you use a site such as Academic Search Complete, make sure you refine your search by selecting *magazine* as the source type. These results can be further refined until you find one or two articles that most closely fit your topic.

Some common English-language magazines related to design are listed below.

Popular Mechanics

http://www.popularmechanics.com/

The Architectural Review

https://www.architectural-review.com/

Make Magazine

http://makezine.com/

Activity A | Read the following magazine excerpt from *University Affairs* titled "'Design Thinking' Is Changing the Way We Approach Problems." As you read, pay attention to the underlined sentences and think about how you might answer the question *What is design thinking?* When you are finished reading, discuss your answer with a partner or small group.

"Design Thinking" Is Changing the Way We Approach Problems

1   A product of the same trends and philosophies that gave us smart phones, laptop computers, and Internet search engines, design thinking is changing the way some academics approach teaching and research, the way architects design classrooms, and how leaders seek to solve the world's most persistent problems. (1)

2   Cameron Norman is a long-time supporter of design thinking (or DT) and an adjunct lecturer at the University of Toronto's Dalla Lana School of Public Health. He notes that designers, especially product designers, are typically experts in conceptualizing problems and solving them—ideal skills for tackling a wide range of issues, from building a better kitchen table to mapping out the plans on a large building. (2) "The field of design is the discipline of innovation," he says. "[Design thinking] is about taking these methods, tools and ideas, and applying them in other areas."

3   Design thinking centres on the free flow of ideas— far-out concepts aren't summarily dismissed—and an unusually enthusiastic embrace of failure. (3) "Design thinkers try to figure out what the key problem is— they look around and try to understand what's going on, and come up with some wild ideas, thinking big and bold, on how to solve it," Dr. Norman says. "They assume they're not going to get it right the first time."

4   If you were looking to build a better mousetrap, you'd prototype a model, test it for weaknesses, then either trash it and start again, or identify the problems and seek to correct them. (4) DT does the same thing, but in an increasingly broad array of areas, from social policy to healthcare to business.

Source: Adapted from Johnson, T. (2016, January 13). "Design thinking" is changing the way we approach problems. *University Affairs*. Retrieved from http://www.universityaffairs.ca/features/feature-article/design-thinking-changing-way-approach-problems/

Activity B | Read the paraphrases for the underlined sentences in the reading on page 175. Then discuss the questions in the notes column with a partner or in a small group. As you discuss the questions, think about how this information might connect with your Unit Inquiry Question.

Paraphrase	Notes
1. Professors, architects, and leaders are solving complex problems with design thinking.	What other professions are using design thinking? What are some examples of world problems that design thinking is solving? How is design thinking different from analytical thinking?
2. Designers are good at understanding and solving problems. These skills can be applied to problems both big and small.	What does a product designer do? How do product designers do their work?
3. Not rejecting ideas that might seem crazy is an important principle in design thinking. Mistakes and failure are seen as positives by design thinkers.	How does the process of design thinking work? Why is failure embraced?
4. When developing an idea, start by building a model and testing it. Then, after testing, either improve the idea, or go back to the modelling.	This article references several steps in design thinking, like conceptualizing a problem, prototyping, and testing. What other steps are involved?

Activity C | Writing Task: Process Paragraph | Write a short process paragraph detailing the major steps in the design thinking process. Use your own ideas, as well as at least one idea from the magazine excerpt on page 175. Remember to use an in-text citation and a reference if you include any ideas that are not your own.

Preventing Plagiarism

Integrating Paraphrases

One way to prevent plagiarism is to paraphrase ideas from another writer, putting them into your own words and then providing an in-text citation and a reference. Paraphrasing is different from quoting because you do not copy the exact phrase or words of the original and you do not need quotation marks.

Paraphrasing Checklist

✓ Use synonyms to change the original text.
✓ Avoid having three or more of the original words together.
✓ Change the word order in the sentence.
✓ Remove and replace examples.
✓ Combine or join sentences.
✓ Use antonyms for variety.

Consider this example of a paraphrase (with an in-text citation in APA style).

Original: Design thinking is changing the way some academics approach teaching and research (Johnson, 2016).

Paraphrase: Johnson (2016) noted that some professors have altered their approach to education and research as a result of design thinking.

Reference Skill

Citing Magazine Articles Using APA Style

Here is the bibliographic information for "Design Thinking," published in *University Affairs*.

Author	Tim Johnson
Date	13 January 2016
Article title	"Design Thinking" Is Changing the Way We Approach Problems
Magazine title	University Affairs
Pages	Not applicable
Web address	http://www.universityaffairs.ca/features/feature-article/design-thinking-changing-way-approach-problems/

If you include any ideas or words from *University Affairs*'s "Design Thinking" in your writing assignment, you will need to write in-text citations and a reference. Here are examples of APA-style in-text citations and an entry for the References list.

	APA Style
In-text citation	According to the article "'Design Thinking' Is Changing the Way We Approach Problems," design thinking is in increasingly more fields of study. (Johnson, 2016).
	In the article "'Design thinking' Is Changing the Way We Approach Problems," Johnson (2016) noted that design thinking is in increasingly more fields of study.
References entry	Johnson, T. (2016, January 13). "Design thinking" is changing the way we approach problems. *University Affairs*. Retrieved from http://www.universityaffairs.ca/features/feature-article/design-thinking-changing-way-approach-problems/

Activity A | Check that you have correctly written in-text citations for the ideas that you included in the paragraph you wrote for Activity C on page 176. At the end of your paragraph, double-check your entry for an APA-style References list. If necessary, make corrections.

Format and Organization Skill

Writing an Ask-the-Reader Introduction

An essay's introductory paragraph should hook readers into reading the rest of the essay. The first two or three sentences of an introduction are critical for securing the reader's interest in the essay topic. Starting an introduction by asking the reader a relevant question and following that with some background details or a brief, related story is one way to create an interesting lead-in to the thesis statement at the end of the introduction. Typically, in this type of introductory paragraph, the question is the hook, the next two or three sentences provide support for the hook (with some background or a short, related story), and the final sentence is the thesis statement.

Activity A | The introduction below describes why libraries are good places for makerspaces. Read the introduction and identify the following parts by underlining them: the hook, support, and the thesis statement.

Why are libraries increasingly opening makerspaces on university campuses? Libraries see the trend for makerspaces as likely to continue. According to a recent article titled "A Librarian's Guide to Makerspaces: 16 Resources" (2017) posted on the Open Education Database, over 135 million Americans were makers in 2015. In fact, campus libraries are a uniquely good place to start a makerspace because of the availability of materials and the diversity of students who use the location. The process of starting a successful library makerspace involves a number of crucial steps.

Reference

A Librarian's Guide to Makerspaces: 16 Resources. (2017, March 17). *Open Education Database*. Retrieved from http://oedb.org/ilibrarian/a-librarians-guide-to-makerspaces/

Activity B | Read each of the essay topics below and the thesis statement for each one. Then create an appropriate ask-the-reader introduction for each topic by adding a question hook and two or three sentences to support the hook.

1. **Essay topic:** Repair café

   Question hook: _____

   _____

   Background sentences or related story (support for the hook): _____

   _____

   _____

   _____

   Thesis statement: A repair café can help the environment by giving clients an easy-to-follow process for fixing broken household items.

2. **Topic:** Tool library

   Question hook: _____

   _____

Background sentences or related story (support for the hook): _____

_____

_____

_____

Thesis statement: People can create a tool library that operates as an equipment lending club by following these simple steps.

Topic Skill

Writing Process Thesis Statements

A thesis statement is usually the sentence in an essay that explains the topic of the essay by answering the inquiry question. It is generally made up of two parts: the main idea and the focus. The main idea is the general topic of the essay. The focus is the specific aspects of the topic that will be discussed in the essay.

In a process essay, the focus of the thesis statement tells readers they are going to read about a process. After reading the thesis statement, it should be obvious to readers what process will be described in the essay. The thesis statement is typically the last sentence in the introduction paragraph. You can state your main idea first, then follow it with the focus, or you can lead with the focus, then follow it with the main idea.

main idea   +   focus

When designing a learning space such as a classroom, it is necessary to survey the layout, choose the furniture, and decide on a budget.

focus   +   main idea

By following these easy steps, students can quickly build their own bookcases.

Activity A | Create thesis statements for each main idea and focus.

1. main idea: building a prototype
   focus: several crucial steps

   _____

   _____

2. main idea: creating a 3D model
   focus: five steps

   _____

   _____

3. main idea: building a bridge
   focus: planning stage, building stage, testing stage

   _____

   _____

4. main idea: engineering design process
    focus: preparing, testing, reflecting

_____

_____

5. main idea: making your own jewellery
    focus: a creative process

_____

_____

Activity B | Read the following introductory paragraph on planning a maker day. Then write a thesis statement that captures the process described using the focus information in parentheses.

Planning a Maker Day

What is a good example of a maker day that works? At the University of British Columbia, instructors hold an annual maker day where innovative young designers build new things. This maker day is described in detail by Crichton and Carter (2013) in their Maker Day Toolkit.

Thesis statement: _____
(choosing a date and location, developing a budget, establishing the tone for the event)

Activity C | Look back at the outline you created for your Unit Inquiry Question in Activity D on page 174. Write a thesis statement for an essay responding to your Unit Inquiry Question.

Activity D | Exchange your thesis statement with a partner. Evaluate each other's thesis statements using the following questions, and discuss any changes or suggestions that could improve the thesis statement.

1. Is the main idea clearly presented?
2. What is the focus of the thesis statement?
3. Is it clear that this is a thesis statement for a process essay?

Activity E | Writing Task: Introduction to a Process Essay | Look back at the outline you created for your Unit Inquiry Question on page 174. Write an introduction that starts by asking the reader a question and then includes two or three sentences of background information or a short, related story. Next, incorporate the thesis statement you wrote for Activity C above and revised in Activity D.

When you are finished, exchange your introduction with a partner. Do your partner's question at the start of the paragraph and the two or three sentences that follow relate to the thesis statement?

Conclusion Skill

Reminding the Reader

Typically, a process essay ends once the process has been described. In a process essay, the conclusion paragraph helps to remind the reader of what came before it. A conclusion also gives the writer one last chance to convince the reader of the importance of the topic and its purpose. Usually, the first sentence of an essay conclusion is the concluding statement. The concluding statement is a paraphrase of the thesis statement.

It is important that you do not simply restate the introduction, as this makes the conclusion repetitive. When writing a remind-the-reader conclusion, ask yourself the following questions.

- Does the conclusion remind the reader of the steps or stages in the process?
- Does the conclusion remind the reader why this process is important?
- Does the conclusion state the information in a different way than the introduction?

Activity A | Read the introduction below related to the process of design thinking. As you read, underline the sentences or phrases that would be important to repeat in a conclusion. Discuss your answers with a partner.

The Process of Design Thinking

    What is design thinking? Businesses have realized the value of design thinking, but it is often a difficult process to learn for a couple of reasons. First, creativity is difficult to teach to others. Therefore, a business needs to start the process by committing time and resources to playing and being creative. Second, creativity without critical thinking does not end in good ideas. Employees must be trained to recognize what critical decisions are needed to produce innovation. Thus, there is a clear process companies must follow if they wish for their employees to engage in design thinking.

Activity B | Create a concluding statement by rewriting the following thesis statement from the introductory paragraph in Activity A. Be sure to paraphrase the ideas so that you are restating the main idea and focus in a new and interesting way.

> **Thesis statement**: Thus, there is a clear process companies must follow if they wish for their employees to engage in design thinking.

Concluding statement: _____

_____

_____

_____

Activity C | Look back at the thesis statement you created in response to your Unit Inquiry Question in the introduction paragraph you wrote for Activity E on page 180. Write a concluding statement that paraphrases your thesis statement.

Activity D | Writing Task: Remind-the-Reader Conclusion | What two or three ideas do you want to remind readers about related to the introduction you wrote in response to your Unit Inquiry Question for Activity E on page 180? Write a remind-the-reader conclusion related to your ask-the-reader introduction. Start your paragraph with the concluding statement you wrote in the previous activity.

WRITING FUNDAMENTALS

Composition Skill

Maintaining Coherence

As you move to longer and more complicated writing, it is important that your writing be coherent. Coherent writing links the ideas from one sentence to the next to ensure that the writing flows smoothly without straying off topic.

There are four types of sentence-level coherence techniques that you can use to achieve more unified writing. These are using transitions and connecting phrases, using pronouns, using words with similar meanings, and repeating verb time and tense. The following chart provides detail on each of the four types of coherence strategies.

Coherence Strategy	Examples	Explanation
1. Making logical connections with transition words and phrases	First of all, designers define the problem. Then they research possible solutions, Next, they choose the best solution. After that, they build a prototype. Once they have a prototype, they test it to see if it works. Then they report the results of the test. As soon as they have feedback from other people, designers reflect on their solution. Finally, they refine the prototype and decide on the final design.	Transition words and phrases connect sentences or phrases together in a logical pattern.

2.	Using pronouns to link topics	<u>Designers</u> are creative people. <u>They</u> use a nine-step process for solving design problems.	Use a pronoun to repeat the topic from one sentence to the next. Pronouns link to the topic without repeating words.
3.	Using words with similar meanings, such as synonyms, to emphasize ideas and create interest, or repeating keywords	A library <u>makerspace</u> where people can create new things will frequently have software and <u>equipment</u>. <u>These tools</u> can be used to build projects that are big or small. Thus, the <u>library</u> can be a good place to go for people who like <u>building things</u>.	Repeat ideas using synonyms and words with similar meanings to make readers more aware of the important information. Reuse keywords as necessary
4.	Repeating verb time and tense to link ideas	Design thinking <u>can be used</u> to solve unfamiliar problems. Analytical thinking, which considers all the parts of a problem separately, <u>can be used</u> to solve problems similar to ones that have already been solved by someone else.	Repeat the verb tense and time to link the content of one sentence to another.

Activity A | Read the following body paragraph on planning a maker day. Decide which of the four coherence strategies—using transition words and phrases, using pronouns, using words with similar meanings or repeating keywords, and repeating verb time and tense—are used in each of the underlined words or phrases. Which coherence strategy is missing? Share your answers with your partner.

> The first step to planning a successful maker day is to organize details related to the date, the venue, and the budget. All three details are critical to the success of the <u>event</u>. It is important to select a date when there are no other activities planned to allow maximum participation in the maker day. <u>Next</u>, selecting the space where <u>it</u> will be held is also important. The <u>space</u> will ultimately determine what types of activities and equipment can be used for the maker day. <u>Finally</u>, developing a realistic budget will help ensure the success of a maker day. It is important to determine the cost of not only the materials, but also any refreshments and advertising for the maker day. Planning these details well in advance will help to ensure that the event will be successful.

Activity B | Reread the process paragraph you wrote for Activity F on page 169. Check your writing to see if you have used any of the coherence strategies discussed in this section. Add some coherence strategies, if needed, to make your ideas flow and connect together. When you are finished, share your paragraph with a partner and explain which strategies you used. Answer the following questions in your discussion.

1. Are there transition words and phrases, including process connectors, in the paragraph?

2. Are more transition words and phrases necessary to hold the paragraph together and make the writing flow?
3. Are pronouns used to make connections to previous sentences?
4. Have synonyms and words with similar meanings been used to add variety to the writing? Have keywords been repeated to create coherence?
5. Are verb tenses used consistently?

Sentence and Grammar Skill

Using Adverbs

Another way to add interest to your process writing is through the use of adverbs. Adverbs give details on the actions in your sentence to better explain what is happening. Adverbs can add precision to your writing by adding more information about a verb, or by adding emphasis to grab your reader's attention. For example, adverbs are useful when describing how steps and stages happen.

Next, the carpenter lightly sands the wood.
The jeweller carefully added the diamonds to the ring.

Adverbs can also provide more information about an adjective or even another adverb.

Following these steps is incredibly easy.
He painted the house very quickly.

Form   Adverbs are commonly formed by adding the suffix -ly to an adjective with some slight changes to the spelling. For example, *lucky* becomes *luckily*, *drastic* becomes *drastically*, and *happy* becomes *happily*. Some adverbs do not have an adjective equivalent (*almost*).

Sometimes an adverb will have a different meaning from a word that appears to be related to it.

He is working hard on his project. (*Hard* means with great effort.)
He is hardly working on his project. (*Hardly* means not very much.)

Function   Adverbs can give various kinds of extra information. Consider the examples in the following chart.

Function	Examples	Sentences
manner (how)	blindly	He blindly followed the instructions.
	carefully	You need to carefully fold the paper.
frequency (how often)	always	Good designers always start with a sketch.
	seldom	I seldom begin my designs with a complete idea in mind.
time and place (when and where)	now	We have to start now.
	here	People should come here to make their projects.

relative time (when)	soon	You will soon know if your prototype has problems.
	already	Our manager has already found a design flaw in our prototype.
degree (how much)	very	This project is very important.
	hugely	The smiles on people's faces were hugely rewarding.
focusing (which one)	even	The new hybrid cars are even more fuel efficient than compact cars.
	specifically	These designs were specifically created for teens.
attitude (how the writer feels)	surprisingly	The steps were surprisingly easy to follow.
	clearly	The new bridge is clearly better than the old one.

Placement   Adverbs often modify verbs but can be found in many places in a sentence. Choosing where to place the adverb can be a challenge. Adverbs of manner are particularly important for describing what the writer thinks about an action. Where the adverb is placed can make a difference in meaning. Note the differences in the three example sentences below.

> Only I completed my process essay assignment.
> I completed only my process essay assignment.
> I completed my only process essay assignment.

In the first sentence, *only* modifies *I*, and the sentence means that no other student completed the assignment. In the second sentence, *only* modifies *my process essay assignment*, and the sentence means that the writer completed that assignment, but no other assignments. Finally, in the third sentence, *only* modifies *process essay assignment*, and the sentence means that the writer had just one assignment to complete, not two.

Activity A | Read the short paragraph below on how to build a bookcase, and fill in the blanks with the best choice from the following list of adverbs.

| carefully | always | seldom | now | already |
| very | even | specifically | surprisingly | clearly |

People _____ make their own bookcases. However, it can be _____ easy. I have _____ taught three of my friends to make their own bookcases, and they _____ like them. First, you should _____ choose some bricks and planks of wood. Next, _____ check for splinters so you don't hurt yourself. Splinters can be _____ painful. _____, you stack two columns of three bricks each and place the planks of wood across the columns of bricks. Do this two or three times to create your shelves. These shelves are _____ designed for books. I think that this kind of bookcase is _____ better than one you can buy in the store.

Activity B | Rewrite each sentence, adding the adverb in parentheses. Then work in pairs and discuss the adverb placement with your partner. Did you place the adverb in the same location?

1. Digital software design tools are useful to designers. (very)

   _____

2. Yuriko set up her own design company. (singlehandedly)

   _____

3. This company has come up with an exciting design for gardens. (really)

   _____

4. Making new buildings accessible for all people is an important design consideration. (particularly)

   _____

5. Strict standards ensure that new and renovated buildings fit with the existing older buildings in the area. (almost always)

   _____

6. The new SUV will not win any design awards, but it's very practical and fuel efficient. (extremely)

   _____

Activity C | Review one of the pieces of writing you have completed so far in this unit to find the adverbs. Underline each adverb used in that piece of writing. Then locate places in your writing where an adverb would be appropriate. Try to add adverbs that represent the different functions. After you have completed your revisions, show your work to a partner. Decide if the new adverbs have been used correctly and effectively. Discuss your feedback with your partner.

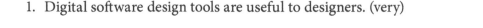

Learning Strategy

Developing Effective Time Management Strategies

I'm tired! I stayed up all night finishing my writing assignment.

I just can't get organized!

Why can't I think of anything to write?

Where do I start?

As you go through the process of writing for an academic audience, you will experience some struggles with time management. This is a normal part of college or university studies. Throughout a term, you will have several assignments, and some may even have overlapping deadlines. In order to meet your deadlines, the following time management strategies are very important.

• Develop a system to keep track of your writing progress.
• Monitor your progress with a calendar that lists start and end times.

- Write a little every day. Waiting for inspiration doesn't always lead to success.
- Set a daily goal to ensure completion of the assignment.

- Finally, create a work environment that helps you to maximize your time. Having your writing materials in one place will help to eliminate distractions.

UNIT OUTCOME

Writing Assignment: Process Essay

Write a process essay of 250 to 350 words on a topic related to design. (Your instructor may give you an alternative length.) You may write on a topic based on your Unit Inquiry Question, develop another topic of your choosing connected to design, or choose one of the following topics:

- What is the most effective process for designing a learning space?
- How can a 3D printer be used to build a prototype?
- How can a school organize its own successful maker day?

Use the skills you have developed in this unit to complete the assignment. Follow the steps set out below to practise each of your newly acquired skills to write a well-developed process essay.

1. **Brainstorm**: Use a sticky note process map to come up with ideas related to your topic.

2. **Find information**: Find some information to support your main ideas. Include information from the unit readings in each body paragraph if appropriate.

3. **Compose a thesis statement**: Develop a focused process thesis statement that includes your main idea and focus.

4. **Create an outline**: Fill in the outline on the next page to plan the first draft of your process essay. You may make changes to the outline as necessary.

Introduction	Hook (question for the reader):
	Supporting ideas (background details or brief, related story):
	Thesis statement:
Main Body Paragraphs (Stages in the Process)	Stage 1:
	Step 1:
	Supporting ideas/details/examples:
	Step 2:
	Supporting ideas/details/examples:
	Step 3:
	Supporting ideas/details/examples
	Stage 2:
	Step 4:
	Supporting ideas/details/examples:
	Step 5:
	Supporting ideas/details/examples:
	Step 6:
	Supporting ideas/details/examples:
Conclusion	Concluding statement:
	Reminder of the importance of the topic:

5. **Write a first draft**: Use your outline to write the first draft of your essay. Do not worry too much about spelling or grammar in the first draft. Try to get your ideas down on paper. If you get stuck, you can skip a part and come back to it later. For example, consider writing the body paragraphs first, then writing the introduction and conclusion.

6. **Self-check**: Read over your essay and use the Evaluation Rubric below and on the next page to look for areas where you need to improve. Think of at least two ways to improve your essay.

7. **Ask for a peer review**: Exchange the revised version of your first draft with a partner. Use the Evaluation Rubric to assess your partner's paragraph and provide suggestions to improve it. Ask questions (as you learned in Unit 4) to help your partner develop the body paragraphs more effectively. Consider your partner's feedback carefully and use it to make changes to your paragraph.

8. **Edit**: Edit your essay for the following:

   • Adverbs: Ensure that you have used some adverbs in your writing to add interest and variety, and that they have been used correctly in the sentence.

   • Coherence: Check that your writing flows smoothly and has a unified feel. Use some of the coherence strategies discussed in this unit if necessary to improve the flow.

   • Vocabulary: Check that you have used some of the AWL and mid-frequency vocabulary from this unit in your essay.

9. **Write a final draft**: Write a final draft of your essay, making any changes you think will improve it. If possible, leave some time between drafts.

10. **Proofread**: Check the final draft of your essay for any small errors you may have missed. In particular, look for spelling errors, typos, and punctuation mistakes. If you used information from an outside source, double-check your in-text citations and your References list to make sure they are formatted properly.

Evaluation: Process Essay Rubric

Use the following checklist to evaluate your writing. In which areas do you need to improve most?

E = **Emerging**: frequent difficulty using unit skills; needs a lot more work
D = **Developing**: some difficulty using unit skills; some improvement still required
S = **Satisfactory**: able to use unit skills most of the time; meets average expectations for this level
O = **Outstanding**: exceptional use of unit skills; exceeds expectations for this level

Skill	E	D	S	O
The essay is organized according to a process essay format and has an introductory paragraph, body paragraphs, and a concluding paragraph.				
The essay introduction hooks readers by asking them a relevant question followed by some background details.				
The essay contains a process thesis statement that clearly introduces the process being described in the essay.				
Transition words and phrases that help illustrate a process are used as needed.				
The essay includes a varied vocabulary with various synonyms used so that no words are repeated too often.				
AWL and mid-frequency vocabulary items from this unit are used when appropriate and with few mistakes.				
The essay conclusion reminds readers of the topic's importance and purpose.				
If required, APA-style in-text citations and References list have been included.				
Various techniques are used to ensure coherence is maintained throughout the essay.				
Adverbs are used where appropriate and with few mistakes.				

Unit Review

Activity A | What do you know now that you did not know before about design and the design process? Discuss with a partner or small group.

Activity B | Look back at the Unit Inquiry Question you developed at the start of this unit and discuss it with a partner or small group. Then share your answers with the class. Use the following questions to guide you.

1. What information did you find in this unit that helped you answer your question?
2. How would you answer your question now?

Activity C | Use the following checklist to review what you have learned throughout this unit. First decide which 10 skills you think are most important—circle the number beside each of these 10 skills. If you learned a skill in this unit that isn't listed below, write it in the blank row at the end of the checklist. Then put a check mark in the box beside those points you feel you have learned. Be prepared to discuss your choices with the class.

Self-Assessment Checklist

☐	1. I can discuss issues related to design and the design process based on what I have read in this unit.
☐	2. I can develop an inquiry question to explore a process.
☐	3. I can choose appropriate synonyms to expand the variety of words used in my writing.
☐	4. I can use the AWL and mid-frequency vocabulary from this unit in my writing.
☐	5. I can identify assumptions and avoid making assumptions that my reader might not understand or agree with.
☐	6. I can use a sticky note process map to brainstorm ideas for my writing.
☐	7. I can create an outline for a process essay, grouping related steps together into stages.
☐	8. I can find and use information from magazine articles to help me better understand a process.
☐	9. I can integrate paraphrases effectively into my writing to avoid plagiarism.
☐	10. I can write an introduction that hooks readers by asking them a question that is relevant to the essay topic.
☐	11. I can write a process thesis statement that is clear and logical, and include it in an effective introductory paragraph that grabs my reader's attention.
☐	12. I can write a concluding paragraph that reminds the reader of my thesis statement.
☐	13. I can use coherence strategies to ensure that my writing flows smoothly and my paragraphs hold together.
☐	14. I can use adverbs to add interest and variety to my writing.
☐	15. I can write an effective process essay.
☐	16.

Activity D | Put a check mark in the box beside the vocabulary items from this unit that you feel confident using in your writing. Make a plan to practise the words that you still need to learn.

Vocabulary Checklist

☐ aesthetic (adj.) 4000   ☐ harsh (adj.) 3000

☐ assemble (v.) AWL   ☐ necklace (n.) 6000

☐ attach (v.) AWL   ☐ overall (adj.) AWL

☐ conceptual (adj.) AWL   ☐ principle (n.) AWL

☐ construction (n.) AWL   ☐ sketch (v.) 4000

☐ copper (n.) 4000   ☐ teen (n.) 5000

☐ delicate (adj.) 4000   ☐ texture (n.) 4000

☐ funds (n.) AWL   ☐ unique (adj.) AWL

UNIT 6

Health Sciences

Wellness

EXPLORING IDEAS

Introduction

Activity A | Discuss the following questions with a partner or small group.

1. How do you define wellness?
2. Which aspect of wellness shown in the picture above is most important to you?
3. How does physical activity enhance well-being?
4. What makes you feel satisfied with your life?
5. Why might there be differences in well-being among students?
6. How important are friends, relatives, and colleagues to having a positive outlook in life?

Activity B | Figure 6.1 shows a wellness wheel with the seven dimensions of human wellness. The column next to the wellness wheel provides definitions for each of the different types of wellness, but in scrambled order. Think about each dimension, then find the most appropriate definition. Write the correct wellness dimension on the blank beside the definition in the right-hand column. The first one, *emotional wellness*, has been done for you.

FIGURE 6.1 Wellness wheel

Definition

A. eating well, being physically active, and getting enough sleep

B. improving the space around you

C. building healthy relationships with others

D. balancing work with life

E. understanding and exploring yourself

F. developing your knowledge and setting goals

G. having values or beliefs that provide a greater purpose to life

Source: Threlfall, J. (2015, January 30). *Fine arts wellness day.* Retrieved from https://finearts.uvic.ca/research/blog/2015/01/30/fine-arts-wellness-day/

Activity C | Work in a small group. Consider the different student activities in the box below.

joining clubs or extracurricular activities	cooking at home	eating out with friends	studying together	volunteering
managing your study time well	meditating	eating local fruits and vegetables	walking in the park	talking with friends or family
playing team sports	working a part-time job	reading books	gardening	

1. Decide which wellness dimension each activity relates to and add the activity to Figure 6.1 beside its dimension. Some activities might fit with more than one dimension.

2. Add in one or two more of your own examples for each dimension. For example, you might write *creating a schedule to balance study and leisure time* beside *occupational wellness.*

3. When you are finished, share your wellness wheel with another group. Discuss where the activities fit best and how these activities contribute to wellness.

FIGURE 6.2 Dimensions of wellness

Fostering Inquiry

Framing a Problem

In everyday student life, you often deal with problems related to wellness—problems such as feeling tired in class or feeling worried because you have a quiz. Personal experiences can be a good place to start looking for topics related to wellness, but not everyone has the same experiences or the same problems you do.

In academic inquiry, your day-to-day problems need to be reframed as more general issues in order to be more relevant for readers. A more general issue can then be turned into an inquiry question, as in the examples below.

Day-to-Day Problem	General Issue	Inquiry Question
tired in class	student lack of sleep	How does sleep affect learning?
worried about quiz	student stress and anxiety	How can student stress be reduced?

Activity A | What do you want to know more about in relation to the topic of student wellness? For example:

- *How does well-being influence student learning?*
- *Is it difficult for students to improve their overall wellness? Why or why not?*
- *How can colleges and universities support student wellness?*

1. Write two or three questions you are curious about related to student wellness.
2. When you are finished, compare your questions with a partner or small group.
3. Choose one question to guide you as you work through this unit. It does not have to be the same question as your partner or group. Your question may change as you learn more about your topic.
4. Write your inquiry question in the space provided. Look back at this question as you work through this unit. This is your Unit Inquiry Question.

My Unit Inquiry Question:

_____

_____

_____

_____

Activity B | Writing Task: Freewriting | Write for at least five minutes on the topic of your Unit Inquiry Question. Do not stop writing during this time. After five minutes, read what you have written and circle two or three ideas that you would like to explore further.

Structure

Problem–Solution Writing

A problem–solution structure is often used when writers want to explain the reasons for specific problems and discuss possible solutions for these problems. Problem–solution writing generally follows the format of first explaining the problem, then proposing a solution.

Activity A | Read the problem paragraph about students' physical wellness below. Then discuss the questions about it on the following page with a partner or small group.

Students' Physical Wellness: Changing Habits

Problem

Students must be very mindful about their physical well-being. One of the main challenges for students in maintaining their physical wellness is related to their attitudes. University and college students will often assume they are healthy because of their age. However, according to the National College Health Assessment (University of Guelph, 2013), less than 20 percent of Canadian students are meeting the recommended guidelines for nutrition and physical activity. In other words, many students are not keeping as well physically as they could be. Not paying attention to physical wellness affects other aspects of wellness. More specifically, we know that the physical dimension of wellness influences emotional and intellectual wellness. Understanding the connection between habits and wellness can start students on the road to better well-being.

Reference

University of Guelph Wellness Education Centre. (2016). *National College Health Assessment: University of Guelph results*. Retrieved from https://wellness.uoguelph.ca/sws/sites/uoguelph.ca.sws/files/public/NCHA_Sept21_16.pdf

1. Where in the problem paragraph is the problem first mentioned?
2. What is the problem?
3. Is the problem outlined in a way that catches your interest? Explain.
4. What tells you that the problem is serious?

Activity B | Read the solution paragraph below to find out the solution that the writer proposes to students' physical wellness challenges.

Solution

Improving university and college students' physical well-being appears challenging. However, modest changes to diet and exercise can produce major improvements. One simple solution for students is to make small changes to their daily routines. Students can look for places to increase their exercise or improve their diets. Small changes, such as getting off the bus one stop earlier, can impact physical well-being. Also, Health Canada recommends choosing lower fat dairy products and whole grains (Health Canada, 2011). Choosing healthier food at the cafeteria can substantially improve overall health and wellness. In short, making small changes to daily routines is a simple and manageable way for students to improve their physical wellness.

Reference

Health Canada. (2011). *Eating well with Canada's food guide.* Retrieved from www.hc-sc.gc.ca/fn-an/alt_formats/hpfb-dgpsa/pdf/food-guide-aliment/print_eatwell_bienmang-eng.pdf

With a partner, discuss the solution that the writer proposes. Evaluate that solution using the questions below. If your answer is Yes, check the box and provide the reason you agree; if your answer is No, make an **✗** and add a suggestion to improve the solution. When you are done, share your evaluation with another pair of students.

☐ 1. Is the solution simple and easy to understand?
       Reason or suggestion:

       _____

☐ 2. Is the solution directly connected to the problem?
       Reason or suggestion:

       _____

☐ 3.   Is the solution practical?

       Reason or suggestion:

_____

Activity C | Read the students' reflections below on wellness. Highlight each student's main personal challenge. Which dimension of wellness is being challenged? With a small group, discuss each student's problem and reframe it as a general issue. Brainstorm various solutions and discuss which may be the most effective and why.

Student A

I have come to realize that wellness is a lot more complicated than I imagined. When I look at my own wellness, I find that generally speaking, I have a balanced lifestyle. In terms of my social wellness though, I have few relationships. If I were to have problems in my life, I am not sure if I'd have someone to talk to.

Student B

As I am not very active, I have some work to do on my physical wellness. I find that I spend a lot of my time studying and so I put off exercising. Improving my overall fitness would help me physically, and it may also help my studying as well.

Language Tip

Introducing Problems and Solutions

There are certain words and phrases commonly used to introduce either a problem or a solution to your reader. The chart below contains some of these useful phrases that you could include in your writing, and provides example sentences to show you the phrases in context.

1. Words and Phrases to Introduce a Problem	
One of the main obstacles to . . . is . . .	One of the main obstacles to wellness is an imbalance between work and leisure time.
The most common problem . . . is . . .	The most common problem related to emotional wellness is that students do not deal with anxiety and stress.
. . . may cause problems for/with/in . . .	Negative emotions from others may cause problems in an individual's emotional wellness.
. . . is a concern for . . .	Anger, as well as anxiety, is a concern for one's emotional wellness.

2. Words and Phrases to Introduce a Solution	
One of the best solutions . . . is to	One of the best solutions for a lack of exercise is to make small changes in activity levels.
It is possible that . . . could improve . . .	It is possible that better eating habits could improve a student's ability to focus on learning.
In general, it seems that . . . is needed to . . .	In general, it seems that a more student-friendly approach is needed to reduce challenges related to wellness.
Understanding the connection between . . . and . . . helps . . .	Understanding the connection between physical and emotional wellness helps students manage their overall well-being.

Activity D | Writing Task: Problem and Solution Paragraphs | Choose either Student A or Student B's reflection (from Activity C on page 199) and reframe the personal problem as a more general issue. Do some reading and thinking about the issue, looking up the sources listed in Activity A if necessary. Then write two paragraphs—a problem paragraph and a solution paragraph—related to the general issue. Use phrases from the *Language Tip* above to introduce the problem and the solution to your reader.

Activity E | Revisit your Unit Inquiry Question on page 197. Now that you have learned more about your topic, you may have a better idea of how to answer your question, or you may consider revising it. Use the following questions to guide you in assessing your Unit Inquiry Question.

- What information have you learned that will help you answer your Unit Inquiry Question?
- What information do you still need to answer your question?
- Do you want to change your question in any way?

ACADEMIC READING

Vocabulary

Vocabulary Skill: Understanding Collocations

Learning collocations, words that frequently appear together, will help you increase your vocabulary. As well, knowing collocations will make your writing more accurate and natural.

For example, the word *health* collocates with the word *wellness*—this means that *health* often appears near the word *wellness* in the phrase *health and wellness*. Collocations can involve several different grammatical combinations. The chart on page 201 shows how the word *health* can collocate with adjectives, nouns, and verbs.

Grammatical Combination	Examples
adjective + noun	poor health, mental health
noun + noun	health care, health concerns
verb + noun	maintain health, improve health

Activity A | The chart below shows words that collocate with the noun *wellness* listed in order of most frequent to least frequent collocation. The most frequent collocation is *wellness centre*. The noun *wellness* acts as a modifier in that collocation, as often happens in English. *Fitness program*, *student wellness*, and *wellness course* are other examples of noun + noun combinations where nouns act as modifiers.

Decide whether you think the word in the first column of the chart comes before or after the word *wellness* and write the expression.

Collocation	Before or After *Wellness*?
centre	after: wellness centre
program	after: wellness program
policy	
personal	
community	
clinic	
promote	
emotional	

Activity B | Complete each sentence below with a collocation from the chart in Activity A.

1. Learning to balance school, work, and social responsibilities can be difficult for students, but it is important to do so. A lack of balance can negatively affect one's _____.

2. An on-campus _____ is a good resource for students looking to overcome various problems. This is a place that helps to _____.

3. The university provides individual counselling to help students achieve _____.

Vocabulary Preview: The Academic Word List

Activity C | The AWL words below are taken from the reading "Well-being in Canada," found on pages 205–207. Study each word and its definition. Then read the sentences below and choose the correct AWL word for each sentence.

access (n.): the opportunity or right to use something or to see something
comprehensive (adj.): including all, or almost all, the items, details, facts, or information
dimension (n.): an aspect, a way of looking at or thinking about something
incidence (n.): the occurrence, rate, or frequency of a disease, crime, or something else undesirable
index (n.): an indicator, sign, or measure of something; a list of such indicators, signs, or measures
integrated (adj.): combined with a number of other things so that they work together
reliance (n.): needing something or somebody in order to survive, be successful
trend (n.): a general direction in which a situation is changing or developing

1. The **dimension / incidence** of medical problems is higher among students with anxiety.
2. When students start university, their health insurance companies should provide a(n) **comprehensive / integrated** list of health and wellness resources.
3. Wellness includes seven **dimensions / trends**: physical, emotional, intellectual, social, spiritual, environmental, and occupational.
4. Campus wellness programs are now giving students more **access / reliance** to medical care.
5. Emotional stability is a good **incidence / index** of psychological wellness.
6. Because there are seven aspects of wellness, the best approach to health care is an **integrated / indexed** one that considers all aspects of a person's life.
7. Self-help groups can decrease student **access / reliance** on traditional health care.
8. Increased interest in yoga and meditation is a positive **comprehensive / trend** in personal wellness.

Vocabulary Preview: Mid-frequency Vocabulary

Activity D | In the following example sentences, the mid-frequency words in red also appear in the unit's reading. Read the two example sentences for each of these words, and identify which word in each sentence collocates with the word in red. Underline it. If you need to check the collocation, use an English dictionary to look up the mid-frequency word. The collocations for the first word, *chronic*, have been done for you as an example.

1. chronic
   a. It is clear that chronic health problems increase with age
   b. Many hospitals have a chronic shortage of beds.

2. composite
   a. Wellness professionals now support composite programs that combine traditional and alternative approaches to health care.
   b. Scientists have created a composite picture of the layers in the brain.

3. deteriorate
   a. Health can deteriorate rapidly if people do not get medical help when they need it.
   b. Health does not have to deteriorate sharply as people age.

4. leisure
   a. It is important to set aside some leisure time for yourself to reduce stress and anxiety.
   b. Universities should promote leisure activities that students find relevant

5. modest
   a. Improving health can be as simple as making modest changes to lifestyle.
   b. Young couples often spend only a modest amount of money on health care.

6. robust
   a. Given the robust Canadian economy, all students should be able to access affordable health care.
   b. Cold water swimming promotes robust physical fitness.

7. soar
   a. Vegetable prices in Canada soar as winter approaches.
   b. Government healthcare costs soared to $28 billion this year

8. vitality
   a. Active young children have a great deal of vitality.
   b. Tiredness robs students of their vitality for learning.

Activity E | Write the mid-frequency words from the activity above beside the best definition in the table below. The first one has been done for you.

Definition	MFV Word
1. lasting for a long time	chronic
2. to rise very quickly	
3. to become worse	
4. energy and enthusiasm	
5. strong and healthy	
6. not very large, expensive, important	
7. made of different parts or materials	
8. time that is spent doing what you enjoy when you are not working or studying	

Reading

The reading "Well-being in Canada" on pages 205–207 contains excerpts from reports by the Canadian Index of Wellbeing (CIW), an index that measures wellness among Canadians. Information from the CIW is used by many Ontario cities and government organizations to evaluate the success of their social and economic development programs. As well, the CIW provides useful background information for social science or urban studies research on Canadian society.

Activity A | The bar graph below is based on the 2016 Canadian Index of Wellbeing National Report. It shows how certain indicators of wellness have changed, positively or negatively, during the years from 1994 to 2014. For example, it shows significant improvements in education, one indicator of well-being. Read the bar graph and then the statements in the KWL chart below it.

In the KWL chart, put a check mark beside any of the statements that are true for you. In other words, in the first column, check anything that you already know, and in the second column, check anything that you want to know more about. When you have finished the reading, return to the KWL chart and check anything that you have learned. Complete the last sentence of each KWL category with one of your own ideas.

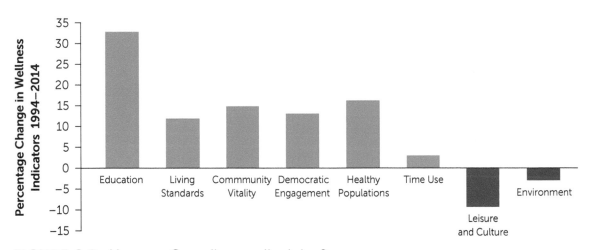

FIGURE 6.3 How are Canadians really doing?

K	W	L
Know	**Want to know**	**Would like to Learn**
☐ I know that the level of education increased.	☐ I want to know why time use has not improved as much.	☐ I'd like to learn about education and well-being.
☐ I know that wellness is related to leisure time.	☐ I want to know why environmental wellness has decreased	☐ I'd like to know more about how healthy communities can improve wellness.
☐ I know . . .	☐ I want to know . . .	☐ I'd like to learn more about . . .

Activity B | Before reading "Well-being in Canada," mark the following statements as true (T) or false (F), based on your current understanding of the topic. After you have read and discussed the text, review your answers based on what you read. Paragraph numbers have been provided to help you check your answers after you are done reading.

1. _____ A wellness index mainly shows if our lives have improved or not. (2)

2. _____ Canadians' quality of life has increased in many areas because the standard of living has increased. (2)

3. _____ A country's wellness index can be used to establish a country's future development goals. (5)

4. _____ A country with a higher GDP (Gross Domestic Product) will have a higher sense of well-being. (9)

5. _____ The biggest challenges to Canadian well-being are the environment and income inequality. (8–9)

6. _____ The CIW shows that well-being in Canada is growing in certain areas, such as education, but declining in other areas, such as in leisure time. (12–13)

Activity C | Read "Well-being in Canada." While you read, notice any problems related to Canadian wellness that the authors discuss. When you find a suitable idea or detail, underline it and write K (know), W (want to know), or L (learned) in the margin. Decide if these ideas might be useful in answering your Unit Inquiry Question.

READING

Well-being in Canada

What Is the Canadian Index of Wellbeing?

1   The Canadian **Index** of Wellbeing (CIW) is a new tool for measuring changes in our quality of life—overall, and in eight specific categories including: our standard of living,[1] our health, the quality of our environment, education, time use, community **vitality**, democratic engagement,[2] and the state of **leisure** and culture. It provides a much more complete picture than narrow economic measures like GDP [Gross Domestic Product].[3]

---

[1] *Standard of living* relates to the money and level of comfort of a particular person or group.

[2] *Democratic engagement* refers to involvement in politics.

[3] the total value of all the goods and services produced by a country in one year

What Does the Canadian Index of Wellbeing Do?

2   The CIW shows if our overall quality of life is going up or down, which categories are making it go up or down, and within those categories, which factors are making it go up or down. For example, the first CIW **composite** index shows that our overall quality of life improved by a **modest** 11 percent in the 15-year period from 1994 to 2008. One of the reasons it went up was that our living standards improved by about 26 percent. One of the reasons why it didn't go up more is that our environment **deteriorated**. Why did our environment deteriorate? Mostly because our greenhouse emissions **soared**.

3   The CIW network also produces detailed reports for each of the important categories of well-being. They show us where we're making progress, where we're falling behind, and what

we can do—both as a society and as individuals to improve the situation.

Why Is This Important?

4   Over the past couple of decades there has been a global movement, led by the OECD [Organisation for Economic Co-operation and Development],[4] to adopt more **comprehensive** and **integrated** ways of measuring the progress of a country. Canada has been a leader in that movement and we are one of the first countries to develop a tool for measuring the well-being of its people in all of its **dimensions**.

5   Now, for the first time in our country's history we have a way of using hard data to judge whether we're moving closer to, or further away from, our vision of ourselves as a people and a country.

What Do You Mean by "Well-being"? Is It the Same as "Health"?

6   We define well-being as the presence of the highest possible quality of life. This includes: good living standards, **robust** health, a sustainable environment, vital communities, an educated populace,[5] balanced time use, high levels of democratic participation, and **access** to and participation in leisure and culture. It's a much broader definition than just health.

How Are Canadians Really Doing?

7   We're doing somewhat better than we were 15 years ago, but not as well as we should be. Our big-picture finding is that, GDP went up a robust 31 percent, but the CIW only increased by a more modest 11 percent. What that means is that much of our economic growth in one of Canada's biggest boom periods did not translate into improvements in our quality of life.

8   While our overall living standards have increased, the lion's share[6] of growth in family incomes went to the richest 20 percent of families. Meanwhile, the gap down to the poorest 20 percent grew larger than ever.

As well, increases in real wages grew considerably more slowly than increases in corporate profits. The income gap[7] is much greater even though family incomes did increase overall on average. This is a troubling **trend**.

9   Something else that the gap between GDP and the CIW tells us is that when you subtract[8] economic activities that are harmful to our well-being—like consumption of tobacco, over-harvesting of natural resources and an over-**reliance** on fossil fuels—as the CIW does, instead of adding them like GDP, you get a much lower number. In other words, you get a much more realistic picture of how Canadians are doing in their everyday lives.

Can You Be More Specific about the Findings?

10   The one bit of good news is that our community vitality has improved in every respect. Both violent and property crime are down. Canadians are more compassionate[9] than ever—we are providing more unpaid help to others and more of us are concerned about the needs of others, in spite of whatever challenges we have in our own lives.

11   Otherwise, it's a very mixed picture. The quality of jobs in Canada hasn't improved but rather gone down, though housing has become somewhat more affordable. Our life expectancy is among the best in the world and getting longer, but we're spending a greater percentage of our life in poor health thanks to increases in obesity and **incidence** of **chronic** diseases like diabetes. Our air is getting cleaner but our greenhouse gas emissions are soaring.

12   Many Canadians are finding themselves caught in a time crunch[10] that is robbing them of peace of mind, keeping them from spending quality time with their family and friends, and leaving them with less time for leisure and arts and culture activities. Our

---

[4] a group of countries that encourages trade and economic growth

[5] all the ordinary people of a particular country or area

[6] *The lion's share* is a figurative expression meaning "the most."

[7] a difference that separates people, or their opinions, or their situations

[8] to take a number or an amount away from another number or amount

[9] feeling or showing sympathy for people who are suffering

[10] a situation in which there is suddenly not enough of something, especially time or money

participation in education is rising, especially high school and university graduation rates, but testing shows that our kids' basic knowledge and skills, and emotional competencies are falling.

Source: Excerpted from Canadian Index of Wellbeing. (2016, November 17). *Frequently asked questions.* Retrieved from https://uwaterloo.ca/canadian-index-wellbeing/resources/frequently-asked-questions

Activity D | Discuss the following questions with a partner or in a small group.

1. How is wellness different from health?
2. What are the three main wellness challenges facing individual Canadians?
3. Where should Canada as a country focus its wellness efforts?
4. Are there any ideas discussed in the text that you do not quite understand? Discuss anything you are not sure about.

Activity E | Revisit your Unit Inquiry Question on page 197. Are there any ideas from the reading that will help you answer your question? Share your ideas with a partner or small group. Use the following questions to help you in assessing your question.

1. How does the information from this reading change your understanding of wellness and well-being?
2. Which ideas from the reading can be used to help answer your Unit Inquiry Question?
3. What additional questions do you have after finishing the reading?
4. Where could you find more information?

Activity F | Writing Task: Problem and Solution Paragraphs | Write two short paragraphs that describe the problem of time management and propose a solution for students who want to improve their time management. Use an idea web, or another brainstorming technique that you have learned, to help you come up with ideas to write about. Try to include five of the vocabulary words from this unit, but make sure the paragraph is written in your own words.

Activity G | Compare your paragraphs to the sample paragraphs in Appendix 2. Notice how the sample paragraphs describe student time management challenges and solutions. Analyze the sample paragraphs, then answer the following questions with a partner or small group.

1. What problem does the writer describe? What causes this problem?
2. What solution does the writer propose? Is the solution directly connected to the problem?
3. Is there a concluding sentence with a prediction or a recommendation? If so, what is the prediction or recommendation?
4. After reading the sample paragraphs, is there anything you would revise in your paragraphs?

Evaluating and Ranking

As you explore the topic of wellness, you will no doubt identify several wellness challenges and several possible solutions. After carefully thinking about the challenges, you will most likely be asked to suggest a possible solution to an important wellness challenge.

To suggest the very best solution, it is important for you to evaluate (form an opinion about the quality of something) and to rank (order from the best to the worst) all the possible solutions. Follow the critical thinking steps in the chart below to evaluate and rank your solutions. Answering the questions at each step will help you come up with and recommend the best solution.

Critical Thinking Step	Questions to Discuss
1. Identify a clear challenge	Can you give an example of an important wellness challenge? Do you agree that this challenge is the most important? Why?
2. Brainstorm solutions	What solutions are there to the challenge? How does each solution relate directly to the challenge?
3. Evaluate possible solutions	How achievable or realistic is this solution? How likely is it that someone else would support this solution?
4. Rank solutions	What makes this solution effective? Is this a good solution for everyone? How so?
5. Choose the best solution	Why is this solution better than other solutions?

PROCESS FUNDAMENTALS

Brainstorming and Outlining

Split-Page Notes Chart

A split-page notes chart is a good way to make important connections linking your thinking, your inquiry question, and the ideas that you come across as you listen to video talks or webinars or read texts.

Organizing a split-page notes chart—to capture your own ideas and others' ideas—is quite simple. On page 209 is an example created by a student after reading "Well-being in Canada." The student started on the right-hand side of the page by noting the date, topic, and source at the top of the page, then made a brief list of main ideas and key points found in the reading. After finishing the reading, the student moved to the left-hand side to list some key ideas and some questions (responses) about those ideas. Finally, in the bottom section, the student has written some notes exploring the connections between the reading and the student's inquiry question.

Key Ideas/Response	Date: 4 May 2018 Topic: Wellness in Canada Source: "How are Canadians _really_ doing?" Canadian Index of Wellbeing, 2014

1. Quality of life + living
   standards
   Q: How are these
   connected?
 	
2. CIW is comprehensive
 	
3. Q: Do other countries
   have _different def'ns_ of
   well-being? Why?
	Main Ideas and Key Points:
	1. 1st CIW index shows _quality of life_ improved by 11% from 1994 to 2008 +
	   living standards improved about 26%.
	
	2. The CIW = _new tool_, measures _changes in quality of life_
	   –8 categories: liv. standards, health, env't, ed'n, time, community, democratic
	   engagement, leisure & culture
	
	3. Def'n. of well-being from CIW: _highest possible quality of life_

Connection with My Inquiry Question:

This information relates to standard of living. This might explain why it is difficult for students to improve their financial wellness.

Possible solution: Having access to financial assistance and part-time employment programs can reduce financial worry in students.

Activity A | On a separate paper, create a blank split-page notes chart of your own, using the same headings as in the example above. Then read the excerpt below from a research study on university student wellness in Canada. As you read the student comments from the study's results, highlight any important details and take notes on your split page notes chart. For this activity, use the inquiry question _What are the most important wellness challenges for students on campus?_ to complete the "Connection with My Inquiry Question" section. When you are finished, share your notes with a classmate. Discuss how your notes are similar or different.

Wellness 101: Health Education for the University Student

Being a University Student

1   With regard to their physical well-being, the most notable barriers were the lack of affordable and accessible opportunities to eat healthy, and the lack of facilities[11] to allow students to bring healthy options from off campus, and store and prepare the foods.

- The on-campus cafeteria[12] should offer more foods that are decent for your body if [the university] is serious about this [enhancing health and wellness].
- I would like to have more healthy food available at odd hours. Often when I am busy and assignments are due I will not have time to get a meal. I need healthy choices available here. I often skip[13] meals because there are no vending machines[14] with healthy choices.

---

[11] a place used for a particular purpose or activity

[12] a restaurant where you choose and pay for your meal at a counter and carry it to a table

[13] to not do something that you usually do or should do

[14] a machine from which you can buy drinks or snacks

2   The majority of comments, however, related to students' psychological well-being and the challenges they faced in managing time and stress when fulfilling their course load demands.

- Wow, school is overwhelming.[15] I try to keep an active lifestyle but have no spare time ever.

- Too much homework and not enough sleep—many nights I miss sleep due to homework.

Source: Adapted from Wharf Higgins, J. S., Lauzon, L. L., Yew, A. C., Bratseth, C. D., & McLeod, N. (2010). Wellness 101: Health education for the university student. *Health Education, 110*(4), 309–327.

[15] very great or very strong

Problem–Solution Essay Outline

In a problem–solution essay, the introductory paragraph gives your reader some background on the problem: the details around the situation and the problem itself. As well, you briefly explain your solution to the problem—your main thinking about how to solve the problem. In the main body, you present more details about the problem and the solution. The concluding paragraph ends the essay and proposes other solutions to the problem.

In a block format problem–solution outline, the problem and the solution are explained in separate main body paragraphs. This format makes it easy for the reader to identify the problem and the solution.

Figure 6.4 shows more detail about the organization of a problem–solution essay in block format and the ideas and information included in each section. Depending on how in-depth your essay is and on how much outside research you do, you may not always include all the ideas and information in Figure 6.4. The questions and statements with an asterisk (*) are the most important to include.

Introduction	*What is the background to the problem? *What is the problem? *What is your solution? Why is this solution a good solution?
Main Body 1. Describe the Problem	*What are the details of the problem? *Why is the problem happening? What other writer thinks that this is a problem? What is the connection between the problem and the solution?
2. Describe the Solution	*What is the solution? *How does the solution solve the problem? Why is this solution the best solution? What other author agrees with this solution?
Conclusion	*Restate the problem and the solution. Propose another workable solution.

FIGURE 6.4   Problem–solution outline in block format

Activity B | Writing Task: Problem–Solution Outline for Unit Inquiry Question | Create a rough outline for a problem–solution essay using the ideas about wellness that you have thought about so far in this unit. Use the inquiry question *Why do on-campus wellness activities not always help students?* provided in the model below, or your own Unit Inquiry Question, to complete the outline. Write your outline on a separate paper.

Topic: Student Wellness

Inquiry Question: Why do on-campus wellness activities not always help students?

Describe the Problem

A.   Say what the problem is exactly and why the problem is happening.

    1.

    2.

B.   Explain why this problem is happening.

    1.

    2.

Describe the Solution

A.   Say what the solution is exactly.

    1.

    2.

B.   Explain how the solution solves the problem.

    1.

    2.

Content Skill

Integrating Information from Online Campus Resources

Libraries and other academic support departments, such as Student Life, often create videos, webinars, and online study guides to aid students. Some of these resources summarize learning information, while others offer independent living strategies. These audio-visual materials and written guides can contain very specific advice and practical examples for students. This information can be very useful to student researchers who are looking for support for their main ideas.

Activity A | The split-page notes chart on page 212 contains notes created as a student viewed an online video, "Things We Wish All University Students Knew: Stress Is Going to Happen," produced by the Wellness Centre at the University of Calgary. Work with a partner to complete the "Key Ideas/Responses" section in the left-hand column of the chart. Use the questions below to help you respond to the ideas and information in the notes.

- Are there any ideas in the notes that are surprising to me? How so?
- Are there any ideas that connect to or differ from what I already know?
- Are there facts that support my ideas? Where can I find additional support?

If appropriate, think about a connection you could make between the key points in these notes and a Unit Inquiry Question—either your question or your partner's question. Add this connection to the bottom of the chart.

Key Ideas/Responses	**Date:** 14 February 2018 **Topic:** Stress and Emotional Wellness, Managing Stress **Source:** "Things we wish all university students knew: Stress is going to happen." University of Calgary. (2014, September 2).
	Main Ideas: –uni experience = multiple deadlines, social life, extra-curriculars (outside school time activities) –feeling stress = normal—think positively, let things go. –diff. between managing day-to-day stressors and having too much stress—important to understand –to cope w/ the demands in your life—use self-strategies –watch for changes in mood, sleep, physical wellness, social activity → ask for help. a sign of mental health challenges? –connect w/ supportive people—remember you are part of a community.

Connection to My Inquiry Question:

Activity B | Read the Sleep and Nutrition tip sheet on the next page. It is an excerpt from online guides created by the Wellness Centre at the University of Guelph (U of G). These guides are designed to provide students with advice on how to manage their wellness so that they can enjoy academic success.

As you read, highlight any ideas that discuss important student wellness problems or solutions to these problems. Consider whether any information would be useful in answering your Unit Inquiry Question.

Healthy Mind and Body
Sleep and Nutrition

What Is sleep hygiene?

Sleep hygiene is a variety of different practices for a normal, quality nighttime sleep and full daytime alertness.

How do I know the best sleep hygiene routine for me?

If you're taking too long to fall asleep, or awakening during the night, you should consider revising your bedtime habits.

Sleep

Students reported a number of sleep difficulties.

	U of G	Canada
Enough sleep to feel rested	59.6%	56.0%
Felt tired or sleepy during the day	62.4%	63.2%
Big or very big problem with sleepiness during the day	22.0%	21.7%

Healthy Sleep Benefits

- improved concentration when you need to study
- better recall of ideas and information
- don't fall sick as much
- feel well rested—your mood is positive

What Is Healthy Eating?

Healthy eating means eating a variety of foods that give you the nutrients you need to maintain your health, feel good, and have energy.

Nutrition is important for everyone. What you eat can affect your immune system, your mood, your concentration and focus, and your energy level.

Nutrition

Canada's Food Guide recommends 7 to 10 fruits and vegetables per day.

Servings per day	U of G	Canada
0	3.5%	5.0%
1 to 4	84.4%	85.5%
5 or more	12.0%	9.6%

Healthy Eating Benefits

- more energy
- more consistent energy levels during the day
- easier to maintain a healthy weight
- fewer headaches or sleep difficulties

Source: University of Guelph Student Health Affairs NCHA Advisory Team. (2016). *2016 National College Health Assessment University of Guelph results* (pp. 2, 4). Retrieved from https://wellness.uoguelph.ca/sws/sites/uoguelph.ca.sws/files/public/NCHA_Sept21_16.pdf

"What is sleep hygiene?" and "How do I know the best sleep hygiene routine for me?" from Sleep and Sleep Disorders: Info Kit (n.d.). Student Wellness Centre. University of Guelph. (pp. 2-3) Retrieved from https://wellness.uoguelph.ca/education/sites/uoguelph.ca.wellness/files/public/Sleep%20and%20Sleep%20Disorders%20info%20Kit_a11y_3.pdf

"What is Healthy Eating?" from Healthy Eating Active Living Information Kit (n.d). Student Wellness Centre. University of Guelph. (p.3) Retrieved from https://wellness.uoguelph.ca/education/sites/uoguelph.ca.wellness/files/public/HEALinfokit_a11y_4.pdf

Activity C | Writing Task: Opinion Paragraph | Consider the ideas that you read about in Activity A and Activity B. Write a short paragraph to answer the question *Why is it important for students to develop healthy bodies and minds?* If you need more information or support for your ideas to write your paragraph, locate the wellness resources from the University of Calgary or the University of Guelph or use any wellness resources from your own campus. When you are finished, exchange your work with a partner. Read each other's paragraph and discuss the following questions.

- What ideas in either of your paragraphs could be explored as a problem in a problem–solution essay?
- What ideas in either of your paragraphs could be explored as a solution in a problem–solution essay?

Reference Skill

Citing Video and Online Resources Using APA Style

To ensure academic integrity, it is important that all ideas and information that you use from any online webinars, videos, or study guides have corresponding in-text citations and reference information.

The chart below contains the bibliographic information for the online video referenced in Activity A on page 211.

Producer	SU Wellness Centre—University of Calgary
Date	2 September 2014
Title	Things We Wish All University Students Knew: Stress Is Going to Happen
File type	video
Retrieved from	https://www.youtube.com/watch?v=DCauapmVFEg&t=29s

If you included any ideas or information from "Things We Wish All University Students Knew: Stress Is Going to Happen" in your opinion paragraph in Activity C on page 213, you need to write both in-text citations and reference information.

Here are examples of in-text citations and a References entry for this video in APA style.

	APA Style
In-text citation	"If you notice changes in your mood, sleeping patterns, physical wellness, or decreased social activity that are impacting your daily life, these may be signs of declining mental health" (SU Wellness Centre, 2014).
	The video "Things We Wish All University Students Knew" from the SU Wellness Centre at the University of Calgary (2014) indicates that one sign of mental health decline may be a significant shift in mood that affects your day-to-day activities.
Reference entry	SU Wellness Centre—University of Calgary. (2014, September 2). *Things we wish all university students knew: Stress is going to happen* [Video file]. Retrieved from https://www.youtube.com/watch?v=DCauapmVFEg&t=29s

Preventing Plagiarism

Using Online Tools to Check Own Writing

Many colleges and universities now use online tools, such as Turnitin.com, to check the originality of assignments that students submit for their courses. Once a student submits an assignment, these tools generate a report to show how original the student's writing is. This report shows how similar the student's writing is to other published documents or to assignments already submitted by other students. Just as instructors can use these tools to check the originality of your writing, you can use these tools to ensure that you have properly cited all the outside sources used in your assignment.

Below are a few top tips for effectively using online tools to check your writing:

✓ Check the originality of your writing using the online tools before the assignment deadline.

✓ Give yourself enough time before the assignment deadline to fix any problems.

✓ Use the results of the originality report to avoid accidental plagiarism.

✓ If your writing is too similar to the wording of another writer's texts, be sure to

• add quotation marks for four or more words copied from another source;

• rewrite any paraphrases or summary statements that are too close to the original text; and

• write in-text citations for all quotations, paraphrases, or summary statements.

✓ Ignore technical words and phrases, common collocations, or author names (e.g., "nutritional imbalance" or "health and wellness" or "Wharf Higgins").

✓ If your writing is too similar to another student's assignment, check with your instructor to see that you have correctly followed your instructor's guidelines around academic integrity. For more information, see Unit 1.

Activity A | To practise citing sources correctly, first proofread the opinion paragraph that you wrote in Activity C on page 213. Have you written in-text citations for ideas or information taken from the University of Guelph study guides on page 213? Did you use APA style correctly?

Next, write an entry for a References list in APA style for one of the sources that you used in your paragraph. Exchange your entry with a partner. Check if your partner's entry correctly follows APA style. Make any corrections needed.

Refer to the chart in Unit 4 on page 139 to check your APA style.

Format and Organization Skill

Writing a Problem–Solution Introduction

A problem–solution introduction sets the context for the essay in four ways.

1. It gives background by explaining the situation.
2. It identifies the problem and explains why it is important to solve.
3. It proposes a solution to the problem in the thesis statement. The thesis statement is often a single sentence that explains the best solution to the

problem. The thesis statement comes out of the writer's careful thinking about the problem.

4. It briefly explains how or why the solution works and gives the most important reason why the solution is effective.

Activity A | The introduction below describes how campus health and wellness services can support wellness among international students. Read the introduction, paying attention to the differently coloured sections of the text. Identify the sections in which the writer discusses the background to the problem, identifies the problem, proposes a solution, and explains why or how the solution works.

Supporting Student Wellness

All students need to adapt to the college or university experience. However, facing many changes in a short time can create both positive and negative feelings. At first, many students might think that their new home seems wonderful. Later, they might develop homesickness. Negative feelings can affect student well-being. Although there are health and wellness services available on most campuses, a recent study shows that many international students do not use these services. They may not even know that these services exist (Mori, 2000). Reaching out to students and giving them information about wellness are difficult tasks for student support services staff. However, to solve this challenge in communicating directly with students, health and wellness staff can better support students by promoting wellness services to students in their courses. This approach is effective because students do not need to seek out health and wellness services.

Reference

Mori, S. C. (2000). Addressing the mental health concerns of international students. *Journal of Counseling & Development, 78*, 137–144.

Activity B | Scan the questions below, then reread the sample introductory paragraph in the previous activity. Work with a partner to answer the questions about the background, the problem, the solution, and the reason why the solution works.

A. Background	B. Problem	C. Solution
1. What is the situation?	4. What is the problem?	Thesis statement:
2. When is this situation taking place?	5. Who is involved in the problem?	7. What is the best solution?
3. Where is the situation or problem happening?	6. Are there any experts who also believe that this is an important problem?	8. Who is involved in the solution?
4. Who is involved in the situation?		Explain why the solution works:
		9. Why do you think that solution will work?

Activity C | Writing Task: Introduction to a Problem–Solution Essay | Look back at the problem–solution outline you created on page 211 for your own Unit Inquiry Question (or the sample inquiry question provided). If you found any useful ideas in "Wellness 101: Health Education and the University Student" (pages 209–210), add these ideas to your outline.

Working from your outline, write a short introductory paragraph introducing the situation and the problem related to your Unit Inquiry Question. When you are finished, exchange your introduction with a partner. Evaluate your partner's paragraph using the questions in the chart in Activity B to guide you. Make two suggestions to your partner on how to improve his or her introductory paragraph.

Topic Skill

Writing Problem–Solution Thesis Statements

In an essay introduction, the purpose of a thesis statement is to present a writer's main idea, or the results of the writer's analysis of a topic. The style of the thesis statement can change depending on the kind of essay. In a problem–solution essay, the thesis statement presents the solution that the writer thinks is the best way to solve the problem.

Consider the thesis statement in the introduction of "Supporting Student Wellness" in Activity A on page 216.

> However, to solve this challenge in communicating directly with students, health and wellness staff can better support students by promoting wellness services to students in their courses.

Notice how the thesis statement states the problem for the reader, mentions who is affected by the problem, and presents the writer's best solution. In this way, the thesis statement prepares the reader to read the main body of the essay. Based on the thesis statement above, the reader knows that the body of this problem–solution essay will discuss

- the fact that information on health and wellness services does not reach students (the problem); and
- the idea that health and wellness staff can visit students' classes to promote their services (the best solution).

Activity A | Read the two problem–solution thesis statements that follow. Underline the problem, highlight who is affected by the problem, and double underline the solution that the writer proposes. When you are finished, share your answers with a partner. Have you identified the problem, the people involved, and the solution correctly?

1. Although talking about wellness may be a challenge, the best way for students to overcome emotional difficulties may be to talk about their concerns with others, including health and wellness service professionals, family members, or friends.

2. The main obstacle to improving physical wellness for students seems to be nutrition. One effective way to help students improve their nutrition is to require on-campus food services to provide specific information about the nutritional value of different foods.

Activity B | Review the topic and the problem statement below. With a partner, brainstorm solutions to the problem, evaluate your solutions, and choose the best solution. Refer to the *Critical Thinking* box on evaluating and ranking (page 208) for help. Fill in the chart as you work.

Topic: Sleep and Student Wellness	
Problem statement: One of the main challenges to physical and emotional wellness is that few students implement nighttime routines.	
1. Brainstorm solutions	
2. Evaluate different solutions	
3. Write the best solution	

Activity C | Review the problem statement and your best solution from Activity B. Write a one- or two-sentence thesis statement for an essay on the topic of sleep and student wellness. Use the example thesis statements in Activity A to help you and be sure to use problem–solution language. (See the *Language Tip* on pages 199–200.)

Thesis statement: _____

_____

_____

_____

Exchange your thesis statement with another student. Give advice on how to improve your partner's thesis statement using the following questions to guide your evaluation. Be sure to say what has been done well and what could be improved.

1. Is clear language used to introduce the problem and present the solution?

2. Is the thesis statement well focused? Does it clearly state the problem, mention who is involved, and propose a solution?

3. Is the solution realistic? Do you think others will agree with this solution?

Activity D | Writing Task: Problem–Solution Thesis Statement for Unit Inquiry Question | Review your Unit Inquiry Question. Identify the problem and brainstorm a solution. Write a one- or two-sentence problem–solution thesis statement for your Unit Inquiry Question. Evaluate your own thesis statement using the questions from the previous activity. Check that you have used suitable phrasing to state the problem and to present your chosen solution. (See the *Language Tip* on pages 199–200.)

Conclusion Skill

Suggesting Other Solutions

The concluding paragraph in a problem–solution essay has two functions:

- to remind the reader of the solution originally proposed in the introduction; and
- to suggest an additional solution to the problem.

Being able to suggest different solutions to your reader shows your deeper understanding of the problem. If the problem is complex, then making your reader aware of other solutions demonstrates your ability to understand and to analyze the problem.

Activity A | The introduction to an essay on sleep and wellness gives this problem statement: *One of the main challenges to physical and emotional wellness is that few students implement nighttime routines.* Read the essay's concluding paragraph below and underline the solution presented and discussed in the essay. Double underline the other possible solution (alternative solution) suggested by the writer.

As we have seen, a key issue for campus health services is how to help students change their sleep behaviours. Sleep clinics are successful in helping students develop better sleep habits because they offer very practical advice on nighttime routines. Another way to promote better sleep habits is to provide students with information on what causes unhealthy sleep. This could include information on how technology is keeping their brains awake and active (University of Guelph, n.d.). Once students understand that sleep is about allowing the mind to rest, they may be more open to letting their minds recharge through better sleep.

Reference
University of Guelph Student Wellness Centre. (n.d.). *Sleep and sleep disorders: Info kit.* Retrieved from https://wellness.uoguelph.ca/education/services/offered/info-kits

Activity B | With a partner, discuss what you identified in Activity A as the other possible solution that the writer suggested. Did you both choose the same alternative solution? Together, discuss the questions below to decide if the other possible solution would work.

1. Is the solution an effective response to the problem? Why?
2. Does the solution show a different perspective or way of thinking about the problem?
3. Can the solution work? Is it achievable? Why? Why not?
4. Do you think that this student writer could find support from an outside source (an expert or an authority) to back up this solution?

Activity C | Writing Task: Solution Conclusion for Unit Inquiry Question | Look back at the thesis statement you created for your Unit Inquiry Question in Activity D on page 219. Review your solution and why it is the best one.

Brainstorm two other possible solutions to the problem expressed in your thesis statement, then choose one that could work to solve the problem. Write a short concluding paragraph of five to eight sentences that proposes another possible solution. Work with a partner to evaluate the solution using the questions in Activity B. What works well in your conclusion? What could be improved?

Note that if you cite an authority to support these solutions, you must include an APA-style in-text citation and a References list. Refer to the APA style sections throughout this textbook.

WRITING FUNDAMENTALS

Composition Skill

Revising and Editing

Starting with an Effective Writing Process Plan   The writing assignments that you will receive at college or university will not be easy to complete in one day. In fact, many assignments may require you to do a lot of research, thinking, and writing. Developing an effective writing process can help you to produce better writing because it ensures that you make good use of the time and brainpower that you need to spend on completing your assignment. Following a clear writing process also makes writing less stressful. The flowchart on page 221 shows the main steps in an effective writing process.

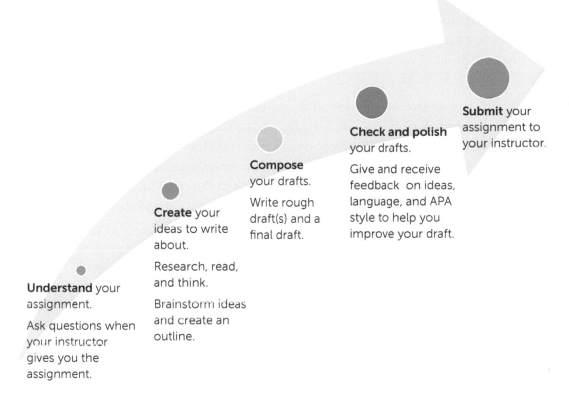

Understand your assignment.

Ask questions when your instructor gives you the assignment.

Create your ideas to write about.

Research, read, and think.

Brainstorm ideas and create an outline.

Compose your drafts.

Write rough draft(s) and a final draft.

Check and polish your drafts.

Give and receive feedback on ideas, language, and APA style to help you improve your draft.

Submit your assignment to your instructor.

Activity A | Imagine that you have 10 days to complete a three-page writing assignment. How will you use your 10 days? With a partner, discuss the four main writing process steps—understand, create, compose, and check and polish—using the questions below.

1. How many days do you normally spend on each main step?
2. Which main step takes the longest for you? Why?
3. Do you agree with the suggested number of days for each main step listed below? Why or why not?
   - understand: 1 day
   - create: 2 to 3 days
   - compose: 2 to 3 days
   - check and polish: 2 to 3 days

Revising   Good writing always requires many drafts. Experienced writers often spend more time revising than editing or proofreading. These writers know that revising requires as much thinking as drafting. To revise, look for essay- and paragraph-level issues: the structure of the paragraph or essay, the organization of ideas, and the connections between ideas.

Comparing the ideas in your outline and in your first draft makes revising your paragraph or essay easier. When you compare, you can notice what is similar or different between your outline and your first draft, and then decide how you could change the draft to improve it.

In the example below, a student has compared her outline and the first draft of her introduction. Notice how she created her introductory paragraph using her outline. As you read her marginal notes, notice how they prepare this first draft for revising. To help herself think about what to write in her notes and what to revise, she considered the following questions.

1. Does my introduction have all the parts needed for a problem–solution essay—background, problem, solution, and reason for the solution?
2. Does my introduction have the same order of ideas as the outline?
3. Are there any extra ideas that I added to my introduction that are different from the outline? Should I keep these ideas in the introduction?
4. Are there any ideas from the outline that are missing and should be added to the introduction?

Outline:

Topic: Nutrition and Wellness

Key Inquiry Questions:

- Why do students have nutritional imbalance?
- How can students and universities solve the nutrition issue on campus?

I. Introduction
   A. Background/Context
      - wellness definition
      - good nutrition definition

   B. Problem
      - students unwell because of unbalanced nutrition
      - being well can positively affect learning

   C. Solution (thesis statement)
      - students be more mindful of nutrition
      - universities provide information on good nutrition and better food choices

   D. Evaluation
      - positive effect on wellness
      - connect wellness to academic success

Draft Introduction Paragraph

Student Nutrition and Wellness

Nutrition is as important to mental wellness as physical wellness. The foods that we eat contribute to our sense of well-being. Many students in residence on campus have unbalanced nutrition, which can affect their learning and academic success. To highlight the important relationship between nutrition and wellness, on-campus food services need to offer students more information and better food choices. These actions will have a positive effect not only on wellness, but also on academic success.

Marginal Notes:

Background OK, but where is the definition of wellness and good nutrition?

Problem is a little hidden. Better to highlight for reader—use phrase "The problem is"

New info added to problem—on campus vs off campus—is there a difference?
Do more research + add sources to problem

✓Solution
add student mindfulness to thesis statement

✓Good reason for the solution—remember to add to conclusion too!
Do I need more ideas about academic success?
—Ask peer reader ☺

Editing   After a text has been revised, the next step is editing. It is always a good idea to wait a while after you've written a second draft before starting your editing. When you edit, you check the second draft for sentence-level trouble spots: sentence structure, grammar, and vocabulary use. Editing does not take as much time as revising because you can focus on your language use without worrying about the organization of ideas or paragraphing.

There are several techniques you can try to become a better editor of your own writing. A mistakes chart is a useful tool for working through the editing process. Below is some general advice on using the mistakes chart set out in Figure 6.5 to develop your editing skills.

1. Know what common writing mistakes to look for.
2. Keep track of your own mistakes to personalize your editing.
3. Study how to fix your most common mistakes.
4. Ask your classmates or your instructor for study suggestions and resources.

Assignment Name: _____			
Type of Mistake	**Code**	**Number of Mistakes**	**Future Study Advice**
word choice/word form	WC/WF		
spelling (especially plurals)	Sp.		
noun–pronoun agreement	NP		
verb tense/verb form	VT/VF		
subject–verb agreement	S/V		
clause structure	CLS		
fragment	FRAG		
wrong word/missing word	WW/MW		
your own personal trouble spots	TS		

FIGURE 6.5 Mistakes chart

Activity A | Reread a paragraph you have written in this unit. Highlight the mistakes you find and record the mistakes in Figure 6.5. If you have trouble finding your mistakes or deciding whether or not something is actually a mistake, ask a classmate or your instructor. Then correct the mistakes you find or ask a classmate or your instructor for advice on how to correct these types of mistakes.

Activity B | Show your chart to a partner, if possible a classmate whose first language is different from yours. Do you have similar or different mistakes? Can you suggest any study/review resources and activities that might help your partner to improve? After your discussion, in the far-right column of the chart, record any advice that might help you in your future editing.

Sentence and Grammar Skill

Using Adjective Clauses

Form and Meaning   Adjective clauses are dependent clauses that begin with words called relative pronouns. Common relative pronouns include *who, whom, whose, which,* and *that.* Writers choose a relative pronoun depending on the antecedent, or what is being described by the adjective clause.

Each example sentence below contains an adjective clause. For each type of adjective clause, read the description, then review the example sentences. Pay attention to how each relative pronoun in bold is used to begin the underlined adjective clause.

1. Adjective clauses that describe people are introduced by *who, whom,* and *whose.*

   Students **who** feel unwell do not always know what to do to feel better.

   University medical professionals, **whom** most students trust, play an important role in promoting wellness.

   A Mediterranean diet is a good choice for students **whose** cholesterol is high.

2. Adjective clauses that describe things are introduced by *that* or *which.*

   A diet **that** is high in fibre and low in trans fat makes people feel healthy and well.

   Student wellness, **which** universities should promote through on-campus programs, is essential to a satisfying university experience.

3. Adjective clauses that provide a reason are introduced by *why.*

   One reason **why** student wellness is so important is that being well helps learning.

4. Adjective clauses that describe activities in a place are introduced by *where.*

   University is a place **where** students can learn to practise healthy habits.

5. Adjective clauses that describe activities during a certain period of time are introduced by *when.*

   The time **when** people can create good healthy habits is during their college years.

Activity A | Read each sentence and the pair of relative pronouns in parentheses. Choose the best relative pronoun to complete the adjective clause. The first sentence has been done for you as an example.

1. Many Canadians experience a time crunch (that/~~who~~) ____that____ is robbing them of wellness.

2. In 2010, (that/when) _____ many wellness initiatives first started on campus, student awareness of healthy habits greatly increased.

3. One reason (who/why) _____ students do not exercise regularly is that they have too many assignments.

4. Research has shown that students living in residences (that/where) _____ they can cook their own food generally eat better.

5. In the survey, students were asked about various preventative measures (where/ that) _____ they participated in, including regular medical check-ups.

6. The Canadian Index of Wellbeing is a new tool (that/which) _____ measures quality of life.

7. Many students stated that they would talk to a health professional (which/ whom) _____ they trust when they have a problem.

8. Students (who/whom) _____ believe that their health is good are less anxious.

Function Academic writers often express ideas in complex sentences (sentences containing an independent clause and a dependent clause). To expand on ideas and add information without writing multiple simple sentences in a row, academic writers use adjective clauses.

Combining ideas

Sentence 1: Students are experiencing a time crunch.

Sentence 2: This time crunch is making students stressed.

Combined: Students are experiencing a time crunch ***that*** *is making them stressed.*

Adding adjective clauses to create a complex sentence that combines ideas is a good way to avoid unnecessary repetition.

Expanding ideas

Sentence 1: The Canadian Index of Wellbeing has a new definition of wellness.

Sentence 2: The Canadian Index of Wellbeing measures quality of life.

Expanded: The Canadian Index of Wellbeing, ***which*** *measures quality of life, has a new definition of wellness.*

Adding adjective clauses to give more information is a good way to avoid writing too many simple sentences.

Activity B | Read the paragraph below about brain food. With a partner, identify which of the simple sentences could be combined into complex sentences to improve the flow of the writing. Use *who*, *which*, or *that* to introduce the adjective clauses in your complex sentences.

> ***Example***
>
> [1] Specific foods can promote brain health.
>
> [2] These foods are very common in the North American diet.
>
> Complex sentence with adjective clause: Specific foods <u>that are very common in the North American diet</u> can promote brain health.

On a separate paper, write the sentences that you think you could put together using adjective clauses. When you are finished, discuss your adjective clauses with another pair of students. Which relative pronoun did you use for each clause? Why?

Brain Food: Better Nutrition for Better Brain Health

[1]Specific foods can promote brain health. [2]These foods are very common in the North American diet. [3]Researchers have studied the nutritional value of foods and have learned how certain chemicals can improve brain health. [4]For example, fruits and vegetables contain antioxidants.[16] [5]These are natural chemicals. Antioxidants can also protect the brain from inflammation[17] even if there is a brain injury. [6]Eating fish also helps people's brains to be healthy because some fish, such as salmon, contains many omega-3 fatty acids.[18] [7]Research shows that some people eat a lot of fish. [8]These people have better brain function. [9]However, many university students seem to have a nutritional imbalance. [10]This means that they do not eat a varied enough diet. [11]Students may eat too many unhealthy foods. [12]These foods may contain high levels of trans fat and few nutrients and therefore do not help brain health. [13]Students should pay more attention to their food choices and have better and healthier brains for learning.

---

[16] vitamins, such as vitamin C or E, that remove dangerous molecules from the body

[17] redness, pain, or swelling in part of the body

[18] a group of acids, found mainly in fish oils, that are important for human health

---

Activity C | Choose a paragraph that you have written for this unit. Check your paragraph for any adjective clauses. If you do not have any adjective clauses, rewrite at least one pair of sentences in your paragraph to make a complex sentence using an adjective clause. Discuss with a partner, explaining why you chose the relative pronoun you used. You may need to refer back to the section on form and meaning on page 224.

Reflecting on Learning and Planning for Future Academic Success

You are likely close to the end of your writing course, so now is a good time to think about your learning to help you improve your own wellness and your academic success. Review what you have learned about student wellness.

- Studying in a new academic community is challenging for everyone.
- Keeping a positive outlook is sometimes difficult when there are so many new experiences.
- Not worrying too much about your studies is important for wellness.
- Making small positive changes in your life promotes wellness and academic success.

Use Figure 6.6 on the right to help you reflect on how well you are doing.

Do you have any "unwell" activities you could stop?
→ **Be mindful and let go of any unwell habits.**

What wellness activities can you continue?
→ **Continue doing the activities you enjoy and being with people you like.**

What wellness activities could you start?
→ **Slowly make time and space in your schedule for new wellness habits in your life.**

FIGURE 6.6 Wellness activities: Stop! Continue! Start!

UNIT OUTCOME

Writing Assignment: Problem–Solution Essay

Write a problem–solution essay of 250 to 350 words on a topic related to student wellness. (Your instructor may give you an alternative length.) You may write on a topic based on your Unit Inquiry Question, develop another topic of your choosing connected to wellness, or choose one of the following topics:

- How do wellness practices support students in their learning?
- What is the value of learning about wellness?
- How can universities and colleges support student wellness through on-campus education?

Use the skills you have developed in this unit to complete the assignment. Follow the steps set out below to practise each of your newly acquired skills to write a well-developed problem–solution essay.

1. **Brainstorm:** Use the split page note charts method to come up with ideas related to your topic.

2. **Find information:** Find some information to support your main ideas. Include information from the unit readings in each body paragraph if appropriate.

3. **Compose a thesis statement:** Develop a focused thesis statement that includes both the topic and the proposed solution.

4. **Outline:** Fill in the outline below to plan the first draft of your problem-solution essay. You may make changes to the outline as necessary.

Introduction	Background: Topic: Thesis statement:
Main Body (Problem Paragraph)	Topic sentence: Problem: Supporting details: Reason for the problem: Connection between the problem and the solution:
Main Body (Solution Paragraph)	Topic sentence: Solution: Supporting details: Reasons why this is the best solution:
Conclusion	Restate the problem and the solution: Propose another workable solution: Integrate support for the solution from another writer:

5. **Write a first draft**: Use your outline to write the first draft of your essay. Do not worry too much about spelling or grammar in the first draft. Try to get your ideas down on paper. If you get stuck, you can skip a part and come back to it later. For example, consider writing the body paragraphs first, then writing the introduction and conclusion.

6. **Revise**: Read over your essay and use the Evaluation Rubric below and on the next page to look for areas where you need to improve. Think of at least two ways to improve your essay.

7. **Ask for a peer review**: Exchange the revised version of your first draft with a classmate. Use the Evaluation Rubric to assess your partner's paragraph and provide suggestions to improve it. Ask questions (as you learned in Unit 4) to help your partner develop the body paragraphs more effectively. Consider your partner's feedback carefully and use it to make changes to your paragraph.

8. **Edit**: Edit your essay for the following:

   - Sentence variety: Check your essay for sentence variety and mistakes in complex sentences, especially adjective clauses.

   - Vocabulary: Check that you have used some of the AWL and mid-frequency vocabulary from this unit in your paragraph.

   - Check use of problem solution words and phrases.

9. **Write a final draft**: Write a final draft of your essay, making any changes you think will improve it. If possible, leave some time between drafts.

10. **Proofread**: Check the final draft of your essay for any small errors you may have missed. In particular, look for spelling errors, typos, and punctuation mistakes. If you used information from an outside source, double-check your in-text citations and your References list to make sure they are formatted properly.

Evaluation: Problem–Solution Essay Rubric

Use the following checklist to evaluate your essay. In which areas do you need to improve most?

E = **Emerging**: frequent difficulty using unit skills; needs a lot more work

D = **Developing**: some difficulty using unit skills; some improvement still required

S = **Satisfactory**: able to use unit skills most of the time; meets average expectations for this level

O = **Outstanding**: exceptional use of unit skills; exceeds expectations for this level

Skill	E	D	S	O
The essay is organized according to a problem–solution essay format, and has an introductory paragraph, two body paragraphs (detailing a problem and a solution), and a concluding paragraph.				
The content is logically organized using a thesis statement, topic sentences, and concluding sentences. The reader can easily follow the writer's thinking.				
The writing shows a good level of idea development and detail.				
Paragraphing is appropriate.				
Words and phrases to explain problems and solutions are used as needed.				
The essay includes an academic vocabulary including natural sounding collocations where appropriate.				
AWL and mid-frequency vocabulary items from this unit are used when appropriate and with few mistakes.				
Adjective clauses are used to create complex sentences where appropriate and with few mistakes.				
Ideas and words from outside sources are clearly marked for the reader with reporting verbs.				
If required, APA-style in-text citations and a References list have been included.				

Unit Review

Activity A | What do you know now that you did not know before about the topic of student wellness? Discuss with a partner or small group.

Activity B | Look back at the Unit Inquiry Question you developed at the start of this unit and discuss it with a partner or small group. Then share your answers with the class. Use the following questions to guide you.

1. What information did you find in this unit that helped you answer your question?
2. How would you answer your question now?

Activity C | Use the following checklist to review what you have learned throughout this unit. First decide which 10 skills you think are most important—circle the number beside each of these 10 skills. If you learned a skill in this unit that isn't listed, write it in the blank row at the end of the checklist. Then put a check mark in the box beside those points you feel you have learned. Be prepared to discuss your choices with the class.

Self-Assessment Checklist

☐	1. I can discuss issues related to wellness, specifically student wellness, based on what I have read in this unit.
☐	2. I can develop an inquiry question to explore a problem and a solution.
☐	3. I can use appropriate phrases to identify problems and propose solutions in my writing
☐	4. I can use appropriate collocations to improve the accuracy of my word choice.
☐	5. I can use the AWL and mid-frequency vocabulary from this unit in my writing.
☐	6. I can evaluate and rank solutions.
☐	7. I can incorporate suggestions made by my peers and instructors in my draft work.
☐	8. I can use a split page notes chart to brainstorm ideas for my writing
☐	9. I can write a block format outline for a problem–solution essay.
☐	10. I can find and use information from online campus resources to support my writing.
☐	11. I can use online tools to check my own writing before I submit assignments to avoid plagiarism.
☐	12. I can organize and write a problem–solution introduction.
☐	13. I can write a clear and logical problem–solution thesis statement.
☐	14. I can work through an effective writing process, including revision and editing stages, to ensure that I make improvements between my first draft and my last.
☐	15. I can use adjective clauses with appropriate relative pronouns to create complex sentences.
☐	16. I can write a short problem–solution essay that explores and analyzes a wellness challenge for my reader.
☐	17.

Activity D | Put a check mark in the box beside the vocabulary items from this unit that you feel confident using in your writing. Make a plan to practise the words that you still need to learn.

Vocabulary Checklist	
☐ access (n.) AWL	☐ integrated (adj.) AWL
☐ chronic (adj.) 4000	☐ leisure (n.) 4000
☐ composite (n.) 5000	☐ modest (adj.) 3000
☐ comprehensive (adj.) AWL	☐ reliance (n.) AWL
☐ deteriorate (v.) 4000	☐ robust (adj.) 5000
☐ dimension (n.) AWL	☐ soar (v.) 4000
☐ incidence (n.) AWL	☐ trend (n.) AWL
☐ index (n.) AWL	☐ vitality (n.) 6000

Appendix 1: Vocabulary

Unit 1

AWL Vocabulary

affect (v.)
aspect (n.)
culture (n.)
dominant (adj.)
generation (n.)
identity (n.)
individual (adj.)
minority (n.)

Mid-frequency Vocabulary

belief (n.)
crisis (n.)
drawback (n.)
dye (v.)
inspire (v.)
jewellery (n.)
reflect (v.)
translate (v.)

Unit 2

AWL Vocabulary

achieve (v.)
capacity (n.)
erosion (n.)
impact (n.)
issue (n.)
perspective (n.)
resource (n.)
technique (n.)

Mid-frequency Vocabulary

commute (v.)
ecosystem (n.)
ideal (adj.)
massive (adj.)
nutrient (n.)
objective (n.)
prosperity (n.)
spiritual (adj.)

Unit 3

AWL Vocabulary

communication (n.)
ensure (v.)
media (pl. n.)
network (n.)
potential (adj.)
promote (v.)
retain (v.)
strategy (n.)

Mid-frequency Vocabulary

device (n.)
enable (v.)
engaged (adj.)
loyal (adj.)
pace (n.)
persuade (v.)
prompt (v.)
retail (n.)

Unit 4

AWL Vocabulary

beneficial (adj.)
diverse (adj.)
economic (adj.)
estimate (v.)
be exposed to (v.)
interaction (n.)
norm (n.)
seek (v.)

Mid-frequency Vocabulary

abroad (adv.)
ample (adj.)
enrich (v.)
majority (n.)
navigate (v.)
optimistic (adj.)
vigilant (adj.)
vital (adj.)

Unit 5

AWL Vocabulary

assemble (v.)
attach (v.)
conceptual (adj.)
construction (n.)
funds (n.)
overall (adj.)
principle (n.)
unique (adj.)

Mid-frequency Vocabulary

aesthetic (adj.)
copper (n.)
delicate (adj.)
harsh (adj.)
necklace (n.)
sketch (v.)
teen (n.)
texture (n.)

Unit 6

AWL Vocabulary

access (n.)
comprehensive (adj.)
dimension (n.)
incidence (n.)
index (n.)
integrated (adj.)
reliance (n.)
trend (n.)

Mid-frequency Vocabulary

chronic (adj.)
composite (n.)
deteriorate (v.)
leisure (n.)
modest (adj.)
robust (adj.)
soar (v.)
vitality (n.)

Appendix 2: Sample Paragraphs

Unit 1

How Is Identity Formed?

In my opinion, **identity** is likely formed by each **individual** person's earliest influences. Where a person was born or how many brothers and sisters he or she has will directly **affect** the **beliefs** and identity that individual will develop. For example, the **culture** someone is born into will help to shape that person's identity. I also believe that parents are an important influence on their children's identity formation. In fact, many people recognize parts of their parents' personalities in their own. Childhood experiences affect many different **aspects** of a person's identity.

Unit 2

Urbanization: Causes and Effects

Not caring about how cites grow may lead to an unsustainable future for many of today's urban centres. The unplanned or poorly planned growth of an urban centre has a great **impact** on its future because rapid population growth can result in unhealthy and dangerous conditions for people and for the environment. One important reason why people move to cities is that there are more opportunities, including jobs and post-secondary education. By moving to cities from the countryside, people can take advantage of new career or educational opportunities—in other words, they are able to achieve greater **prosperity** in their lives. However, in some modern cities, rapid urban growth has a negative impact on the environment. Air pollution is one major consequence of **commuting**. Pollution changes the air quality. In fact, the city grows hotter and smoggier. In this way, people's health and overall wellness are affected. The growth of cities also results in the loss of farm land. As cities expand, new buildings are constructed on land that had been used for growing food. In many cases, without a local source of food production, people in the cities eat food that is grown elsewhere and brought to the city stores. Shipping food long distances results in additional air pollution. All in all, people will continue to move to cities for economic reasons. However, if a sustainable city is considered an **ideal** city, then city planners and land developers must act to preserve resources for future generations. One important **perspective** must not be forgotten: the growth of today's cities has to be planned carefully.

UNIT 3

Two Main Differences between Online and In-Person Shopping

Shopping online has two main benefits over shopping in person. First of all, online **retailers** offer a wider selection of products. This wide selection **enables** customers to find exactly what they want to purchase. Secondly, online retailers can **promote** their products and **communicate** more effectively with shoppers. For example, online shoppers can read product reviews right on a retailer's website, and they can **engage** with other customers through social media. On the other hand, shopping in person is not nearly as convenient. Bricks-and-mortar stores are limited by what they can fit into their physical locations. Thus, they cannot offer as many options as online retailers. Also, shoppers in physical stores have to depend on salespeople for information, which may be limited compared to the information they can find online. All in all, it seems like online shopping is a better choice than traditional bricks-and-mortar shopping.

UNIT 4

International Students and Friendship in Canada

Making new friends helps international students to feel at home in Canada. Many international students arrive in Canada alone. It seems then that the challenge for international students is finding opportunities for social **interactions** with local students. Canada is **diverse**, and so many students are **optimistic** at first that making friends with different people will be easy. According to Morrison (2014), on-campus staff should be sure to arrange for local and international students to get to know each other outside class. However, despite the chance to interact with local students, some international students may find it challenging to fit in and feel at home. Because people of different cultures have different ways of **navigating** the world, cultural differences can become very noticeable and can cause unpleasant feelings, such as culture shock and homesickness. Sometimes, these feelings make it more and more difficult to adapt to Canadian life. Therefore, it is important for students to make friends early on in their studies **abroad** (Morrison, 2014). In particular, at the start of the new school year, the **majority** of first-year students, including local students, feel homesick. This is the best time to meet new people because everyone is **seeking** new friends. In short, noticing cultural differences is normal, and accepting these differences takes time, but the opportunity to develop lifelong friendships **benefits** all students, encouraging everyone to feel at home on the international campus.

Reference

Morrison, I. (2014, January 13). Study abroad challenges. *iStudent Canada*. Retrieved from https://web.archive.org/web/20140419040500/http://istudentcanada.ca/study-abroad-challenges/

Unit 5

Three Key Decisions in the Design Process

For many people, creating a quality product can happen only if the various interconnected decisions related to the design process are carefully made. First, the **overall** purpose of the product must be considered. Knowing how a consumer will use the product is critical to its eventual design. Once a general purpose has been decided, then the designer must think about how to **assemble** the product. Finally, the design should consider the **aesthetic** quality of the product. The look and the **texture** of a product create a strong impression in the mind of the consumer and cannot be ignored. There is a **delicate** balance between each of these three decisions in the design process and all must be considered to guarantee a high-quality product.

Unit 6

The Challenge of Time Management for Students

Time management is a **chronic** challenge for students. They have to decide how to spend their free time. Because time outside of class is unstructured, social activities and academic assignments often compete for student time. Saying "no" to friends and "yes" to homework can be a difficult thing to master. In fact, balancing study and **leisure** time seems to be the most difficult part of time management for students, but maintaining this balance can keep their grades and emotional well-being from **deteriorating**.

One of the best solutions for students to balance their time is getting organized. Students need to organize their time so that they complete assignments without giving up activities they enjoy. Using a calendar with a daily to-do list is a simple way to plan. The calendar is a vital tool that gives an overview of upcoming due dates for assignments, and the to-do list includes the tasks required to complete these assignments. If students plan their assignments first, then they will be able to see how much leisure time they have to enjoy social activities. In this way, students can become better at **integrating** both study and leisure activities in their lives.

Credits

Literary Credits

Dictionary definitions in *Academic Inquiry* were taken or adapted from *Oxford Advanced Learner's Dictionary*, 9th Ed. by Margaret Deuter, Jennifer Bradbery, and Joanna Turnbull., 2015, Oxford: Oxford University Press. Reproduced by permission.

12 Adapted from "Understandings of Globalization," *In Living in a Globalizing World* (pp. 25, 30-31) by Pamela Perry-Globa, Peter Weeks, Victor Zelinski, David Yoshida, and Jill Colyer, 2007, Don Mills, ON: Oxford University Press Canada; 19 Adapted from Greenwood, S. (2015).*Misunderstood Subcultures*. The Brock Press; 40 O'Neill, D., 2004. Threats to Water Availability in Canada. National Water Research Institute, Environment Canada. NWRI Scientific Assessment Report Series No. 3 and ACSD Science Assessment Series No. 1, p. 128; 43 Adapted from Bridgestock, L. (2012, March 9). Green Universities. QS Quacquarelli Symonds Limited; 45 The Human Population. In Environmental Science (p. 227) by Michael Heithaus and Karen Arms, 2013, Orlando, FL: Houghton Mifflin Harcourt; 48 Pamela Perry-Globa, Peter Weeks, Victor Zelinski, David Yoshida and Jill Colyer, *Living in a Globalizing World*. © 2007 Oxford University Press. Reprinted by permission of the publisher; 51 Pamela Perry-Globa, Peter Weeks, Victor Zelinski, David Yoshida and Jill Colyer, *Living in a Globalizing World*. © 2007 Oxford University Press. Reprinted by permission of the publisher; 57 Adapted from "Green Guide" (p. 5) by Christian Brum, 2014, Waterloo, ON: University of Waterloo.; 60 "Green Guide" (cover page) by Christian Brum, 2014, Waterloo, ON: University of Waterloo; 63 Adapted from The Human Population. In Environmental Science (p. 226) by Michael Heithaus and Karen Arms, 2013, Orlando, FL: Houghton Mifflin Harcourt; 85 *Marketing Dynamics* (Canadian Edition, pp.121-130) by Greg Gregoriou, Jessica Pegis, Brenda Clark, Jennie Sobel, and Cynthia Gendall Basteri, 2013, Don Mills, ON: Oxford University Press Canada; 88 Greg Gregoriou, Jessica Pegis, Brenda Clark, Jennie Sobel and Cynthia Gendall Basteri, *Marketing Dynamics* Canadian Edition © 2013 Oxford University Press. Reprinted by permission of the publisher; 102 Adapted from Marketing Dynamics (Canadian Edition, p.123) by Greg Gregoriou, Jessica Pegis, Brenda Clark, Jennie Sobel, and Cynthia Gendall Basteri, 2013, Don Mills, ON: Oxford University Press Canada; 128 *A World of Learning: Canada's Performance and Potential in International Education.* (p. iv and p.9) by Jennifer Humphries, Karen Rauh and David McDine, 2013, Ottawa, ON: The Canadian Bureau for International Education; 129 Excerpted From Study abroad challenges. by Ian Morrison, January 13, 2014, Study Advice from the Canadian Bureau for International Education. https://web.archive.org/web/20140419040500/http:/istudentcanada.ca/study-abroad-challenges/ Reprinted with permission by the author; 136 *A World of Learning: Canada's Performance and Potential in International Education.* (p. 29) by Jennifer Humphries, Karen Rauh and David McDine, 2013, Ottawa, ON: The Canadian Bureau for International Education; 137 Adapted from excerpts in: The Daily (2015, December 10). A summary of conclusions in International students who become permanent residents in Canada, 1990-2013. by Feng Hou and Yuqian Lu, 2015, Ottawa, ON: Statistics Canada; 175 "Design thinking" is changing the way we approach problems: Why researchers in various disciplines

are using the principles of design to solve problems big and small. Johnson, T. (2016, January 13). University Affairs. {http://www.universityaffairs.ca/features/feature-article/design-thinking-changing-way-approach-problems/}; **180** Adapted from Crichton, S. Carter, D. (2013, Nov 198) *Maker Day Toolkit*. pp.20-21; **197** National College Health Assessment University of Guelph Results (2013). Student Health Services: Wellness Education Centre. University of Guelph; **198** Eating Well with Canada's Food Guide. (2011). Health Canada; **205** Adapted from Canadian Index of Wellbeing. (2014). How are Ontarians Really Doing? A Provincial Report on Ontario Wellbeing. Waterloo, ON: Canadian Index of Wellbeing and University of Waterloo; **209** Wellness 101: Health education for the university student" (p. 318 and p. 319), by Joan S. Wharf Higgins, Lara L. Lauzon, Ann C. Yew, Christopher D. Bratseth, and Nicole McLeod, 2010, in Health Education, 110 (4), 309-327. With permission from Emerald Publishing Limited; **212** Summarized from video "Things we wish all university students knew: Stress is going to happen." University of Calgary. (2014, September 2) Retrieved from https://www.youtube.com/watch?v=DCauapmVFEg&t=29s; **216** Summarized from: Mori, S. C. (2000), Addressing the Mental Health Concerns of International Students. Journal of Counseling & Development, 78: 137–144; **223** Adapted from TESOL Resource Center, "Charting Writing Errors to Improve Editing Skills" by Laurie Hartwick, 21 Aug 2013.

Photo Credits

Index